Grand Prix mechanic turned author, columnist, editor and television broadcaster, Steve Matchett is an exceptionally rare commodity – a commentator of genuine insight; a man that has prepared world championship-winning machinery with his own hands. Standing alongside Ross Brawn and Michael Schumacher, Matchett worked the pit lanes of the world's most challenging sport throughout all of Benetton's glory years. He is currently both technical editor to *F1 Racing* magazine and technical analyst to North America's *SPEED* Channel, a key member of their broadcasting team. He is the author of *Life in the Fast Lane* and *The Mechanic's Tale*, both of which have been highly praised; this is his third book – the final lap of his F1 trilogy.

The Chariot Makers

ASSEMBLING THE PERFECT FORMULA 1 CAR

STEVE MATCHETT

ORION

An Orion paperback

First published in Great Britain in 2004
by Orion
This paperback edition published in 2005
by Orion Books Ltd,
Orion House, 5 Upper St Martin's Lane,
London WC2H 9EA

A CIP catalogue record for this book
is available from the British Library.

ISBN 0 75286 524 2

Printed and bound in Great Britain by
Clays Ltd, St Ives plc

www.orionbooks.co.uk

Contents

Acknowledgements		viii
Prologue		2
Introduction: A Farewell to Arms		4
1.	Pea Soup in Fifth Avenue	10
2.	A Remedy for Terminal Boredom	17
3.	From Birdcage to Autoclave	30
4.	Quenching the Dragon's Thirst	51
5.	Suck – Squeeze – Bang – Blow	70
6.	Ah, Yes ... But is it Art?	99
7.	Shifting Times	118
8.	Turning Things Upside Down	142
9.	High-Speed Suspended Animation	160
10.	Down a Bit ... Down a Bit More ...	190
11.	Coffee in Saint Germain des Prés	216
Index		224

For Sam Posey:
Artist – Architect – Writer – Racing Driver –
Extreme Model Railroader.
A man of adventures. My Hemingway.

Acknowledgements

Eternal gratitude goes to:

Ross Brawn – technical director, Ferrari.
Jock Clear – chief engineer, BAR.
Frank Dernie – special projects engineer, Williams.
Alastair Gibson – chief mechanic, BAR.
Alan Permane – chief race engineer, Renault.

My appreciation extends to many others from within the F1 paddock, of particular note for their continual help: team members from BAR, Ferrari, McLaren, Renault and Williams.

And from within the broadcast booth, I am forever indebted to Frank Wilson and Bob Varsha, for their guidance and for opening the door to a whole new world. My sincere thanks to David Hobbs: colleague, mentor, sparring partner, friend. Your philosophical advice – that we should always dine late and expensive – has provided countless headaches, endless inspiration.

Thanks also to Ian Preece, my publisher at Orion, for his optimism and belief in the project.

Finally, it goes without saying, my apologies to J.

A Day at the Races

'It was a period in which many victories befell the Reds, a time of palms and laurels. In October they won XXV races in Circus Maximus, a string of XXV without fail. The hexes of the other stables proved weak and the Whites, the Greens and Blues could only settle for lesser rewards as Gaius Diocles drove forward.

'On that 8th November, from the tenth tier where I sat, the chariot of the Reds looked a percentage of the others, or was this a trickery of light and shadow? In any event, be it smaller or the same, the chariot of Diocles was lower to the sand, I wasn't alone in seeing this.

'At race's end the Reds were quick to reward their horses with water, and their chariot was swiftly adorned with heavy drapes of scarlet and gold. Before we had properly celebrated the victory, the garlanded chariot had already left the arena, pulled from view.'

Tribune Pliny (the younger) – Rome – 8 November AD 91

Prologue

In his book *Repairing Old Clocks and Watches*, Anthony J. Whiten writes: 'I feel the prologue to a book is merely the author's excuse for what is to follow. Whether this is true or not, here are my excuses.'

Here, then, are my own excuses.

My intention in writing this book was to share with you all I've learned, all I have picked up over the years, to show you exactly how we have arrived at the car designs currently used in Grand Prix racing. Why they look as they do, how they are built and pieced together, how the engines are installed, how the suspension works and how it is set-up for each track.

In scheming out the chapters, however, it quickly became apparent that compromise would be called for. Formula 1 engineering is a colossus of a subject. For example, with sufficient research I could easily fill every page with nothing more than information concerning the material specification and method of manufacture of just the carbon brake discs alone. But what good would that do? Sure, come the end of the final chapter we'd all know a lot more about composite brakes, but the vast majority of us would be bored rigid and never want to read anything else ever again.

Consequently, what I've done is to show you around the cars in some detail but not to dwell on the intricacies of everything; we'll pause, have a look and move on. For many readers this may well prove sufficient; for those who wish to linger and study longer, however, those that really want to feel the carbon splinters piercing the fingers, then I hope this book serves as an introduction, to whet your appetite and make you run to the nearest research library – I'm sure you'll forgive the rest of us for moving on.

On a final note, the reader will soon notice that the precise timing of that day in New York, and the dates in some of the subsequent conversations prove impossible to tally – I raise my hands. I only hope you'll forgive my playing the artistic-licence card so soon. The happenings of those foggy twenty-four hours are all based on real events, but in order to include and discuss the most contemporary ideas and thoughts of what is truly a fast-moving business, I have included certain reminiscences from more recent times. I really must thank my three friends for their kind and patient indulgence; they readily accepted these sporadic shifts in the time/space continuum without so much as the blink of an eyelid – although the occasional sideways glance from George Wingrave made me suspect he knew there was something fishy going on.

Steve Matchett
Bimini
17 September 2003

Introduction

A Farewell to Arms

'There are only three sports: bullfighting, mountaineering
and motor racing; all the rest are merely games.'
Quotation (erroneously?) attributed to Ernest Hemingway

I had resigned my Benetton commission in February, 1998. We had
finally won the elusive Constructors' Championship in 1995, the
one ambition I had so passionately craved. Now, campaign concluded, colours forever pinned to the trophy, I was happy to call it
a day. My spanners had been cleaned and polished meticulously,
wrapped in velvet and stowed away. A symbolic gesture – I felt like
a cavalry officer retiring his pistol and sword from active duty. My
pit-lane battles were over.

Leaving my team gave an odd sensation, though not particularly
melancholy – the scent of change was heavy in the air, had been
for some time. Benetton had undergone substantial change. I had
changed, too. What once was, was no more, and I parted without regret. I knew my next goal, I also knew that to stand any
chance of reaching it would require a complete change of personal
circumstance.

One evening, while pondering life over a rather nice Bordeaux, I
calculated that if I sold everything of value I owned (which on
summation turned out to be alarmingly little) I could just about
afford a place in France. Nothing grand, and certainly something
in need of work but it would, nonetheless, be paid for – mine in
both name and deed. That was the important thing; I'd be debt
free, rid of that damnable millstone called Mortgage, once and for
all. Indeed, I'd be out of the soul-sapping rat race altogether. Even

allowing for the prejudicial influence of the wine, the idea of a fresh start in a foreign land definitely appealed. It seemed like a terrific adventure.

The planning and implementation from original thought to decisive action took two years. Twenty-four months during which I saved everything I could, and searched for a house to buy. Eventually, I discovered the perfect project, an abandoned farmhouse standing amid the grapes of Cognac. Structurally the place was sound, though clearly it had not been occupied for decades – the most recent date on a stack of yellowed newspapers was 26 October 1970. All it needed was lots of tender loving care and a hundred years of renovation work. Negotiations with the owners took less than ten minutes; they had no interest in the place. A deal was concluded with handshakes and smiles all round. The vendors seemed absolutely thrilled with the sale, and several glasses of fiery *eau de vie* – strong, nasty and ready to ignite into shimmering blue flame with unnerving ease, an indication, so I'm told, of its superior quality – sealed the transaction.

With everything in place, I was in a position to tender my resignation. Joan Villadelprat, the team's operations director, wished me luck and promised to find me work should I ever need to retrace my steps. I was touched, but assured him I would not be returning. The day after quitting Benetton I took the cross-Channel ferry to Saint-Malo. On the drive to Portsmouth I stopped to buy petrol and a couple of language cassettes, thinking it might be useful to learn a smattering of French.

My days were split between renovation and writing. My publisher had asked if I'd care to record the years I'd spent with Benetton. I worked on the house in the sunshine and when it rained I worked on the book. Unhindered by the inconvenience of regular work, I made reasonably quick progress on the first draft. My only problem was that being free of the inconvenience of regular work also meant that I was free of the convenience of regular income. It was true that I had reduced my outgoings to an absolute minimum, but I was amazed at how quickly my meagre savings were slipping away.

In helping to put bread on the table and cement in the mixer, I'm for ever indebted to *F1 Racing* and *On Track* magazines. On hearing of my move to France the editors of both contacted me (quite independently, I should add) to ask if I would consider contributing. Both were keen on the fact that I understand the cars, know how they're assembled, how they operate. They hoped I might offer some insight into the nuances of the cars' behaviour. I was delighted to help, and the extra money allowed me to buy oak timbers instead of pine. I celebrated by buying some cheese wrapped in vine leaves – not plastic; then, in an act of total decadence, threw caution to the wind and put *two* logs on the fire.

What pleased me most, however, was that the magazines had approached *me* – not the other way round. For the first time *I* wasn't doing the pushing, raising a hand and asking for a chance to prove myself, this time others were doing the asking. I mention this not through any erroneous sense of self-importance, God forbid, but rather to highlight the fact that a significant change had occurred. Leaving Benetton had freed me of the inevitable editorial constraints of working for a Formula 1 team; I was no longer obliged to toe any party line. Editors approached me knowing that my circumstances had changed. I felt honoured.

The Mechanic's Tale was published in the spring of 1999. My publishers said they were pleased; I told them I was pleased, too. From the mail I received it was evident that people were fascinated by life behind the scenes of Formula 1: the details of the daily grind of Grand Prix racing, something which has received surprisingly little attention throughout the sport's fifty-odd-year history.

Life was good in France, there was much sunshine, and as the year pressed onward so did the renovation of the farmhouse. Catch it in the right light and (occasionally) it looked more like a house, less like an abandoned wreck – though, admittedly, the 'right light' was usually at its best just before the sun gave up for the day and dropped out of sight altogether.

Yes, on the whole life was good – the transition from the relentless push of paddock life, to this distinctly more tranquil existence had been easier than expected. I tried to blend with my surroundings and bought a beret. An old man told me he thought my beret too big but I didn't mind; at least he'd made conversation, something I took as a sign of acceptance.

I was comfortable, I was happy, I was at ease and yet ... I did miss something from my racing days. I missed being part of a team. Moreover, I missed the camaraderie that permeates and binds any group of like-minded souls. And while I certainly didn't miss the drudge of 4.00 a.m. alarm calls, twenty-four-hour flights, and bleary-eyed, sleepless nights spent nursing some awful piece of machinery back to health, I did miss the comradeship – the all-for-one solidarity. I missed the after-hours fun and the high jinks – the *craic*, as the Irish call it.

And then, one rainy evening in May 2000, an e-mail popped on to my laptop screen: 'Steve, my name is Frank Wilson,' it began, 'I'm the producer of Speedvision's F1 broadcasts in the US, I got your e-mail address from the *On Track* folks. I was wondering if you'd be interested in doing some television commentary for the Canadian GP. Our announce team consists of Bob Varsha, David Hobbs and Sam Posey – however, Hobbs and Posey will be covering Le Mans and we need someone to work with Varsha. I hope this interests you, I have read your work and I think you offer a perspective that our viewers will find interesting. Thanks, and I look forward to hearing from you. Frank.'

I read the message several times, thinking I must have missed the punchline somewhere. It must be a joke, a prank sent by some bright wit back in England. An offer of work, to travel to America and become a TV announcer overnight, with absolutely no experience of the profession ... well, it simply doesn't happen, does it?

However, the offer turned out to be perfectly genuine. It was as though someone or something had sensed my longing and had carefully arranged a series of random events to unfold in such a way as to bring Frank Wilson and me into contact. I've said it before but it stands repeating as this was a classic example: how odd, the twists and turns of life! You can never tell what awaits around the next bend. Really.

The Speedvision studios were located in Stamford, Connecticut, which, depending on traffic, is either forty-five minutes or three hours north of New York. Frank and I hit it off from our first handshake, a wonderful, easygoing chap on a personal and professional level. Actually, I've never found any starched primness when dealing with Americans – everything's friendly and informal, within minutes it's like talking and working with a gang of old friends.

His advice for the show was reassuringly simple: 'Don't worry about the TV side of things, Steve, that's *our* business. Varsha'll get us in and out of commercial breaks,' he said. 'What you're going to see on the monitors – that's *your* business. You know that stuff inside out, you know the people inside the garages, you know what those guys are doing, *exactly* what they're looking at on the cars. And our viewers would love to know, we'd like you to tell us the story that you see unfolding, point out the things your eyes go to.'

Sitting alongside Bob Varsha in the commentary booth was an enlightening experience. Bob is the consummate broadcaster: a man able to follow his script, sift his notes, call the race, and listen attentively to the producer, director and his fellow announcers ... all at the same time. It is the skill of the professional juggler, he remains poised, relaxed, and in complete control while all about his head spin an array of flaming torches.

Participating in live television provides a wonderful mix of excitement and anxiety: you see the action, you call the action. There's no time to ponder and evaluate things as there is with after-the-event reporting – no 20/20 hindsight to prove those masterly retrospective predictions: 'Ah, yes, and both Minardis crossed the finish line ahead of the Ferraris ... just as I fancied they would.' Live television is like simultaneous translation, the only difference is that these skilled translators can only work for twenty minutes before needing to rest, such is the level of stress, but an F1 show lasts for three hours, and the ninety-plus minutes of actual racing unfolds at 200mph; one blink and something – perhaps something of vital significance – has been missed.

During the flight home, reflecting on the events of the weekend, I realised I'd thoroughly enjoyed the experience; more than anything, being part of a team again. Frank Wilson seemed happy, too. Later in the season I was asked to help cover the Belgian and Malaysian races. It was then that I met Sam Posey and David Hobbs, the other two members of the regular announce team. Both had enjoyed long and successful careers behind the wheel, and both had made the successful transition from fast driver to insightful announcer. Along with Bob, it was clear that the chemistry was right, each complemented the other perfectly; not only were they friends but they worked well together. As the newcomer, I wondered if they might resent my joining them in the studio, yet nothing could have been further from the truth.

Towards the end of 2000 I was asked if I'd like to join Speedvision, as a member of their F1 crew. The question was unnecessary, I told Frank I'd be delighted. I wanted to keep my base in France, however, so the job would involve some serious transatlantic commuting. That was the only downside. I hate flying, always have. It's not airsickness, just a mild dread of confined spaces. Cocooned inside a 747 for nine hours, four times a month ... who was it that said 'It's best to face one's fears head on'?

1

Pea Soup in Fifth Avenue

'I like to walk everywhere, it's really fashionable in New
York these days, you know; they call it strolling.'
Pseuds Corner – *Private Eye*

It's difficult to pinpoint why exactly, but from my first trip I was
smitten by Manhattan. A combination of things, I guess, but one
thing's certain, New York is special; it weaves a spell. The archi-
tectural scale of the place is staggering; nature stands abashed
before it. In comparison to the scale of their surroundings the trees
more resemble blades of grass, while the city's inhabitants scurry
the avenues with little more than antlike presence.

Back in the 1930s, several of New York's foremost architects
had the vision and the powers of persuasion to convince their
'moneybag' clients to allow for the inclusion of detailed stonework
when financing their projects. The lasting legacy is that many of
Manhattan's whopping structures remain worthy of applause: the
gothic spires standing atop the Woolworth Building are prime
examples. The simple, rising splendour of the Empire State is
another, an icon of design and one of the most identifiable sights
in the world. And for interior detailing, look at the immense vaulted
ceilings of Grand Central Station, where carefully positioned spikes
of sunlight are allowed to pierce the roof, shining like stars mapping
out night-time constellations.

For me, however, Manhattan's overall winner is found on East
42nd Street – the magnificent Chrysler Building; William van Alen's
lush styling is elegant beyond compare. This art-deco masterpiece
stands as living proof that there is no inherent need for skyscrapers

to be born ugly, merely that we consciously choose to engineer them that way. There's no denying, of course, that it's always going to be cheaper to mix vats of cement than to quarry and carve blocks of granite and marble, and therein lies the fundamental reason for the global plethora of suicide-inducing architecture: profit. In most cities it's the turrets of royal palaces or buildings dedicated to art and faith that dominate the skyline. In Wall Street Dow-Jones is king and Nasdaq queen. The dominant buildings in the kingdom of Wall Street are dedicated to commerce; not a single church spire stands free of shadow. Even at midday, at the height of the sun's prowess, the looming dollar-factories for ever cast their gloomy shadows.

My knowledge of New York is growing all the time, I can now navigate the subway from Grand Central to Wall Street in under thirty minutes. From here I walk to George's Diner, a couple of blocks west of the station. I don't know George, don't even know if there is a George – perhaps he moved on decades ago – but it's in George's Diner that I usually order lunch: a tuna melt, a glass of half-and-half, and a cup of coffee. George's Diner isn't particularly chic, far from it, but it's always busy and that says a lot.

If I'm unaccompanied I try to sit at the counter. There's something rather fun about those pivoting stools fixed to the floor, where the tiles have been buffed to a brilliant patina by a million leather soles. Sitting at the counter to eat breakfast, or lunch, is an American tradition; it doesn't really happen on the other side of the Atlantic. Of course Europe has its bars and cafés, but they're not the same; the concepts are different.

Each time I've visited George's Diner I've been served by the same waitress. I don't know her name, although I once overheard her telling a customer, '. . . Since you ask, I'm from Croatia,' she said to the off-duty policeman sitting in a booth. 'But I'm wondering if you know where Croatia is, eh?' she asked, smiling, topping up his coffee.

'Sure I do,' said the policeman, 'it's Yugoslavia – the *former* Yugoslavia. Croatia's part of what was Yugoslavia, right? I know that … you take me for a dummy?'

'Okay, okay,' said the waitress, her dark eyes sparkling. 'I'll bring you cheesecake, on the house, it's your prize, but don't tell the boss you got it for free, okay?' Maybe the boss was George, I don't know and she didn't say.

After lunch I like to walk: habit takes me left out of the diner, then south, to Battery Park, the very tip of Manhattan Island. Looking over the bay I can see both Ellis and Liberty Islands; the former used to house New York's immigration centre, the first port of call for twenty million new Americans. The second is home to Madame Liberty herself, arguably the most famous landmark in the world. Right arm held aloft she grips the torch of freedom, the shattered chains of oppression strewn at her feet; proud and defiant she stands at the very gateway to America. As the thousands of ships arrived from Europe, she beckoned the masses of exhausted immigrants – welcome to the New World.

The last time I travelled the subway to Wall Street, to have lunch at George's and walk to Battery Park, was in the autumn of 2001, 3 September to be exact, I remember it well. It was Monday morning, the day after the Belgian Grand Prix at Spa. Sunday's GP had proved memorable, the race where Luciano Burti suffered a frightening shunt at Blanchimont, spearing his Prost AP03 into the tyre barrier at close on 175mph. It was also the race where, prior to the restart, the Williams mechanics had left Ralf Schumacher's car stranded on low-stands, unable to leave the grid while the others pulled away on their formation lap.

I remember Sunday's race and I remember visiting Battery Park on the Monday morning. I remember sitting on a bench and looking out across the bay, the walls of Castle Clinton behind me. It was sunny. There was a light sea breeze, I could taste the salt. I remember two women next to me, sharing the bench, they looked like sisters, one relacing her training shoes, the other reading a guidebook. Two children, arms wide, ran in circles chasing gulls, squealing at the excitement of it all.

I remember the day well, it would be my last trip to New York before the twin towers of the World Trade Center would be razed to the ground and the lives of three thousand people would be destroyed along with them.

The next time I visited Manhattan was in late November, a wet and foggy Thursday. The 2001 racing year had concluded earlier that month in Japan, with Michael Schumacher taking his fourth crown, and Ferrari their eleventh Constructors' trophy. I had been asked by Frank to fly over from France to contribute to the F1 review show: two taped programmes scheduled for transmission in early December. It would also be my final assignment for Speedvision. What had originally started as a small, niche company had steadily grown to become a highly respected member of the American cable industry. Speedvision's owners had been approached by the Fox empire, one of the biggest players in American television, and a deal was agreed whereby Fox would take control of the company. For the start of 2002, the station would be renamed Speed Channel, and the whole operation would relocate to Charlotte, North Carolina.

Speedvision recorded their final F1 programming in Stamford, Connecticut, on Tuesday, 27 November. The following day was a time of mixed emotions; of parties and goodbyes. Many familiar faces would be joining the new company but, inevitably, not everyone wanted to move south, to start a new life in a new city. I'd been invited to stay, to continue with Speed Channel's planned F1 coverage, and was more than happy to do so. However, the fact we would operate from Charlotte meant that this would likely be my last business trip to New York. That saddened me. Nevertheless, I wasn't due to fly out of JFK until the next evening; the eleven o'clock Air France 747 bound for Paris. I was determined to enjoy my remaining time in Manhattan.

Taking the late flight, I could spend all day in the city, and this is exactly what I'd planned. I didn't visit George's, I really didn't feel I had any business being so close to the crumpled towers so soon after that awful day. The roads around Wall Street had reopened but I felt no desire to see such brutal wreckage.

Today I'd arranged to have lunch with Kimberly DeNike, an assistant producer with Speedvision. A New York girl, Kimberly knows some fantastic restaurants and happily volunteered to drive us into town. It had started to rain almost immediately, the first drops splashing off the windscreen as we cruised along the Henry Hudson Parkway into Manhattan; to our right occasional wisps of mist played over the river. We crawled south along Broadway, through Times Square and down towards Fifth Avenue at an elegant five yards a minute. The rain grew progressively worse the further we drove. Kimberly's answer was to open the sunroof. 'How cool is this?' she said, beaming. 'We're in New York ... in the rain. Can you believe it? Look up, Steve,' she urged, 'look straight up, I bet you can't see the top of the buildings!'

She was right, I couldn't, at best forty floors were visible, the rest lay hidden in the growing fog. And, I have to admit, it was fun to be driving in New York in the rain even though we were both pretty wet by now. With its noises and smells, its steaming storm drains and its tangoing traffic cops at every intersection, Fifth Avenue looked more movie-set than reality.

The shadowy interior of Union Square Café heaved with lunch-time diners. A long timbered bar stretched the length of the wall to our right, every stool occupied. The rest of the clientele gathered in small gossiping groups around linen-draped tables. A colourful selection of macs and umbrellas dripped from the hatstands.

Great pasta, excellent company; yet the occasion wasn't without a tear. Kimberly had decided against the move to Charlotte and was saddened to leave the company. She enjoyed her work and loved the Speedvision crew, but her life was here in New York, not in North Carolina. She was happy to be staying put and I wished her well. Everything about Kimberly is positive; her conversations are gift-wrapped in optimism. I'd miss her.

Replete and satisfied, it was with more than a little reluctance that we dragged ourselves back into sodden Manhattan. Standing on the reflection-filled pavement we chatted for another thirty minutes before parting. Finally, arm stretched through the sunroof, waving goodbye, Kimberly drove off into the growing swirl of yellow cabs and sparkling tail lights. She was soon lost from sight, her car consumed by the damp, hazy city.

Suddenly I was distracted by a commotion over my right shoulder. On the opposite side of the street a man, wrapped in a gabardine and sheltering under a brolly, was shouting and gesturing manically at a bedraggled-looking chap sitting cross-legged on the pavement. Regardless that he was both soaking wet and suffering a tirade of verbal abuse, the dripping vagrant looked quite unruffled. A handwritten sign was propped against his knees: YELL AT ME FOR TWO BUCKS! Only in America.

The heavy rain had receded over lunch, it was now a steady, persistent drizzle. The fog, however, had become more dense, another ten storeys had vanished from view. It was only three o'clock but the diffused lights of the traffic made it seem like evening. This wasn't turning into a good day for sightseeing, my shoes were squelching. Coat buttoned and collar turned up, I splashed my way through the crowds. The weather was perfect for a trip to the cinema.

The theatre on West 42nd has seven floors and twenty-five screens, it's a ten-minute escalator ride from the foyer to the screens at the top – everything's big in Manhattan. A huge advertising hoarding larger than a basketball court was draped high on the outside of the building. A famous young wizard was visiting America. From down on the street level the top of Danial Radcliffe's head was lost to the creeping mist; I could just make out two large eyes peering out from behind round specs.

The drizzle had stopped by the time I emerged from the cinema but the mist had thickened; dense soupy clouds of yellow fog nuzzled through the creeping traffic. The opposite side of 42nd Street was lost to the near-impenetrable gloom. As I made my way towards the nearest bar I wondered how bad the weather was at JFK. My flight was still a few hours away but this fog looked as though it was here to stay.

Speedvision had arranged for a car to take me to the airport. At five to eight a black limo glided to a halt next to me. I climbed into the back, the driver closing the door smartly. The smell of leather permeated the car, the seats were luxurious and soft. I folded my coat, kicked off my shoes and played my damp feet over the heating vents. The driver asked if the music was agreeable. Ella Fitzgerald's silky voice floated on the air: 'Just a Simple Melody'. Perfect. The ideal song to accompany an evening drive through the misty avenues of New York.

Warm and comfortable in the back of the limo, my mind began to wander ... memories returned of my days as a race mechanic, of those endless minibus journeys we endured, ferrying ourselves to and fro between circuit and modest hotel; nearly always in the early hours. Twelve mechanics to a bus; sweating, streaked with carbon dust, rattling around on bench seats as we raced over the hills and winding roads of Imola, Monza, Bandol and a thousand other backwaters. We were always tired, often irritable, after yet one more twenty-hour stint at the track. Boy, those trips were horrid! I gave an involuntary shudder at the memory.

'You cold, Mr Matchett?' said the driver, smiling in his rear-view mirror, 'I can turn up the heat if you like ...'

I was miles away, his voice made me start. 'No ... no, it's fine, thanks. Believe me, things could hardly be better ... don't change a thing.'

We trundled north before turning east, leaving Manhattan by way of the Queensboro Bridge. As we headed towards the Van Wyck Expressway the black waters of the East River surged beneath a slithering blanket of fog.

2

A Remedy for Terminal Boredom

'There is only one thing worse than suffering today's mass-
produced injection-moulded air travel, and that is suffering
the traditional handcrafted delay before it happens.'
Alan Grange – *The Grand Tour Encore*

The cavernous check-in hall at Terminal 9 was almost deserted. It
was true that transatlantic traffic had slumped dramatically following the terrorist attacks of September, but this was the quietest
I'd ever seen New York's principal airport. *JFK International – Where
America Welcomes the World!* proclaims the sign. It wasn't wel-
coming much of the world tonight, that's for sure. Probably the
locals had taken one look outside and decided to stay warm and
snug at home: better to rebook than risk waiting for flights destined
to be cancelled. There were very few American accents amongst
the small number of passengers milling about the terminal; some
French, a few Brits, but not many from anywhere.

'No, sir, your flight has *not* been cancelled, Mr ... May ... shay
...?' The girl behind the desk squinted slightly as she read my
passport. Her tan was a subtle golden brown and her face looked
free of cosmetics. 'Keep your eyes on the information screens, sir,
you'll be advised of any changes or delays. Okay, you're all set,
have a nice flight,' she indicated the way to the Air France lounge.

I was taken aback by her stunning features, a natural complexion
made her remarkably attractive, with waves of shimmering auburn
hair, bright eyes and a picture-perfect smile. She also had a small
spider dangling from one ear, meticulously anchoring a minute
silver thread to her left shoulder. I wanted to tell her but just

couldn't bring myself to do so. Besides, a touch of imperfection is never a bad thing, don't you think? The spider kind of enhanced the overall effect.

The lounge was deserted but for three chaps talking around a table adjacent to the bar. We were the only occupants in a lounge designed to hold at least a hundred. Leaving my coat and briefcase – at another table well away from the others – I poured myself a Scotch from the self-service bar and dropped wearily into a seat.

I thumbed through a favourite dog-eared paperback, occasionally pausing to pore over random passages; I knew the story by heart. Most of the pages have fallen victim over the years to scribbled annotation or yellow highlighter and even the Day-Glo ink now looked pale and jaded. Friends have offered to buy me a replacement copy, but I would never give up such a faithful travelling companion.

My neighbours continued to chat and laugh together, obviously relaxed and enjoying each other's company. All three nursed tumblers, ice cubes chinked as their shoulders moved up and down. These three were total strangers to me and yet, the more I observed them surreptitiously over the top of my book ... there was something familiar about them, something I couldn't quite put my finger on ... I know one shouldn't but I simply couldn't resist; I leaned a little, discreetly, and tried to eavesdrop.

'... Yes, well, that's as maybe, Carl, old man,' said one, in plummy English. 'Quite possibly these newfangled V10s have got more power than the old twelves, all I'm saying is that they don't *sound* like it, not to my ears. Remember Mansell's Ferrari at Silverstone a few years ago? Now, that was an engine ... piercing! On the point of explosion every damned lap!'

Grand Prix enthusiasts. What a bizarre coincidence, to be sitting in an American airport, three thousand miles from Europe and the only other passengers in the departure lounge are engrossed in F1 talk, the very subject that brought me to New York. Perhaps I'd seen these chaps at a race track somewhere?

There's an old expression that suggests there are no such people as strangers, merely friends that have yet to be introduced. I put down my book and walked to the bar, poured a Scotch and called over to the chaps at the table, asking if I could fix them a drink. The one with the plummy accent turned to me, 'Yes,' he said, 'absolutely!' A grin spread across his face as he nodded and tipped his empty glass. 'A fine idea and a splendid gesture!' he added, before reaching down to retrieve his tweed jacket that had fallen from the back of his chair.

One of the others jumped to his feet. 'Absolutely, what a fine idea, and please' – he gestured towards an empty chair – 'come join us, why don't you? We could certainly use the company, this place is more morgue than international airport tonight.'

I put the fresh glasses on the table and shook hands. 'Hentschel, by the way, Carl Hentschel. And this is Wingrave and Paul Kelver,' he added, by way of introduction.

'Wingrave has a first name, too, it's George, but he won't let us use it,' said Kelver.

'George makes me sound old. Wingrave, on the other hand, makes me sound like an important banking-type of a chap.'

'But you *are* a banker, Wingrave,' said Kelver.

'Yes, I am a banker,' said Wingrave, 'and Wingrave makes me sound like an important one, too.'

Carl leaned across the table and dropped his voice, ' "Important" means they have to leave him alone to sleep between nine and four during the week, but on Saturdays they're allowed to kick him out at twelve.'

'Actually, that's not far from the truth,' Wingrave laughed.

'We know it's not, we've tried ringing you at that blasted bank!' Kelver exclaimed.

I liked them, they were easygoing and fun. As we talked I discovered that all three were keen motor-racing enthusiasts. Every summer they planned a three-month trip together, arranging their holidays around the Formula 1 schedule: each year a different country; a different race track. This year they'd decided on America, arriving in Indianapolis in late September, in perfect time for the US Grand Prix. The next eight weeks had seen them exploring eight states. Now, late November, it was time to head home.

On their way back to England the three were planning a stopover in Paris. 'To buy the most pungent cheeses available to mankind, and take them with us on the train to London!' explained Carl, with a mischievous schoolboy's smile. I suppose there are certain advantages in having cheese as a travelling companion.

Paul Kelver asked what circumstances had brought me to New York on such a grim day, and they beamed as I explained about the Formula 1 shows I'd recorded with Speedvision. Wingrave visited the bar, returning with bags of peanuts and mini-pretzels to toast our chance meeting. The peanuts were gone in minutes, the mini-pretzels remained unopened. Half an hour later Paul exchanged them for more peanuts.

The first announcement came just after ten o'clock. The arrival of the Boeing 747 scheduled to take us to Paris had been delayed because of the adverse weather conditions; it had finally taken off from wherever and was currently heading towards New York. Inevitably, there would be a delay to the departure of flight AF009. We would be advised of the new departure time. I glanced over at the bank of television monitors – half the listed flights had CANCELLED flashing in the last column. Looking through the lounge windows towards the silent runways, the oozing fog seemed well settled.

'I strongly suspect, gentlemen, that we haven't heard the last of her voice,' said Wingrave with a long sigh. 'Methinks we are destined to be here for some time yet. Scotch, anyone?'

Carl dropped his empty tumbler into his friend's hand. 'Well, listen, Steve,' he said, 'seems we've got some time to kill. Now, just before you arrived we were busy amazing each other with our lack of understanding. We're all pretty passionate about racing, love the sport, always have … but I don't think I'd be doing any of us an injustice by suggesting we know very little of what actually makes

these wondrous cars tick. What say you chaps, fair comment?' Both
Kelver and Wingrave nodded their agreement.

'We were playing a little game over dinner in Indianapolis one
night – Saint Elmo's, down in the centre. Their shrimp cocktail ...
mmm ... never tasted horseradish like it, hottest bloody thing
I've ever eaten! Delicious ... *but my God!* Well, we were amusing
ourselves by trying to piece together the perfect car – a dream team
car, if you like. Best chassis, best engine, best gearbox ... you name
it. Best of everything over the years. How do you feel about giving
us the benefit of what you know?' Carl paused.

'Personally, I'd love to know what's hiding under those covers
the mechanics put in our way!' said Paul.

'And another thing,' added Wingrave, 'all of those tiny adjustments ... they seem so insignificant. In comes the driver, a quick
turn of the mechanic's screwdriver and off the car goes again, half
a second quicker! I mean, can things really be that precise, can the
drivers really feel such small adjustments?'

'You got an opinion on that, Steve? We quite understand if you'd
prefer not to talk shop, just thought it might help to pass the time,'
said Carl, looking at me over the rim of his glass.

I had no objection to their suggestion, far from it. I'm always
willing to talk motor racing, I'll gas on till the cows come home if
people are interested, but where to begin? Formula 1 engineering
is a big subject – a vast subject. Not only that, but to piece together
the perfect car? How does one go about doing that? It's by no
means a new question, of course; nor is it the reserve of Formula
1 enthusiasts. Cricket, baseball, football, golf – it's the sort of
conundrum for which winter nights, log fires and good pubs were
invented. But, in so far as the question relates to motor racing,
there is one major difference to all other sports: the equipment.

If we look back over the last sixty years, there has arguably been
no significant change to the equipment used in world championship golf, or cricket, or baseball, or a hundred other such
sports. And when enthusiasts of these sports talk of assembling

'dream teams', they're really looking only at the performance of the athletes themselves; it's merely accepted that the equipment used by the participants through the years has remained comparable. For example, the size and weight of the baseball pitched by Whitey Ford to win the 1950 World Series is identical to that pitched by John Lackey to win the 2002 World Series: five ounces in weight and nine inches in circumference. I'm reliably informed those dimensions have remained unchanged since 1872.

Motor racing, however, is very different. Sixty years ago there was no such thing as the Formula 1 World Championship; now, following its 1950 inauguration, it has grown to become one of the leading sports/businesses in the world, a colossal multi-billion-dollar industry. And each year the equipment used by the protagonists constantly changes. In the early days these changes appeared as insignificant, but as the science of motor engineering became better understood, and as the racing itself forced the advance of technology, so the seasonal changes became more noticeable. Other than both sharing the honour of being Formula 1 race cars, there is virtually no similarity between the Alfa 158 driven by Giuseppe Farina to win the 1950 World Championship, and the F2002 Ferrari in which Michael Schumacher stormed the World Championship in 2002.

When discussing Formula 1's colourful history – who was hot and who was not: machines, teams and drivers – it's really necessary to split the last fifty years into decades and treat each ten-year period as an individual era. The great names of the 1950s are not the same great names of the 1960s. Each decade is different. Everything changes in this sport: constant revisions to circuit layouts are induced by safety concerns; constant revisions to the cars are induced by design innovations and consequent amendments to the technical regulations. Drivers come and go, either by virtue of retirement, dismissal, injury or, sadly, occasionally through being killed in action.

Carl was right. Piecing together the perfect car did seem like a fun way to pass a few hours but, when he and his mates were playing the game over dinner in Indianapolis, they had missed one very important ground rule: it doesn't really work if you mix 'n' match different eras; it's important to stick to a defined period of the sport's history. What intrigued me most about Carl and Wingrave's question, however, was that they wanted to discuss the equipment as much as the drivers. Their question wasn't the tiresome 'Who's best?' Fangio or Clark? Clark or Lauda? Lauda or Senna? Senna or Schumacher? Fangio or Schumacher? The simple answer here is that there is no answer. Different eras produced different cars, and in any given era, the sport's drivers required different attributes; physical and mental strengths in order to make their mark in history.

At the media launch of McLaren's MP4-16, during a pre-season test in Valencia, I remember Ron Dennis pondering the issue of drivers-through-the-years. A reporter had asked Ron to expound on the longevity of the Coulthard/Hakkinen partnership, seeing how the pair were about to embark on their sixth season as team-mates. (Their sixth and final, as things transpired, with Hakkinen electing to retire at the end of 2001.) Dennis gave the man his quotes and the reporter shuffled off with sufficient material to write and file his copy.

Then Ron began to reminisce a little, illustrating the diversities between different periods. How there was so little money available, even just a few years ago, and how meagre the annual budgets were as a consequence. How it seemed a constant struggle, even to buy sandwiches for his mechanics at the track, and how today every team member is presented with an array of sumptuous dishes, prepared by the team's lavish catering facilities. How pristine the pit garages have become, a place for everything and everything in its place, whereas two or three decades ago the trackside facilities really were nothing more than inspection pits in the ground.

I was fascinated by Ron's reminiscences, and, in a business where tomorrow is the only date that matters, McLaren's team leader was clearly enjoying the chance to ponder the past. He then moved on to the subject of drivers, explaining how it was impossible to compare Fangio's skills, or that of others from the same era, with the skills of today's drivers; and how we'll never know if Fangio would have coped successfully with the complex array of electronics, and the myriad permutations of settings available to both engine and transmission needed to extract the maximum from a contemporary car.

How confident, how relaxed would a champion such as Farina or Ascari or Fangio feel if they were driving in contemporary competition? How would they react to the endless pressure, the constant demands on their time by the international media, team sponsors and the hundreds of millions of fans? Sure, the sport was popular in the 1950s, but the stars of yesteryear were subjected to but a fraction of the psychological stress and invasion of privacy endured by today's multi-millionaire global icons. The bottom line is: how would the burden of such intense, unceasing demands influence their concentration, their confidence, their on-track performance today? The answer, of course, is that we'll never know.

I agreed with Ron's assessments, but the variations between the drivers of different generations can be extended still further. How comfortable would Fangio be, a man of impressive physical stature, if he was squeezed into the tight confines of a contemporary car's cockpit? And if Fangio would feel the pinch, then dear old Jose Froilan Gonzalez, his bulky Argentine compatriot, would stand absolutely no chance. His would make Mansell's efforts of trying to get comfortable in the 1995 McLaren seem insignificant by comparison.

We could spin this hypothetical situation around and ask how well the light and lithe Schumachers and Trullis of today, would fare against the Fangios and Gonzalezes of the 1950s, if racing the machinery of bygone days. Would our contemporary stars even dare to risk racing one another in the open-sided, tin- and aluminium-sheet cars of fifty years ago? No roll-hoops; no side-impact protection; no head restraints; no wheel tethers; no on-board extinguishers – pretty much nothing at all in the way of safety. Fuel sloshing down the drivers' backs; boiling oil spraying over the screen; and a wildly spinning prop' shaft a mere half an inch below their testicles.

Even if our modern-day drivers were courageous enough to face the challenge, would they possess the upper-body strength and stamina to fight these cars around a track? No power steering; no paddle-shift transmission. All manual and all brute strength. Although not every driver of these pioneering days was built big and stocky – Nuvolari's diminutive physique would make wee Allan McNish seem burly – there was good reason why so many of them were: the design characteristics of the brutish cars demanded it. Exactly as the design characteristics of a contemporary machine require its driver to have the body of a steeplechase jockey combined with the leg-strength of a Soviet weightlifter.

I readily appreciate, of course, that for many enthusiasts the drivers will always be the focus of their interest – perfectly understandable. They are, after all, modern-day Ben Hurs; gladiators racing their chariots around the coliseums of the world, their heroics watched and adored by millions. At battle's end the gladiators stand proudly to attention, graciously accepting laurel wreaths and wine and splendid trophies beaten from precious metals. Prizes awarded with polite praise by the organisers of the games, while down below surges a raucous crowd ... *Ave Caesar! Ave Caesar!*

But there is more to this sport than trumpets and streamers and colourful banners. Much more. And those whose eyes are concentrated solely on the derring-do exploits of the charioteers are missing out. Their attention is being misdirected, to some extent deliberately so. For no sooner are the victorious warriors accepting their silver, than silk covers are being pulled securely over the chariots to shield their secrets, and the stable doors are gliding firmly closed, the muffled cries of the euphoric crowd excluded. Now safe and secure from prying eyes, the gladiators' employers begin to plan for the next games, but days away. It is here, inside the stables, where the shining chariots are crafted and polished, that the real story of Formula 1 unfolds.

The drivers are strong-willed, competitive individuals, but, if they want to succeed in Formula 1 (which presumably they all do), then they must establish an intimate working relationship with their team. But of far greater importance, they must form a synergy with the car. It is not enough that the driver merely feels at ease in the car; moreover, it is *essential* that he becomes a part of the whole: the four corners of the car must become sensitive extensions of his nervous system.

A driver is employed by a team because it is hoped he will be of advantage to them, and if he works well he will be amply rewarded for his efforts. He will be allowed to drive the car until the day he shows he is no longer an advantage, at which point he will be plucked from the car and replaced. It stands to reason that an exceptional driver may decide of his own volition to move to another team; he may drive for several teams throughout his career – he may go on to win five, six, even more world championships – but regardless of how exceptional his abilities are, the day will always come when a sharper or quicker driver arrives on the scene and the whole process starts over. The once shining star has lost his sparkle, he no longer provides the chariot maker with any advantage, and his achievements are consigned to the history books.

The same is equally true for a team's choice of engines. A team will make use of a particular supply of engine until a faster, more reliable alternative becomes available, at which point the slower units are removed from the car. Naturally, a team with a tight budget may decide to make use of those engines. By the same token, a team with a smaller budget may also decide to utilise the discarded driver. Eventually the engines will become so outdated, so off the pace that they will be scrapped and will disappear from the sport altogether – so will the driver. It may be a harsh way of looking at things, but Grand Prix racing is a harsh business. I can make no apology for that.

This isn't to say that the drivers play anything less than a major part in the sport – I have no desire to detract from their worth – all I'm suggesting is that in an holistic evaluation, a driver's contribution to his team is exactly that – a contribution. Great teams such as Ferrari, McLaren and Williams have been successful for decades – even when not winning regularly. Ferrari have been at the forefront of Grand Prix racing since the first race of 1950. Great drivers, however, play an active role for but a few fleeting years. Certainly they leave their mark, but they are nevertheless transient players of the sport. Michael Schumacher's phenomenal career with Ferrari will form but a single chapter in the team's illustrious history. Before Schumacher races his last for Ferrari the team will have already made a carbon seat for their next driver.

Arrivederci, Schumi, grazie tantissimo . . . Forza Ferrari!

Inside the industry of Formula 1 everything is subservient to the unassuageable hunger of the chariots. Everything.

Similar difficulties also confound any attempt to compare the technology of Grand Prix racing. Evaluating the technical highlights of different eras produces an intangible fudge. For example, there's little to be gained by comparing the size, weight and performance of the turbocharged 1.5 litre, 4 cylinder, 1000bhp engines of the 1980s to the normally aspirated 3.0 litre V10s of today. The only reason the current engines don't use turbos is because they've been outlawed from the sport for over a decade. However, should the FIA suddenly reverse that ruling (which they won't, this is purely hypothetical) then every team in the pit lane would almost certainly attempt to have a turbocharged engine in the back of their car for the very next race. Time constraints would result in the initial installation being a mite crude, but by the second race the integration would appear seamless.

We can all appreciate the awesome power produced by BMW's mid-eighties turbo engine, and we can all marvel at their latest V10 power plant, too. But it's really impossible to say which is the better engine. If tomorrow morning they started with a clean sheet of paper, how much power could BMW produce if the rules allowed them to supercharge the induction system? How much again if the current restrictions on fuel composition were rescinded and the chemists were given the freedom to blend more of those crazed toluene-based cocktails that were used in the mid-eighties?

The same is equally true when we consider aerodynamics. Notwithstanding frequent amendments to the technical regulations in an attempt to curb downforce levels, the current crop of F1 chassis are producing considerably more downforce than the revolutionary ground effect cars of twenty-odd years ago. This is a remarkable achievement considering that those earlier cars, for example the Lotus 79, the Williams FW07, the Ferrari T4 to pick just three (not entirely at random), were largely unrestricted aerodynamically; cars specifically designed to benefit from under-body wings and venturi-profiled floors, their bodywork 'sealed' to the tarmac with sliding skirts.

Chatting with Patrick Head one day, in the Williams museum at their Grove factory, he explained that the Williams FW07 produced around 1500 kilos of downforce. Impressive for the time, no question, but the latest generation of Grand Prix cars, with all of their aero restrictions – smaller, lower rear wings; raised front wings; stepped floors et al – regularly produce between 35–40 per cent more downforce than the FW07. And the FW07 was no slouch aerodynamically, far from it. It was the cream of the F1 crop of 1980, handing Alan Jones his one and only drivers' crown and Williams their first constructors' championship.

Nevertheless, irrespective that the FW07 proved so dominant in 1980, if that same chassis was to compete against a car of current design, the pride of the ground effects era would, lamentably, be hopelessly outpaced, blown into the weeds by even the most lacklustre of today's machines. And that is based purely on the cars' differing levels of aerodynamic efficiency, not to mention every other performance gain that's been made over the years. The reason that contemporary cars are far more efficient is because the principles of aerodynamics are now better understood. Engineers possess a vastly enhanced appreciation of how to manipulate airflow and harness the resulting forces: more implementation of proven science, less gut-feeling and instinct.

All of which leads overwhelmingly to the question, exactly how much downforce would the cars of tomorrow produce if the technical regulations allowed the sport's contemporary engineers, with their improved appreciation of aerodynamics, to reutilise ground effect styling?

On and on it goes, an unending, unanswerable conundrum: chassis, electronics, suspensions, transmissions . . . drivers. Different eras are different eras, and the subsequent comparisons produce more questions than answers.

'. . . Steve . . .? Sorry . . . you seemed quite lost in thought!' It was Carl. I must have been miles away, pondering drivers, thinking about the thrills of the chariot racing at Circus Maximus. 'So, what do you say?' he tried again. 'Willing to chat and pass the time with us?'

'Of course, why not? Here's what I suggest: let's not go down the road of comparing F1 through the ages, I can see all kinds of pitfalls there. I'll share what I know about the different parts of a contemporary Grand Prix car, and we can go through the whole thing, section by section.

'We shouldn't compare eras but it might be fun to follow the progression of certain ideas, to see why current cars are built the way they are. We'll piece together our own machine taking the best solutions from everything in the pit lane and either do a deal with an engine manufacturer, or, build our own; we can decide that when the time comes. Same with the gearbox and the chassis, too; buy the best or put together our own design. So, what do you say . . . you up for it?'

'Here's to the fog!' toasted Wingrave. We chinked glasses, the game was on.

3

From Birdcage to Autoclave

'He was a genius of racing ... the main good things of Jano
was to design simple things. And in my opinion it's the
best thing you can do in a racing car.'
Mauro Forghieri, talking of Vittorio Jano

Many books have been published on the subject of race car engineering. Understandably, the majority have been written with the
professional race car engineer in mind. Such volumes play an
important role, of that there is no question, but to those seeking
an introduction to the mysteries of racing, many of these books
appear to be written in a foreign language – technical legalese rather
than everyday English.

Consider the following: 'If the "height" of a rectangular plate is
denoted by value x, and its "width" is denoted by value y, then the
aspect ratio of that rectangular plate can be defined as x/y. If the
value of x/y = 1.0, the plate will be square, not rectangular. The
normal drag coefficient of a rectangular plate is affected by its
aspect ratio, x/y. If for a square plate the drag coefficient is 1.18,
the drag coefficient will increase in value as x/y decreases.'

If you're a person who delights in such detail as that, well, you
may wish to ascertain the net mass of the book you're holding –
by means of some perpendicular balance equipment fitted with
suitably accurate integral instrumentation – annotate your findings,
then investigate the labyrinthine corridors of the Bodleian and
peruse those volumes with a minimum calculated mass in excess
of five times greater.

Be assured, you're not going to find any of that sort of language in this book. Not all Grand Prix enthusiasts are doctors of mechanical engineering, but I suspect many enthusiasts do possess an interest in mechanics and a desire to know more. Moreover, debating F1 should be an enjoyable experience, it's a vibrant sport and it's supposed to be fun. Race cars shouldn't be festooned in the cobwebs of mathematical equation. Personally, I find digesting pure logic for pleasure has the same effect on me as downing an infusion of wormwood and powdered root of asphodel.

There's no question that F1 is an intense, multi-million-dollar business, but from the enthusiast's perspective its purpose is to be entertaining – something that was reaffirmed to me while talking with Wingrave, Kelver and Hentschel. And if the trick to learning is to take things one step at a time, then let's do that. To better appreciate how a Grand Prix car works – and why it sometimes fails – it will help if we pull the car apart, split the thing into its various components and examine them one at a time.

When considering Formula 1 car design, the first and last thing to remember is that *everything* is a compromise. There are a million examples to underline this but here's just one, the first that springs to mind: the designer drawing the monocoque, the carbon chassis, wants it to be as strong as possible, resistive to both twist and flex (the reasons why we'll cover a little later). To help him achieve his goal of creating a stiff chassis he has no desire to include provision for any access holes. Holes remove material and that creates a potential weakness – the bigger the hole, the greater the potential weakness.

However, to allow the mechanics to gain access to the inside of the car, to attach the suspensions, install the fuel tank, assemble the pedals and steering rack, et cetera – and for the electricians to route their wiring harnesses around the car – then the monocoque's design *must* include a number of access holes. Inevitably, the chief designer will grumble about this but he is, nonetheless, persuaded to see the validity of the argument: if the mechanics can't assemble the car, then the team cannot go racing. Consequently, the designer's drawings will include access holes; small ones – often too small – but they do exist. Stage one of the negotiations is complete.

Now it's the mechanics' turn to moan, complaining that at least one of the access holes is 'way too small', offering insufficient clearance to allow component x to pass through. The designer huffs, remeasures component x, remeasures the hole, recalculates the stress loads, and begrudgingly agrees to enlarge the hole a tad more. Finally, even the most sceptical of mechanics has to concede that component x does now fit through the hole. Agreement reached, all parties go their separate ways, amid dark mutterings as to why these negotiations need to be so protracted. Every year it's the same ... without fail.

Successful race car design requires an holistic approach – one component touches another, all parts touch each other. Compromise is everywhere and the most successful Grand Prix cars are those built in harmony. Next time you look at something on a car and wonder why they designed it in such a strange way, well, now you know: part A affects part B affects part C.

And there are two more themes, philosophies if you like, and again, both are interconnected. Irrespective that the combined weight of the car and its driver must not be less than 600kg (known in the FIA's technical regulations as the 'racing weight'), it remains essential to manufacture everything as lightweight as possible – though not to the extreme that its strength is compromised, of course.

The car should be as light as possible, well below the 600kg minimum weight. Leading teams have managed to get their car/driver weight below 525kg; the car is then ballasted to bring it up to 600kg. The ballast is located as low to the ground as possible, improving the car's centre of gravity, often referred to as C of G. However, remembering that the driver should be considered as much a component of the car as the transmission or the fuel tank or the engine, then already we can see why diminutive drivers have found favour with the sport's designers: the lighter the driver, the more ballast can be fitted low to the ground.

Considering that we've just been discussing access holes within the chassis, I suggest that the chassis is the ideal place to begin our look at the current state of car-build technology. The chassis is the primary building block of a Formula 1 car, the foundation point from where all further construction begins. Its correct name is a monocoque, although both tags are common to the industry (I've used both terms already, so forgive me as I chop and change). Monocoque is French in origin, one of countless words the English language has embraced over the centuries: mainly, I suspect, because it's easier to steal from the French than to invent words of our own. Besides, they did exactly the same with Calais (the port of, I mean, not the word) so I guess it's a case of fair exchange, no robbery. *Mono* meaning singular, and *coque* meaning shell. Actually, the word chassis is also French, but we'll never make any progress if we continue playing word games.

It is of paramount importance for the chassis of a race car to have as much torsional rigidity as possible, meaning it must resist both twist and flex. To illustrate this, take a baguette, hold both ends, then twist your hands in opposite directions. First the bread loses its rigidity, then breaks. The same applies if you hold both ends of the baguette and flex the bread up and down; again, the bread frets, weakens, then breaks in two.

Back to our race car. If the chassis were to twist and/or flex sufficiently, then it too, just like the bread, would fret, weaken and break. With current construction techniques, today's monocoques tend not to break in this fashion but they still twist and they still flex. It's something that can never be fully eliminated, so the trick is to control it. As Ross Brawn of Ferrari once explained to me, 'Everything flexes on a car, *everything* ... the important thing is how much.'

The desire to reduce chassis flex goes beyond the basic need to prevent the car from collapsing midway through a Grand Prix (though this in itself is a fine reason), but in terms of general performance, a weak chassis will severely affect the handling of the car. Throughout the race weekend, the engineers and their drivers will set up the car by continually adjusting the suspension settings, changing the springs and roll bars, tweaking the dampers, etc. – all of which we'll discuss in more detail later.

In one way or another, all the suspension components are connected to the chassis, the car's foundation stone. If our chassis has a mind of its own, however, if it wants to twist and flex and wiggle from side to side (and it doesn't need to move by very much), then the handling of the whole car will become equally erratic. From time to time you may have heard teams say that they have retired chassis number such and such from service because it has grown tired? What this means is that over a period of time – six, seven, eight races – the chassis has lost some of its torsional rigidity; the time has come to phase it out. We all get tired, and race cars are no exception.

Before we look at a contemporary F1 car it might be useful to step back in time, just to illustrate a little of the evolution of race car construction. I don't wish to dwell in the past too much but we really should look at two landmark cars; designs of colossal importance, a pair of Einstein's giants, for they reveal the whole story as to why today's cars are built the way they are.

Our contemporary chassis is really a monocoque because it's a single shell; that is, the chassis (or frame of the car) and the body of the car are combined. It's important to note here that the body or bodywork of the car means the permanent (or near-permanent) parts of the car that collectively form the driver's area (the cockpit if you like), but it doesn't refer to any number of non-structural, removable panels such as the engine cover, for example. To turn that into an analogy of the family saloon car sitting on the driveway, the body really means the floor-pan, the roof and its pillars; not the doors, the boot and bonnet.

Up until the early 1960s a race car's chassis was a tubular steel frame to which everything else was fixed, including the bodywork. The chassis was very basic, like a steel bedstead, and a version of it remains in use today. Have a look at a truck or coach, the two parallel girders beneath the cab, running back towards the rear axle – that's the most basic chassis there is. This rudimentary design has remained a steadfast of the heavy haulage industry since the dawn of the first automobile.

It wasn't so long ago that a truck's cab could be unbolted from its chassis, leaving both the steering and pedals in place. Bolt a seat to the chassis and the truck could still be driven. As a kid I can remember new coaches being delivered this way to the local body shop; their windswept drivers wrapped in great leather jackets, fur boots and flying helmets.

The race car designers of the 1950s had considerably refined this elementary flat-bed concept, the machines of the period featured an elaborate lattice-work chassis constructed from myriad tubes; a concept known as a space-frame. When welded together, some of these space-frames were so intricate they looked more birdcage than car chassis. Indeed, so striking was this resemblance that the 1960 Maserati, the Tipo 60, became known as the Maserati Birdcage. In recent years these cars have proved a fine investment, too. Currently, on the rare occasion they fall under the auctioneer's hammer, they've commanded bids way above the million-dollar mark.

In the early part of the space-frame era, the engine was mounted on rubber bushes, slung within a cradle at the front of the car; the body itself formed by using thin-gauge sheets of steel or aluminium; screwed, riveted or welded to the framework – near-permanent panels but adding only marginal additional strength to the finished car. The lattice-work of tubing was expected to supply the vast majority of the rigidity.

Alfa Romeo, BRM, Maserati, Ferrari. A sample of the great constructors of the period, teams that built and raced the brutish chariots in which the likes of Fangio and Moss, Collins and Hawthorn battled for glory. They were frighteningly quick machines. Well, they were frightening in every respect, really – fabulous, certainly but frightening! Safety played little, if any, part in the design process back then.

That was the state of play in the 1950s. Now we move into the next decade, and it was Colin Chapman, the founder of Lotus, and a name synonymous with innovative design, that did much to pioneer the use of the monocoque chassis in Grand Prix racing.

Other designers of the period had already made use of the concept (the engineers at Jaguar's Coventry plant had adopted a similar principle for their D-type, a car developed for endurance racing at Le Mans) but, so far, no cars featuring a monocoque had entered the F1 arena.

For his next project, the Lotus 25, which would become his Grand Prix car of 1962, Chapman wanted to research an alternative construction method to the complex space-frame chassis. Chapman was a revolutionary. If there was an advantage to be had he would refine a concept to its absolute end, but if he thought further development was pointless, or if he thought a concept was inherently flawed, then he'd happily scrap the system and invent something better, something that he knew would work.

Chapman had grown frustrated by the shortfalls in performance offered by what he saw as wearisome technology; of having to fabricate a chassis from tubing, then, to create the car's body, having to dress the already heavy framework with sheets of otherwise fairly ineffectual cladding. However, that's not to disparage the continual development work on the space-frame chassis carried out by all the teams. Towards the end of its era, in its most sophisticated form, the engineers had gained significant additional strength by careful placing and fixing of the bodywork. Nevertheless, even allowing for this natural development, at the end of the day the basic concept of such a chassis resulted in a burdensome car, one that would always offer insufficient integral strength for its inherent weight and complexity of build.

Everyone was searching for a lighter, stronger car, Chapman amongst them, but making a space-frame any lighter would reduce its strength still further. It was a case of catch-22. No matter how beautiful the stitching, a handbag made from a pig's ear will never be a silk purse. Chapman knew the time had arrived to sell the pigs and move into silk production.

It was this desire – of increasing his car's torsional rigidity and of reducing its overall weight as far as possible – that prompted Colin Chapman to rethink the entire concept of F1 chassis construction.

Legend has it that he sketched the initial design on a restaurant napkin one day during lunch.

His wish was to take the aluminium sheets used to form the add-on body panels and incorporate them within the structure of the chassis, making the skin of the car an integral part of the whole. And his solution to the conundrum proved a stroke of pure genius.

Chapman set about the task by fabricating a series of aluminium box-sections, designed to run the length of the car, sitting either side of the driver's legs. These box-sections were laterally fixed, tied together using a series of four bulkheads. The forward bulkhead would also mount the front suspension; two in the middle would double as the dashboard and the driver's seatback; while the one at the rear would also mount a small space-frame, acting as a cradle for the gearbox and rear suspension. The engine sat inside the monocoque behind the driver, resting between the seatback and rear bulkheads.

Chapman used aluminium sheet to form the floor of his car, carefully folding it underneath and around the two box-sections before riveting it firmly into place. In this way the floor became of vital importance to the car's overall strength; it had become, as the industry parlance has it, a 'stressed member'. With the sides and the floor of the car taken care of, all that remained was to enclose the cockpit surround. This he achieved by a simple fibreglass moulding; it had no need to be strong, merely aerodynamic. Relatively lightweight, it simply dropped over the car and was clipped shut. Job done. In essence it was extremely simple, yet the results were absolutely astounding.

Chapman's first attempt at an F1 monocoque weighed close on 35kg and reportedly offered twice the torsional rigidity of a space-frame car. These figures are derived by securing the front of the chassis to a test rig, in such a way that the front is solidly fixed, while the rear of the car remains free to move. A weight or force is then applied to the rear of the chassis, acting at a right angle to its longitudinal axis, and observing how much torque (lb/ft or N/m) it takes to deform or twist the chassis by one degree. The greater the required torque, the better the chassis' torsional rigidity.

Again, to help the mind's eye to visualise this, the torsional rigidity test is exactly like holding one end of that bread baguette in a clamp or bench vice and seeing how much effort it takes to twist the bread with your hand. Rooting through my piles of notes and books, I unearthed one paper which rates a generic space-frame chassis of the period as having a torsional rigidity of 1000 lb/ft per degree, and rates the Lotus 25 at 2400 lb/ft per degree. Even allowing a suitable margin of error, the conclusion of these results, the obvious difference in rigidity between the two construction techniques, speaks for itself. The future had arrived.

The launch of the Lotus 25 turned the science of race car design upside down. What had been the industry's state-of-the-art technology suddenly seemed utterly prehistoric. The reign of the space-frame was over. Overnight more than 90 per cent of the welded tubular chassis had been scrapped. Only the transmission/rear suspension sub-frame remained, and it wouldn't be long before that went the same way. The dawn of the fully stressed engine wasn't far away – this another of Einstein's giants – and another laudable first for Colin Chapman and Team Lotus.

Lotus had shown the way, the future was clear and the principle of the monocoque was subsequently adopted and developed by all the teams. As a result, over the following five years the average torsional rigidity had risen above 3500 lb/ft per degree of flex, and, naturally, the engineers continued to develop and further develop the box-section monocoque, forever searching to unlock even more strength and to shed even more weight.

Towards the end of the 1970s, engineers began to move away from the Lotus style of box-section/stressed-floor monocoque design. The shape of the cars was changing, the long slender aerodynamics of the sixties and early seventies were being superseded by the distinctly square-cut 'ground effect' styling, where the profiling of the underside of the cars became more important than the top.

Teams began to build their monocoques using a new product. These preformed panels of aluminium-honeycomb were produced by bonding a sandwiched layer of small aluminium pockets (that look exactly like bees' honeycomb, hence the name) between two thin-gauge sheets, also of aluminium. These slab-like panels were reasonably light and far stronger than a single skin, however, the drawback was that they couldn't be contoured. Consequently, the monocoques of the ground effect era were squat, angular tubs – every surface was flat as though they had been assembled from sections of plywood.

These block-sided monocoques weren't particularly pleasing on the eye but they did offer another significant increase in rigidity, we were now seeing figures in the region of 4500–6000 lb/ft per degree of flex. And unlike their predecessors, to create an aerodynamic shape they needed to be *fully* enclosed within easily removable body panels.

So, that was the state of the union as we leave the seventies. And as we enter the 1980s we really need to visit Woking, in Surrey, the home of a newly formed company: McLaren International. The result of a merger between the old (and struggling) Team McLaren and F1 newcomers, Project 4, a team that had previously only competed in junior formulae of motor sport.

Project 4 may have been new to Grand Prix racing but its leader himself had extensive F1 experience. A former Grand Prix mechanic with the Cooper outfit back in the late fifties and early sixties when Jack Brabham was driving for them. The head of what was Project 4 is the same man who continues to this day to head-up the mighty McLaren International. He is, of course, Mr Ron Dennis.

And Ron's new engineering talent, fresh back to England after working in America was Mr John Barnard, another man who, along with Chapman, has played an insurmountable role in transforming the way Grand Prix cars are built today; perhaps will always be built. Chapman may have pioneered F1's first monocoque chassis, but it was John Barnard that we can thank for producing the very first carbon fibre chassis. Groundbreaking work, and Barnard's success in introducing composite materials to Grand Prix racing has had a knock-on effect throughout the whole motor sports industry.

When Barnard's original composite chassis was first unveiled in the early days of March, 1981, his detractors were swift to decry what they considered to be a bizarre invention: 'Carbon fibre is the material of the aerospace industry, not the race car industry!' 'What happens when it hits the Armco? It'll disintegrate, that's what'll happen!' 'Forget it, the thing is a folly, nothing more.' They laughed. If ever there was a case of 'He who laughs last, laughs longest', then surely this was it.

Within the space of two or three seasons everyone had followed suit, producing their own version of Barnard's pioneering design. (In fact, Lotus themselves were only just pipped at the post by McLaren International.) And now almost all major series within single-seater motor sport have adopted the carbon fibre chassis, it has become the industry standard. Indeed the technical regulations governing Grand Prix racing are written in such a way as to *insist* that the constructors build nothing but carbon fibre chassis.

John Barnard, just like Chapman before him, could see that current technology was fast approaching its zenith, the era of the aluminium tub, in all its guises, was nearly finished. Once again, there seemed little point in continually refining something that had reached its natural demise. It was time to start over.

The reason that Barnard was so taken with the concept of using carbon fibre (for what would become McLaren International's first chassis, the MP4-1) is due to the material's exceptional strength-to-weight ratio. Basically, the stuff blows everything else into the weeds, 'Twice as strong and five times lighter', as they say. I admit, though, I'm not entirely sure from where that maxim originates but it does sum up things pretty accurately.

For John Barnard, producing that first carbon chassis proved highly problematic. The main stumbling block was that other than basic fibreglass work, the use of exotic composite materials in the automotive industry simply did not happen. Okay, undoubtedly there must have been the occasional non-structural component produced here and there for some outlandish prototype sports cars, but no one had ever conceived of anything as major as manufacturing a car's primary building block from composites. Up until that point, such sophisticated technology had remained the sole domain of highly specialised aircraft manufacturers.

It would be a steep learning curve for everyone at McLaren, a time requiring patience and great determination. Looking back on those pioneering days John Barnard himself said, 'It was a big thing at the time, we didn't really know if it could work, never mind if it *would* work!'

The theory of engineering and proposed construction methods behind that first chassis were entirely different to anything that had gone before. Barnard wasn't merely proposing to replace the aluminium-honeycomb panels with ones faced with carbon fibre instead of alloy sheet (though this was something that Lotus were toying with), and then build his new car in the same, time-proven way. Far from it. What he intended was to machine a series of moulding tools and 'lay-up' his chassis over the tooling, using multiple layers of unidirectional carbon fibre cloth. Unidirectional cloth, as the name suggests, is exceptionally strong when stressed in one plane, but *only* in one plane.

The way to ensure optimal strength from this material is to offset the weave of the different layers or plies by 45°. As a rough guide to how this works, imagine the mould tooling as a clock face, then the first ply of carbon cloth is laid over the tooling with its grain running straight up and down between the hours of twelve and six. Resin is brushed over the cloth before the second ply is added, the grain of which runs between two and eight o'clock. More resin and the third ply is added, the grain now running between four and ten. More resin ... more plies ... and so on.

After eight plies of unidirectional cloth have been laid-up, sections of honeycomb are cut to shape and laid over the mould to form a core, followed by eight more plies of cloth. The whole thing is then slow-baked in a huge oven, known as an autoclave, to cure the resin. Once hardened, the tooling, around which the chassis has been made, must be dismantled and withdrawn, the separate pieces pulled from the cockpit opening.

Now, it's important to note that this form of mould tooling is known as a 'male' mould because the cloth, etc. is laid-up over the *outside*. A 'female' mould is where the cloth is laid-up on the *inside* of the moulding. (For the purpose of distinction, this male/female thing crops up everywhere in engineering: a bolt is considered male, while a nut is female; an electrical plug is male, the socket is female. I'm sure you get the idea.)

To ensure the project had its best chance of success and to find the necessary expertise, Barnard knew he would have to curry favour with the aerospace industry, the people most familiar with such advanced materials. After a string of unsuccessful talks with British companies (most of whom seemed completely under-whelmed by such a strange scheme), a deal was eventually struck with an American firm – Hercules Incorporated of Utah; a company that specialised in 'missile rocket motors'. Hercules agreed to make the McLaren/Barnard carbon fibre monocoque. The finished pieces were flown back over the Atlantic, and the cars were assembled and finished at McLaren International's headquarters in England.

And the bottom line, after all the pontificating by Barnard that this revolutionary new monocoque could/should/would be the best thing since sliced bread; when the McLaren engineers weighed it and conducted a torsional rigidity test, was it any better than what had gone before? You bet it was! Not only did it prove 25 per cent lighter than a contemporary flat-panelled aluminium-honeycomb chassis but, after double-checking their figures, the results still showed the MP4-1 to be more than 100 per cent stronger, too. That first chassis was so stiff that it resisted torsional flex at the rate of 14,500 lb/ft per degree. In fact, the results were so impressive that future examples were produced using less carbon cloth, something which lowered the mono-coque's weight by a further five kilos – tipping the scales at just 36kg, almost exactly the same as Chapman's aluminium box-section monocoque – and still strong enough to withstand 12,000 lb/ft per degree of flex.

The McLaren/Hercules partnership proved a great success, in deference to their contribution and faith in the project, each MP4-1 monocoque carried a prominent 'Chassis Made by Hercules' sticker, on the dash bulkhead. Just as happened with the unveiling of Colin Chapman's Lotus 25, the arrival of the McLaren MP4-1 changed everything that had gone before – changed it for ever. The other teams stood back a while and watched McLaren's progress, but all knew that they would soon have to follow John Barnard's lead. With the launch of their first carbon chassis, the 126C4, Scuderia Ferrari capitulated in 1984. The following season Williams Grand Prix Engineering followed suit with their own version, the FW10; and by the halfway point of the decade not a single F1 car would be constructed using any other material. Once again, the future had arrived: first the monocoque, then the composites monocoque. Carbon fibre and Grand Prix motor racing had become inexorably linked.

Of course, it would be totally wrong for me to suggest that the design principle of every Grand Prix car we see today is solely due to the pioneering efforts of just two visionaries. Such a claim would be a terrible injustice to the scores of others who have helped to drive the business forward. Nevertheless, there is no question that a very great deal of thanks is owed by the whole motor sports community to Messrs Chapman and Barnard for their brilliant contributions and services to the industry.

I should just add that since the dawn of McLaren's landmark MP4-1, there was one other major refinement to the procedure of manufacturing carbon monocoques. The majority of teams shied away from Barnard's male-moulding technique, opting instead to use female moulds. The primary disadvantage of the male mould was that the perfectly smooth finished surface was on the *inside*, where the driver sat; the outside face of the monocoque was only as smooth as the composite specialist could apply the final ply of cloth. Consequently, the male technique resulted in the outside of the monocoque looking a little messy ... perhaps *textured* would be a kinder word? The car still needed to be entirely clad in additional body panels to supply the aerodynamics. This smooth-face/rough-face scenario affects anything produced in a mould, even apple tarts – the side baked against the pie tin is smooth, while the top of the tart is rough.

It was the low-key, somewhat maverick Gustav Brunner (currently working as chief designer with Toyota) who was the first to produce a carbon monocoque using a female mould. His 1983 ATS became the very first Grand Prix car with a monocoque made with a perfectly smooth, 'finished' exterior. True, the car failed to score so much as a single championship point all season, but it did so with a great sense of dignity and aplomb. Brunner's ATS was another significant milestone because its moulded shape, the contours of the monocoque were made to follow the desired aerodynamics. Considerably fewer add-on body panels were needed as a result, all of which saved weight and production time.

The female-mould technique has now been universally adopted; has been for more than a decade. I've asked several composite specialists for their opinions of what the future holds, and all seem settled on the idea that we have reached the end of the line in terms of revolutionary chassis design. Naturally, there will be continual advancements in the science of composite materials: revised molecular structures, offering more strength for even less weight, and there is no question that such materials will be exploited the split second they become proven and available.

Nevertheless, the overwhelming conclusion within the industry is that there will be nothing in the future to cause a fundamental re-evaluation of the carbon fibre monocoque. The cars of tomorrow will be finely honed evolutions of Brunner's 1983 ATS. Of course, it was at exactly such a juncture in time (the 'we-can't-possibly-advance-any-further stage') that the Chapmans and Barnards got out their biros, scribbled the future on table napkins and proved us all wrong. And, I guess, we should never say never, but, on this occasion, I think it's reasonably safe to do so.

The torsional rigidity of a contemporary monocoque is quite staggering. Talking with the engineers it is not uncommon to hear them suggest figures in the region of 23,100 lb/ft per degree of flex – nearly double that of the McLaren MP4-1. Impressive, sure, but now just compare that to the paltry 1000 lb/ft per degree offered by the original space-frame cars of the 1950s. Today's cars are more than 2300 per cent stiffer – that's serious progress!

In terms of weight, a new chassis tips the scales at an average 50kg. That's significantly heavier than Barnard's first attempt. This extra mass is a result of the FIA's crash test requirements. In order to compete in the World Championship, each monocoque is subjected to, and required to pass, a series of structural tests where the roll-hoop, bulkheads and sides of the tub are compressed with hydraulic rams.

The FIA likes to refer to the monocoque as the 'survival cell', that part of the car designed primarily to protect the driver in the event of a shunt. The only way for a team to build a monocoque capable of passing these compulsory tests is by including extra material around the test areas and by bonding additional crushable structures to the cockpit sides. This extra material doesn't necessarily increase torsional rigidity, it isn't added through any engineering desire, but there's no question that it does offer more driver protection.

The precise methods used to manufacture a chassis will vary from team to team; no two chassis are alike, irrespective of aerodynamic considerations. Everyone has their own idea of how to go about the job. That said, however, all the teams do follow a very similar recipe. A cordon bleu chef will assure you that no two omelettes are ever alike, indeed that such a thing is a complete impossibility! Yet all omelettes are made by beating eggs in a bowl, before cooking over a gentle heat. Basically, it's the same in the Formula 1 kitchens, too; the master chefs all possess individual ideas of how things must be done, but the basic culinary skills remain the same.

The first thing to happen is the design stage. The chief designer and his team get their heads together and focus on what were the fundamental problems with the previous year's chassis – not the whole car, just the monocoque. The most likely answers here will be that the chassis was too heavy; too weak, it flexed too much; and it didn't produce sufficient downforce. There might be other problems to address, too. The team may have signed a deal with a different engine manufacturer and the design of the next generation of chassis will have to take the installation of a different engine into consideration. It could be that last year's chassis kept breaking its suspension mountings, or that the fuel tank was too small – or too big – and that the design of the fuel tank housing will need to be rethought. Whatever the shortfalls of last year's car, the new, all-singing, all-dancing replacement will not feature the same failings.

Assisted by the latest version of their computer-aided-design system, the designers set to work, producing drawings and writing the software program that will allow the team's five-axis CNC mill to machine a precise copy – from modelling block – of the outside shape of the monocoque.

The cutting arm of a five-axis mill has all the articulation of a human hand (with none of the shake). In lay terms, the cutting tool can move up, down; forward, backward; in, out; and traverse along both diagonals. Programming the mill to machine along a line comprised of coordinates from any of these five axes will produce any desired shape. The process is a bit like reading a map and making a model of a mountain from careful study of its contour lines. The software program plots the contour lines of the new chassis, the mill's brain reads them and instantly gets to work to make the life-sized copy. And it does so with sublime speed and accuracy; watching a five-axis mill at work is a fascinating experience.

Using the finished model, the composite workers then make their female moulds. The carbon monocoque itself is made in two sections, bonded together like the halves of a chocolate Easter egg. The monocoque is divided either into top and bottom sections, or front and rear sections, a preference of the individual team.

The sections of the monocoque are laid-up in stages, ply by ply, still very similar to how John Barnard's team worked on that first carbon tub more than twenty years before. Once the outer plies, the honeycomb core, and the inner plies are in place, the whole assembly is sealed in a heatproof plastic bag and a vacuum pump is used to extract as much air as possible – air that was unavoidably trapped between the plies during assembly. Any persistent air bubbles would result in tiny pockets, or voids, reducing the integral strength of the laminate construction.

The vacuum bag needs to be heatproof because, again, just as with the MP4-1, the sections of today's monocoques need to be baked in an autoclave in order to cure the bonding agents; the pumps remain in operation throughout. The curing process takes approximately four hours, the ovens set between 120–160° Celsius, depending on the requirements of a particular material.

One significant improvement from those pioneering days of the early eighties is that the vast majority of today's carbon cloth is manufactured with the necessary bonding resins already impregnated within the weave, a material known as 'pre-preg'. There is no need to seal the individual plies with additional bonding agents, and this pre-preg cloth remains malleable, workable until heated within the autoclave. Nevertheless, the composite specialists have to be acutely aware that the bonding agents within the pre-preg cloth will begin to cure, albeit slowly, at ambient room temperature. They have a finite time – carefully monitored – to prepare their chassis.

In order to preserve the condition of this cloth prior to use, it must be stored below minus 18°C. The teams' composite departments have refrigerated storerooms designed especially for this. Even allowing for the stringent precautions on time and temperature, the pre-preg cloth is still subject to a shelf life. Any cloth remaining after its expiry date will not be used for monocoque production; understandably, the teams are somewhat loath to discard such extravagant stock. It usually ends up with the race mechanics, to manufacture various pieces of pit equipment such as cowlings for the cooling fans taken to the grid; basically anything where structural strength is of superficial significance.

As a guide, the whole process to produce *one* monocoque (not including production of the initial moulds from the five-axis model) takes approximately 1280 hours of labour. And this is a *bare* chassis I'm talking about, not a complete, ready-to-race car. There are on average five people working on each chassis. It takes them a week to laminate the outer skins, and a further week to cut and assemble the honeycomb core and 'hard patches' for the suspension mountings. Another week is used to prepare and laminate the inner skins, too, and a further seven days to install the bulkheads and unite the two halves of the monocoque. A similar period of time is taken up by machining the multitude of precision holes, brackets, pick-up points and bolt locations. Oh, yes, and it takes about half a second for the driver to get the car out of shape and slam the thing into the Armco, rupturing the core and tearing a suspension mounting on impact and reducing this once magnificent racing chassis to an utter useless pile of space-age scrap. Still, there's always another one in the back of the truck.

'There's more, of course. Mountains of stuff we haven't covered,' I said, looking at the three eager faces around the table. 'But at least that gives an idea of how and when. All the teams use carbon monocoques, or chassis, or whatever you want to call them ... now you know the reasons why. What is important, though, is that we've talked about the basic differences, you'll be able to identify them at the historic meetings. Hunt out a Lotus 25 and give it a little pat. You should do the same with one of those early male-moulded McLarens, too – you'll be touching history! A few years from now they'll be locked away in glass cases, the preserve of museum curators. You want to take your chance while it's still possible!'

'I will,' said Carl, 'I jolly well intend to do exactly that! Wingrave, make a note in that posh diary of yours: *Silverstone, next historic meeting*. You can drive, Paul.'

Returning from the bar, Paul dropped more peanuts on the table. 'I don't mind driving,' he said. 'But, I'll never be able to look at another wrecked car in the same light again! Being hoisted off the track like that. How long did you say it took those poor guys to make a chassis?'

'Between three to five weeks,' I told him. 'It really depends on how many people you throw at it. Nowadays, most teams make two sets of moulds, so the composite chaps can be busy making two monocoques at the same time. Most teams – the top teams – make an average of ten, maybe twelve tubs a year: two race cars, the spare car (or t-car) and an emergency spare chassis in the back of the truck, all for the race team.

'Then there's the test team cars as well. Most teams have two test cars, though I think Ferrari are up to six; they run three entirely separate test teams. One concentrating on tyre development; the next on chassis set-up and aerodynamics; and the third specialising in engine development. Okay, even allowing for the fact that Ferrari are a bit of an exception to the rule, it doesn't take many shunts before a team's annual chassis production reaches double figures.'

'So,' said Wingrave, 'what about a chassis ... sorry ... *monocoque*, for our dream machine? Which team are we going to borrow it from?'

'Call it a chassis if you like,' I smiled. 'I nearly always do. It doesn't matter to be honest, it's just a tag, that's all. The only thing that matters is that you can tell the difference. As to our dream team chassis ... I'm going to insist that we produce our own. We shouldn't beg, borrow or steal another team's chassis – absolutely not.

'In my eyes, Grand Prix racing is what it is, the king of motor sports, primarily because all the teams build and race their own creations. The Formula 1 Constructors' trophy is the most prestigious automotive engineering award in the world. For the hundreds of designers, engineers, mechanics, machinists, fabricators, electronics experts and composite specialists from each and every team in the pit lane, the fact that they are competing for such an eminent global prize by racing *their* cars – machines produced with unending care and attention, designed and built by their own skill and effort – is of insurmountable importance.

'Now, on saying that, we have just been discussing how Hercules were asked to produce the tub for the MP4-1. From every team there are countless examples of outside contractors adding their contribution to the mix; but there is no question that the MP4-1 was a product of McLaren International.

'There was a time, of course, when teams did race cars supplied by rival constructors; for example, Enzo Ferrari used to race Alfa Romeos before he got his own act together. Ken Tyrrell made use of Marta and March chassis prior to building his own. Frank Williams raced both Brabham and De Tomaso cars – to name just two – before Patrick Head finally penned the FW06 (which is generally regarded as being the first "real" Williams car). But that was then and this is now. Times have changed.

'We should – *must* – manufacture our own design. We'll assume we have the best facilities at our disposal, certainly on a par with the top teams, so we can do anything they can. However, I think we should leave the actual aerodynamic styling of our chassis until a little later. We should study the current trends in aerodynamics before committing ourselves; we can't afford to change our minds halfway through the season over something so fundamentally important as the design of the chassis. Currently, there are two schools of thought concerning airflow around the front of the car, and we must choose one before we set the five-axis mill in action and fire the autoclave.'

I glanced at my watch, the hands were just shy of midnight, in another two minutes it would be tomorrow; two hours had passed since we'd started chatting. The fog, however, remained as thick – as impenetrable – as before.

4

Quenching the Dragon's Thirst

'If that fireball [in the Benetton pits at Hockenheim, in
1994] was less than a gallon of petrol, it's a good job you
didn't lose the whole tankful and have a really big one...'
Josh Reid – *The Chequers*, Chipping Norton

At the beginning of the previous chapter I described the chassis as
the foundation stone of the car, the starting point for further
construction. So, for the purpose of moving the conversation along,
let's assume we now have our chassis ready to go. The composite
specialists have delivered it with much pride and loving care to the
race shop – the area of the factory given over to 'car build' –
and it's now resting at knee height atop two high-stands (looking
something akin to the hinged legs of a trestle table), awaiting our
attention. The aerodynamic lines can be finalised later, that's the
beauty of a project born of imagination; later on we'll meld the
profile of the chassis to become whatever shape we desire. If only
reality were so amenable.

The race shop is the domain of the race mechanics – a curious
breed. Requirements for the post include: thick skin and a deep-
rooted sense of humour; the ability to thrust and parry cutting
comment with rapier speed and precision; to have an unconditional
trust in one's colleagues; and a willingness to put one's private life
on permanent hold. When the team isn't away testing or racing,
the race shop is the mechanics' home.

The composite chaps hand over their work, and from here on
the chassis belongs to the mechanics; it will stay with them for the
rest of its competitive life. The mechanics will build the chassis

into a complete car; they will make any changes to it during the practice and qualifying sessions; they will maintain it in between sessions; and they will rebuild it overnight. The mechanics will learn the car from top to bottom, front to rear, and inside out. Working on the car will become second nature to them. They will become familiar with the size of every washer, the length of every bolt, the pitch of every nut. They will memorise every component and know exactly which tiny bracket goes where; which O-ring seals which oil pipe. The car will become a part of them. The only time it is let out of their complete control is when the driver takes it on to the track, and all the mechanics can do is watch ... and wait. The relationship between mechanic and driver is a very special one.

The chassis is finished, sitting in the race shop, and the engine is the next major consideration. However, before we go any further along that route I want us to back up just a little. Before we can unite the engine to the chassis we first need to install the fuel cell and all of its associated paraphernalia. Some aspects of a Grand Prix car's fuel system are on show for all to see; some, however, are hidden from view, deep within the confines of the car. I think it's well worth spending a little time delving into this important, though much overlooked, aspect of the car.

We see the F1 pit crews refuelling their cars at various stages throughout a race, perhaps as often as three times per car depending on strategy and tyre wear. The mechanics attach the hose to the car and we watch the fuel being safely delivered from the pit lane fuel rig into the car's tank. At least that should be the case if everything works correctly: Hockenheim 1994 being the extreme example of when things don't go according to plan.

At a delivery rate of twelve litres per second, the fuel enters the car through a two-stage valve mechanism, opened and closed via the operation of coupling and decoupling the delivery hose. Initially, as the mechanic engages the nozzle into the car's valve, only the primary stage is opened – a breather or vent creating a free-flowing connection between the car's fuel tank and the pit rig. No fuel flows from the rig at this time. Then, as the mechanic leans forward and pushes down again, the delivery valve itself is opened and the predetermined charge of fuel is injected into the car's tank. As the fuel is delivered, any air or vapour inside the car's tank is displaced and forced out through the vent hose, back towards the relative safety of the rig.

The reason we see only one hose during the pit stops for both venting and delivery, is because the smaller diameter delivery hose runs within the larger vent hose. This venting action is a vital safety feature, as it allows not just air and vapour to escape but it also allows any surplus fuel to flow back to the rig. Without this venting action the pressure of the incoming fuel has the potential to crack the fuel tank bulkhead, mounted behind the driver's back.

Michael Jakeman once told me an interesting story concerning this very scenario when the pair of us worked at Benetton. Michael currently manages the transmission department at Jaguar, but prior to joining Benetton he worked for many years as a race team gearbox mechanic for Frank Williams. Michael explained that in the early 1980s, as the cars blasted towards their pit slots to be refuelled, the drivers used to slacken their shoulder straps beforehand. The cars' bulkheads, then constructed from aluminium-honeycomb, used to bulge with the incoming charge, deforming the bulkheads sufficiently to cause the drivers to gasp!

With regard to mid-race refuelling, these were pioneering days. Teams would attempt to refill their cars in under four seconds utilising such curious schemes as coupling two beer barrels together: one filled with fuel, the other pressurised with air. Flow was accomplished by opening a tap and allowing the pressure from one barrel to enter the other, displacing the fuel and slamming the fresh charge into the car at a frightening rate ... mmm ... the good old days, eh?

Anyway, back to the present and the business at hand. The equipment used and the actual process of delivering fuel into the car can be seen with the naked eye. It's a different story, however, once the fuel is actually inside the car's tank. Now everything is out of sight and the fuel's serpentine route to the engine's injectors is distinctly less obvious. One might suppose that the fuel is merely dumped into the car, then pumped directly to the spray-rail feeding the engine, job done. Well, in very basic terms that *is* what happens, but things being what they are in Formula 1, there is much more to it than that.

The biggest concern for the engineers is that their car should not run out of fuel before its next scheduled pit stop. They need to ensure that every drop of fuel can be used, that the engine is supplied with a constant flow regardless of the high g-loading the car is subjected to. At Indianapolis, for example, it wouldn't be much fun suffering a misfire from fuel starvation when the car turns right at the banking leading on to the main straight; a misfire caused by the engine's fuel pump pickup having been mounted in the right-hand side of the tank, while all the fuel is gaily swashing around and climbing up the left side of the tank under a 3-g side loading. In fact, we don't want the fuel to be sloshing anywhere, we want its movement contained as far as possible, eighty kilos of fuel sloshing around the tank will significantly affect the car's handling. We're trying to build a prima ballerina here, a car with poise and grace and accuracy, not some great drunken sailor, tanked-up and weaving along the quayside. No, we need to control the fuel, we need to keep it steady, to hold it in place over the fuel pump, ready to be used.

The space inside the fuel tank is filled with a series of internal chambers, each equipped with two, one-way trapdoors. The fuel from the rig rushes into the tank, pouring into the chambers, their trapdoors swinging open allowing the fuel to flow freely. What the fuel doesn't realise, however, is that it's been tricked, has fallen victim to a cunning trap, for once the fuel has entered a lower chamber, the trapdoor swings closed; it can never flow back, there is no escape, the only way is down … a concept somewhat reminiscent of the labyrinthine traps inside an Egyptian pyramid.

The fuel has no option but to drain ever lower, downward and to the centre. Eventually the fuel finds its way inside the middle chamber at the very bottom of the tank. Here sits the Collector, a two-litre carbon fibre container, resting at the heart of the fuel system. It is from the Collector, a painstakingly supplied central reservoir, that the engine-driven, high-pressure mechanical pump draws the fuel that feeds the engine's injection system.

At the start of a race, or immediately following a pit stop, when the fuel tank is full, the Collector's low location within the tank ensures it remains immersed in fuel for some time. 'Some time' is a tad vague, I know, but exactly how long depends on the quantity of fuel in the tank and the rate of its consumption, and this will vary from track to track. With the tank full, keeping the Collector supplied with fuel presents no problem, but to ensure it remains fully charged as the tank's level slowly decreases, the Collector is constantly supplied with fuel by two relatively small, low-pressure electronic pumps. Known as primary pumps, one is mounted in each corner of the lower rear chamber.

These two pumps are capable of delivering more fuel to the Collector than the engine will consume, even during sustained periods at full throttle. They are designed this way so that the Collector should be oversupplied, any surplus fuel from the electronic pumps will merely overflow the Collector and pour back into the main tank, where it will, once again, be picked up by the primaries and again delivered to the Collector. As long as the Collector remains full, this surplus fuel will continue to recycle around the system in this way.

Inevitably, however, as the race progresses, the tank's level will drop as the fuel is consumed by the engine. A point will be reached when there is no surplus of fuel; we are now down to the remaining two litres, the quantity held within the Collector. Now the job of the primary pumps is to scavenge any last dregs of fuel from the main tank and keep feeding it to the Collector. And if the engineers have got their calculations correct, there should be just enough fuel to allow the car to drive back to the pits and be replenished; the second or third stint of the race begins and the whole process starts over.

The car's fuel consumption is carefully monitored by the engineers. There is no in-car fuel gauge, the driver's job is to drive fast and not shunt, he has more than enough to occupy his mind without fretting over an empty tank. There is no fuel level sensor within the tank either; fuel consumption is monitored by a flow-meter housed within the spray-rail. The engineers (should) know precisely how much fuel the car started the race with; so, by subtracting the amount of fuel consumed by the engine from the quantity that was originally in the tank, they can calculate precisely how many laps the car can continue to run without spluttering to a rather undignified stop halfway round the circuit ... well that's the theory.

There's no doubt that the fuel system is reasonably complex. Its masses of pipes and trapdoors, along with its electronic pumps, wiring looms, Collector, mechanical pump, and all the various seals does take a considerable amount of time to install in the chassis – at least a full day, if not two. Access is the biggest problem; working in the fuel tank is like operating through a letter box. Not only is it very tight in there, but the work is usually accompanied by the constant stink of fuel. Not much fun.

Unlike any road car that I'm aware of, the fuel tank inside a Formula 1 car is not a rigid prefabricated structure, made from welding or riveting sheets of steel or aluminium together. Instead the teams use a flexible bladder to store their fuel, known in polite society as a fuel cell, or in pit lane parlance as a bag-tank. The FIA's technical regulations are written in such a way as to require the teams to have these fuel cells manufactured for them by specialist companies; the FIA have a list of officially approved suppliers. In theory, any company wishing to build and supply these tanks can apply to the FIA to have their name added to the list but they are required to meet some pretty formidable standards. Basically, you don't want to get involved unless you are absolutely convinced that you can mix it with the best. The idea behind this stipulation – that the teams must use a bladder, as opposed to, say, a tank fabricated from titanium or aluminium sheet – is that in the event of an accident where the monocoque is damaged, the bladder should deform rather than rupture, preventing fuel leakage. The minimum (safety) design specification for these tanks is governed by the FIA, detailed in their paper: FIA/FT5-1999.

The regulations refer to the tank as 'a single rubber bladder'. In these days of sophisticated composite materials, I can't help thinking that rubber is a somewhat outdated substance. I can imagine the Lotus 25 having rubber tanks but surely not our contemporary state-of-the-art machines? Well, they do – they all do. As quaint as it may seem, it appears as though the space age material that can better the inherent qualities of processed tree sap has yet to be developed. Even synthetic rubbers are but man-made latex copies of the organic version. Rubber is the specified material, and when a heavy weave of Kevlar mesh is coated with rubber the resulting fuel cell is both pliable, exceptionally strong and will, I've heard it said, contain a gunshot at close range, but I've never felt tempted to put that particular claim to the test.

The tanks are manufactured as bespoke items, made by specialist companies to dimensions specified by the team. The maximum capacity of the tank depends on the requirements of an individual team. How thirsty is the engine they are using? How many laps will their tyres last before they are forced to pit? A small tank will help save weight and aid the aerodynamic profiling of the chassis, but it will also compromise the team's pit-stop strategies, forcing them to stop more often to replenish the fuel. Obviously a larger tank will hold more fuel, but the price paid for this is the penalty of extra weight and the limitations on chassis profiling. Compromises ... always compromises.

In most forms of motor sport, certainly in Formula 1, fuel is not discussed in terms of its volume but rather its mass. The same is true of the aeronautics industry: a refuelled aircraft will behave differently, react slower because of the added mass of the extra fuel. In a similar way, a race car will also react differently on 'full tanks' (use of the plural is still commonplace in the pit lane regardless that the contemporary car has only one tank).

Race engineers are concerned with how much difference any on-board fuel makes to their car's weight; the actual volume, the space the fuel occupies inside the tank is largely immaterial. Consequently, fuel is added to, or removed from, the car by kilogramme increments ('Fifty kilos of fuel in Michael's car, please'). As a guide it's safe to assume that a generic, F1 specification racing fuel, tips the scales at 750g per litre, and a generic F1 fuel tank/fuel cell/rubber bladder/bag-tank, call it what you will, holds approximately 100 kilos of fuel. Some are larger, some smaller, but that's a reasonable average.

Housed within the monocoque, the fuel cell sits directly behind the driver and ahead of the engine. And this is the only place that the regulations allow fuel to be housed. The technical regulations require that the fuel-flow and -return lines running between the tank and the engine must be equipped with frangible couplings, basically an *intentional* weak link, designed to 'fail' before the fuel lines themselves are stretched to breaking point. In the event of a shunt big enough to rip the engine from the back of the tub (God forbid!) a section of these couplings will snap off, decoupling the lines and causing a fail-safe ball and spring mechanism to operate, sealing off the flow of fuel.

Furthermore, the regulations do not allow any fuel to be stored ahead of the driver's seatback bulkhead. The aim of these regulations is to ensure the on-board fuel is contained in a single, carefully controlled environment, minimising the risk of leakage or fire as far as is practicable. Contrast these contemporary requirements with those of bygone days: have a look at our photo of Chapman's Lotus 25 in the plate section: the removable cap and pipe-work sitting just ahead of the dashboard was used to fill the two on-board fuel tanks nestling each side of Jimmy Clark's legs. No dry-breaks in those days, of course, and the fuel pipes are sealed with simple hose clips. Just another example of different eras, different priorities.

Installing a bag-tank within the tight confines of the monocoque is one of the most awkward, strenuous, patience-sapping tasks a mechanic has to endure. Without any of the trapdoors, pipes, pumps and associated paraphernalia fitted inside the fuel cell, the access hole to the monocoque's internal chamber is *just* big enough to allow the bladder inside, providing the bag has first been squeezed down and rolled up and secured with straps to prevent it springing back again. The mechanics have to push and shove and curse and sweat as they persuade the tank, inch by inch, through the hole and inside the chamber.

The shape of the bladder perfectly follows the profile of the chassis. Once the mechanics have the bag inside the chamber, they will unstrap it and coax it into place. When installed there isn't an inch to spare, the bladder fills the whole area. There are a number of location studs bonded into the outer wall or skin of the bladder, these (after a lot more coaxing) will eventually align with holes machined through the walls of the monocoque and are used to fix the fuel cell into position.

With the bladder secured, the chassis' access hatch is closed with a strong carbon plate and ring of bolts, helping to replace some of the torsional rigidity lost to the monocoque by virtue of the necessity for the hatch's inclusion in the car's design. Remember, that in an ideal world the designers would prefer not to have any access hatch at all, but seeing how they must allow for the fuel tank's installation, then they want to make the resulting hole as small as possible, ensuring that it compromises the integral strength of the monocoque as little as possible. And this is what makes the fuel system such a painful task for the mechanics. The whole operation from start to finish is a pig of a job; I can think of no better way to describe it.

The monocoque's access hatch to the fuel-cell chamber will be in one of three places. Depending on design preference of a particular team, it will be either inside the cockpit – part of the driver's seatback bulkhead; or underneath the chassis, directly below the chamber; or it will be a part of the rear face of the chassis, forming part of the engine bulkhead. And if it's the latter, then this is one reason why the fuel tank must be installed before we focus our attention towards the engine; with the engine in place there is no way to get to the fuel tank access hatch.

The drive for the injection system's mechanical pump is supplied courtesy of a crankshaft-driven jockey gear housed inside the front cover of the engine (hence the name 'mechanical pump' as opposed to the two electronic primary pumps, powered by the car's battery). Mounted inside the bag-tank, the mechanical pump sits with its input boss protruding through the skin of the tank and flush against the engine bulkhead (the pump is sealed to the bladder with O-rings and a ring of bolts to prevent leaks, of course).

It is imperative not to overlook the mechanical pump when the engine is mated to the chassis. Forgetting to install the small coupling shaft (merely the size of a stubby pencil) between the jockey gear and the pump's drive will result in no fuel pressure – no fuel at all – when time comes to start the engine. I think most teams in the pit lane would hold up their hands and admit to stumbling over that little faux pas at some point. Usually these things happen in the early hours of the morning, after twenty-odd hours at the track, and give rise to another character building exercise when the engine is removed to allow the drive coupling to be connected.

It is possible to engineer substantial gains in horsepower by creative fuel chemistry. Back in the early 1980s, at the outbreak of the turbo era, Renault designed a water injection system for their engines. The original thinking was that supplementing an atomised mist of water to the incoming fuel/air mixture charge would help to reduce temperatures within the cylinders, helping to control excessive heat build-up, aiding both combustion stability and engine reliability. The new system worked, just as the engineers had expected, but the water injection did something else, too, it increased the power performance of the engine.

It appeared that the finely atomised water spray was somehow acting as a combustion stimulant. I've never heard a scientific reason for why this happened, but perhaps – and this is merely guesswork – the pressure and heat of the burning fuel/air inside the cylinders enabled a percentage of the oxygen held within the water molecules to be released and contribute to the combustion process. Whatever the reason, water injection certainly made a difference to horsepower production and it wasn't long before Ferrari, in partnership with Agip, were developing their own system.

This new-found horsepower seemed an inspiration to the fuel chemists and they soon began to experiment with different fuel mixes and exotic distillations. Although these concoctions were relatively simple at first – a modest percentage of commercially available aviation gas (Avgas) blended with forecourt automotive fuel – they soon became far more complex. After all why stop at Avgas? Sure, in the quest for power, an aircraft is an extremely powerful beast, no doubt about that, but there must be something else, something even more exciting? How about rockets? Now, rockets really do pack a punch! Okay, you don't get much of a bang for your buck, but invest enough bucks and you get a really very impressive bang indeed. It was time to call in those favours from the chaps down at NASA. By the mid-1980s the only fuel to have in your Formula 1 race car was a subtle blend of 80 per cent toluene rocket fuel, delicately diluted (presumably at arm's length) with 20 per cent 'regular petrol'; this is a mix of pump fuel boosted with whatever other chemical ingredients were required in order to get the whole simmering brew to comply with the technical regulations and declared legal by the FIA.

By the time I arrived on the Grand Prix scene, in February of 1990, the FIA had already acted to outlaw these outrageous mixes and the heady (surreal?) days of 'rocket fuel' were over. Nevertheless, there was still sizeable room for manoeuvre within the scope of the regulations and considerable power gains were still being obtained courtesy of the men and women at the fuel labs. When I say considerable, I'm talking in the region of 30–50 horsepower.

During one testing session late on in that year, held at the Estoril circuit in Portugal, reports filtered back to the Benetton factory in Witney that merely by introducing a new fuel to the Cosworth V8, Nelson Piquet had shaved 0.6 seconds from his lap time, and increased his straight line speed past the pits by 6.0 kph. Piquet was amazed at the performance gain, as we were all. I was reasonably new to things back then, young and enthusiastic, and I remember being so excited by our new-found horsepower that I made a point of jotting those figures in my notebook. Talking to a senior engineer from Cosworth some years later, I mentioned this story to him and asked if he could remember it; he had actually been present at that very test, I hadn't. He said he could remember it only too well, and confirmed the numbers: point-six improvement in lap time, six clicks faster past the pits. He also added that the fuel had shown a forty-horsepower advantage during dyno-testing.

The fuels of the early 1990s used to stink – something awful. Not just the Benetton pits, but everyone's garages used to smell frightful whenever the fuel churns were being filled or emptied. Ferrari's garages were particularly bad as I recall. At that time Benetton used to have the garage adjacent Ferrari's, and I remember an occasion when one of their mechanics knocked over a drum of fuel, the stuff sloshing under the dividing wall (at that time merely a wire grid-work strung with the teams' banners). There were cries and apologies from the other side of the banners and both crews of mechanics set about mopping up the fuel as quickly as possible. Clearly it's never a good thing to have racing fuel washing around the pits. But it proved impossible to work near the fuel for more than a few seconds at a time, the evaporating vapours were so thick and heavy, I could taste the clammy chemicals at the back of my throat, my eyes were streaming and I could feel my head pounding in complaint. Terrible. It might not have been the height of the fuel madness era but they were still pretty crazy, heady days, and I was more than happy to see the back of that particular period of the sport's history.

These days, however, the FIA is *exceedingly* strict with regard to the actual compound make-up of its Formula 1 fuel: what is allowed, but more importantly, what isn't. These are enlightened times and, as I understand it, the FIA's current policy is to encourage the use of ecologically friendly, very low emission fuels. They want the fuel used by racing cars to be the same specification to that which you and I can buy at the local filling station. Thus, the governing body of this seemingly decadent sport are seen to be promoting the idea that the chemists working on racing fuels are helping to produce the best, the most advanced green fuels for everyone – more country meadows and swooping swallows, less thunderous launch sites, scorched earth and flames. We all win ... well, nice thought, I guess.

The basic premise behind the contemporary fuel regulations is that today's Grand Prix engines must only use unleaded, minimal sulphur 'pump petrol'. Once again, however, we mustn't forget that this is F1 and the regulations will always be exploited to the maximum. In terms of specifics the word 'petrol' is pretty meaningless, perhaps even more vague in definition than 'food' or 'music'. There are literally hundreds of individual chemical elements blended together to form an automotive petrol; in a fuel made exclusively for motor sports most of the elements are purely aids to an increase in engine power, of course, though others are included to help lubricate valve stems, lower combustion temperatures and prevent pre-ignition.

As a consequence of the multitude of ingredients available to the chemists, there is an entire section of the technical regulations devoted to the meticulous clarification of the fuel; the exact wording governing precisely what constitutes a permissible 'petrol' is wonderfully long-winded and studying them at length is sure to provide a wonderful cure for insomnia. They'll tell you, for example, that the definition of a Naphthene is a 'monocyclic paraffin (with five or more atoms in the ring) and saturated aliphatic side chains'; or that Aromatics are 'monocyclic and bicyclic aromatic rings with and without saturated aliphatic side chains and/or fused naphthenic rings'.

The regulations go on to say that, 'The total concentration of each type of hydrocarbon group in the total fuel sample (defined by carbon number and hydrocarbon type), must not exceed the limits given in the table below ...' Believe me, if you're planning on driving the kids to school, or operating heavy machinery, you don't want to be reading 'the table below'. And there's much more of that sort of stuff, too. That the chemists are fascinated by it is sufficient for me, and I'm thrilled if you wish to investigate it all in much more detail, but, for the sake of the rest of us, go get your own copy of the regulations – they're freely available to download from the FIA website. You won't find any further extracts of them here, at least not the ones concerning fuel composition.

The fuel used in Formula 1 is not distilled by a sole supplier (which would certainly be the easiest way to ensure compliancy with the stringent regulations), the teams are free to sign technical partnerships with any petrochemical company they wish. Big names such as Shell, Castrol, Mobil, Elf, and Agip have long been involved with Formula 1. It's wonderful advertising for a fuel company to be associated with a winning team, which, of course, is the reason why they're prepared to take on such a costly exercise.

You might be surprised to learn that irrespective of the current repressive regulations governing their science, the fuel chemists of today expend more effort in developing and blending their fuels than ever they did ten, even twenty years ago. The research and effort is greater but the spoils are significantly less, throughout the course of a racing season the net gain in power from fuel development is between 2–5bhp. Those figures were given to me by an engineer at Cosworth, but I have heard that back in 2001, Honda's engineers apparently unearthed a further ten horsepower from fuel refinement. The question this raises, however, is how comparative were the companies' different fuels to begin with; did Honda's 'new brew' merely lift them to the same rung of the fuel-development ladder that Cosworth had already attained? I suspect we'll never know. I seriously doubt either company would be willing to swap fuels, dyno-test their engines and publish the results purely to satisfy *our* curiosity. In Formula 1, there are always more questions than answers, aren't there! Personally, I think this is a good thing, it's what keeps everyone motivated, on their toes … keeps the sport alive.

The regulations are stringent but the chemists are encouraged to push ahead with their research. Throughout the season, the teams are free to develop as many different fuels as they deem necessary, and are at liberty to introduce them at any point during the season, providing the fuel has first been approved by the FIA. Prior to the first race of every season, the teams must donate a sample of any fuel they are intending to use in their cars. The FIA have the samples checked by a chemical laboratory to verify that the fuel conforms with the regulations; when the fuel is approved its 'fingerprint' (the fuel's precise chemical composition) is recorded and held on file by the FIA.

At any time during the race weekend the FIA's technical delegate reserves the right to take from any competing car a spot-check fuel sample for analysis (actually, two one-litre samples are taken). The lid of one sample can is lead-sealed by the FIA and given back to the team, in case of any later disputes over the legality of the fuel, and the other is carried off for inspection. This check is carried out at the track – there and then – using a gas chromatographer, which although sounding a bit like something out of a *Doctor Who* adventure is actually a real machine that separates and identifies the fuel's individual elements.

If the fingerprint of the fuel taken from the car matches the fingerprint of the original sample given to and approved by the FIA, then all is well. If not, then the team can expect all sorts of frightful penalties, not the least of which could be exclusion from the event and/or the race results. Furthermore, should the fingerprint of the fuel taken from the car during a spot-check not match any of the team's previously approved samples, it makes little difference to the FIA that the fuel complies in every respect with the technical regulations concerning its composition. It may well be perfectly legit but if it's not been pre-approved by the FIA, then the team are at fault, and accordingly will have to suffer the consequences.

The rules are the rules are the rules.

Tough crowd, the FIA. Nevertheless, providing the exact wording of the rules is interpreted fairly and any subsequent penalties are just and without prejudice, then I don't think we have reason for complaint.

As a note to finish this talk about fuel and the car's fuel system, it might be useful to have a look at the per-lap fuel consumption of a Grand Prix car. The rate in which the fuel is depleted from the tank depends on several factors, primarily: the length of a particular track; the full-throttle demands of that track; and the prevailing weather at the time (rain will significantly reduce fuel consumption by virtue of the reduced speeds). As a rough guide, in dry, sunny conditions, Monaco produces the lowest fuel consumption, approximately 1.8 kilos per lap; while Spa produces the highest, in the region of 3.8 kilos per lap.

Earlier on I mentioned that the pit lane refuelling rig delivers its charge at 12 litres per second. The engineers will interpret that figure as 9.0 kilos of fuel per second, sufficient to allow their car to circulate for between 2.5 and 5 laps depending on track and pre-vailing conditions. Below is a simple chart which gives a cross-reference between delivery time, weight of the replenished fuel, and the number of laps the car should cover as a result of the pit stop. Again, the indicated one, two, or three stop strategies are but a rough guide.

Seconds of fuel delivery	Weight (kilos)	Sufficient for number of laps
4	36	12
5	**45**	**15 (three stop strategy)**
6	54	18
7	**63**	**21 (two stop)**
8	72	24
9	81	27
10	90	30
11	**99**	**33 (one stop)**
12	108	36 (full tank)

It's worth remembering, too, that just like driving in the rain, any laps driven behind the Safety Car will also reduce a car's fuel consumption, by as much as 30 per cent per lap; allowing the engineers the chance to recalculate and extend their pit stop windows by one lap for every three in which the Safety Car remains in use.

As to which fuel company we'll use, I think it's all pretty much of a muchness, to be perfectly honest. From what I've seen, all the big petrochemical companies are more than capable of producing the quality of fuel we need to stay on terms with the leading teams. Every oil company has its share of gifted fuel chemists, and, as we touched on a little earlier, it will prove exceedingly difficult – I hesitate in saying impossible – to get any worthwhile comparison between the different products on offer. More than anything, the link-ups between individual Formula 1 constructors and their fuel/lubricant suppliers seems to be primarily based on the needs of sponsorship or long-standing commercial partnerships in the road car industry.

'Goodness!' exclaimed Carl Hentschel, looking from me to his two friends, his eyes wide.

'Bet you had no idea there was so much to a fuel tank, eh, Carl?' Wingrave chuckled. 'Amazing. I'd always assumed a Grand Prix car's petrol tank was just a carbon box or something. Never occurred to me it was a big rubber balloon!'

'Me neither,' said Paul Kelver. Then, leaning towards me conspiratorially, he said, 'I've got a Ferrari at home, nothing posh mind, had it for years, a 308. Nice little car, actually – on carburettors, not fuel injection. Anyway, I had a leak from the petrol tank, the one on the right – it's got two, one each side – and I thought I'd have a go at getting it out myself. Talk about a nightmare! Wheels off, fibreglass wheel arch panel out – snapped every bolt getting it out – all seized. Bloody air con' pump perfectly in the way, I mean *perfectly* in the way ... hands cut ... drenched in petrol; and my neighbour watching over the fence, giving free advice. Gave up in the end, wish I'd never started the bloody job; ended up calling the garage, cost me a fortune. Nightmare, total bloody nightmare!'

Carl looked at Paul, quizzically. 'Fascinating, old man, I'm sure, and we all feel sorry for you; truly we do, but your point is ...?'

Wingrave chuckled again, 'Leave him alone Carl ... he's bonding!'

'Bonding? Well, let him do something useful. Why not go and bond with the bar; my glass is empty, so is Steve's – yours too, Wingrave, we're all empty.'

'Paul, off you trot, there's a good fellow,' said Wingrave, 'and see if you can find out what's happening about this damn plane – we're going to be all night at this rate.'

Paul sighed, rolled his eyes and without further word set off, albeit a little unsteadily. His two friends chuckled good-naturedly as he went.

'Right,' said Carl. 'Let's get on and decide which engine we're going to use in our dream team car before Paul gets back. Engines are his big thing, you see, the last thing we need is Kelver waffling on about how he tried to replace the camshaft belts on that bloody awful 308 of his. How he spent a week adjusting the tappets, how sweet it *would* have run if he hadn't made such a hash of it all and had to call Bob What's-his-name in to sort it all out.'

George Wingrave turned in his chair, looking back towards the door of the lounge. Paul Kelver, four empty tumblers in hand, was deep in conversation with the girl on duty at the reception desk. 'One minute, chaps,' said Wingrave hauling himself up. 'I'll be right back, don't carry on without me ... all this ice we've been drinking, I need to ... won't be more than a minute.'

I didn't think it was entirely the fault of the ice but I also felt the need to 'not be more than a minute' and I padded off after Wingrave, who, I noticed, walked with just the hint of a limp.

The facilities in the Air France lounge are like those I'd expect to find in a private health club – all marble tiles and gold taps. There are showers, bathrobes and masses of plump towels, too. George seemed equally impressed, as we ambled back he said he was going to take some photographs of the place and get some interior decorators to refurbish his bathroom in the same style, but with just the one loo, not six.

We sat down again and Carl told us he had 'some good news and some not quite so good news'. The good news was that a table at the side of the bar had been laid with a selection of bread and cheeses, fruit and cold meats. The bad news – well, in light of the arrival of the buffet, the bad news came as no surprise – the 747 that was to become our transport to Paris had circled over New York for thirty minutes, was unable to land and had flown away again. Flight AF009 was cancelled. With a single word Wingrave summed up things perfectly: 'Bugger!'

Carl added that the assistant at the reception desk had asked that we remain in the lounge, help ourselves to something to eat and that she was 'looking into' what Air France could do for us. True enough, the girl that Paul Kelver was talking with had been joined by three female colleagues, two of whom I hadn't seen before, the third I recognised from the check-in desk. I couldn't tell if her pet spider was still in residence. Two of them gazed intently into a computer screen, a bluish glow shading their faces, the only sound a curiously reassuring clicking of nails catching plastic as a keyboard was worked with efficient speed.

5

Suck – Squeeze – Bang – Blow

'The power output of an engine [equals] the size of the
bangs, times the number of bangs per minute that you can
manage to get.'
Keith Duckworth – Cosworth Engineering

The power plant; the motor; the mill; the lump; the gear-bag spacer. There are a multitude of names for the engine, ranging from the most complimentary to the most derisory. The chosen tag largely depends on whether one builds the chassis or the engine. Naturally, the engine manufacturers believe their creation to be the most important part of the car: 'What chance does our engine have of winning races when it's got to push that clonking brick-like monstrosity along?' Naturally, the chassis constructors believe exactly the same of their own work: 'Our car could have won that race if that stinking lump of yours hadn't grenaded itself on the last lap . . . again!'

Such playful exchanges are usually out of public earshot, of course, and when chassis/engine partnerships are winning races, then it's an entirely different matter. When things are going well, then it's all sweetness and light and pass the champagne.

Horsepower, reliability and talent behind the wheel: three essentials if a team is to stand any chance of winning races. Ask any engineer in the pit lane what he would like to have more of and he will likely say, more power from the engine; more grip from the tyres; and more money for himself – though not necessarily in that order. Ask him off the record and he might add a 'technically more savvy driver' to his wants list, too.

Any gain in engine power is worth its weight in gold. A fifty-horsepower advantage over the competition will help to mask many shortfalls in the chassis; the car is able to run more wing (helping its cornering stability), while relying on the extra grunt to overcome the additional drag and keep its straight line speed comparable to the opposition.

Here's a classic example to highlight the need for power and talent. The 1988 McLaren MP4-4 chassis was no particular masterpiece of innovative design; carbon monocoque, yes, but the opposition had now caught up with this earlier advantage. Attached to the back of the chassis was the mighty, 950bhp turbocharged 1.5 litre V6 Honda RA168E, arguably *the* power plant to have at the time. It may not have been the most sophisticated car but it was very powerful, consequently they could afford to run whopping wings, and that made it very stable. And – the icing on the cake – the car proved reliable, *extremely* so. And driving this engine/chassis combination round the circuits were two of the sport's most gifted talents of all time: Ayrton Senna and Alain Prost.

Huge power, wonderful reliability, brilliant skill behind the wheel. Result: fifteen victories from sixteen races. Almost the perfect season but not quite … something which to this day has never been achieved, perhaps never will be. Ferrari came close in 2002, managing to equal McLaren's record of fifteen wins in one year, but 2002 was a seventeen-race season, so I guess Ron Dennis can still hold his head high.

The only race the McLaren-Honda MP4-4 failed to win in 1988 was the Italian Grand Prix, held in the north at Monza, the cathedral of Italian motor racing. And the events that transpired at that race proved pretty bizarre, too: Off bolt the two McLarens, with everything looking like business as usual. Then Alain Prost retires with engine failure (it was destined to be Honda's only race failure all year). With just two laps remaining, Ayrton gets into an altercation with a backmarker – his car clipping wheels with Jean-Louis Schlesser's Williams – resulting in the McLaren becoming beached on the kerbing at the side of the track. Quite understandably, the young Brazilian superstar-in-the-making looks totally bewildered by these happenings – his team seemed a tad nonplussed too. Falling out of the race in such an ungainly fashion had not been part of Ron Dennis's pre-race briefing.

With both McLarens out of the frame, the way is clear for Ferrari to score a one-two victory on home turf. Not only that, but this unbelievable victory fell into the team's lap mere days after the death of the team's legendary founder, the great Enzo Ferrari himself. There are many great stories associated with Grand Prix racing but this is my all time favourite; I hope you'll indulge me if you've heard me talk of it before.

Turbocharging is now a banned practice, McLaren-Honda's nearly perfect season of 1988 was the end of the era. Everyone was having too much fun; the FIA decreed the cars were going way too fast, too much grunt available for insufficient grip. Something had to be done to control the speeds, and the turbo was banished. Since the start of 1989 the engineers have been forced to design their engines using 'normal aspiration' induction systems.

In basic terms, a turbo is an air pump, boosting the engine's induction system with a pressurised supply of air. More air equals more fuel/air mixture in the cylinders, which in turn will generate more power. Remember, Honda's turbo-charged engine that we mentioned earlier on, that minute 1.5 litre V6, was producing in the region of 900–950bhp in race trim. The turbo era will be remembered as a very special time – certainly it was. There are many reports suggesting that the power output of the top qualifying engines soared as high as 1300bhp. Breathtaking!

If you're new to the principle of turbos, here's an illustration to show you the difference between normal aspiration and turbo-charging: Sit back, relax, take a deep breath. As you breathe in, your lungs are filled with air under atmospheric pressure, at sea level this is 14.7 psi, or 1 Bar, in new money. And this is the pressure that a non-turbo engine breathes at: the piston descends inside the cylinder and the incoming mixture is pushed into the cylinder under atmospheric pressure, in exactly the same way that air is pushed into your lungs. Normally we refer to this process as 'sucking', but the reality is that 'suck' doesn't really exist; it's a word that frequently upsets college lecturers, makes them go all shaky. They'll tell you that we don't *suck* air into our lungs, rather we create a vacuum, courtesy of our diaphragm, and that atmospheric pressure forces air inside our lungs to fill the void we've made. But that's lecturers for you.

Turbocharging, on the other hand, is similar to breathing from a pressurised bottle. (By the way, don't try this at home kids because it would be both very dangerous and very, *very* stupid.) The turbocharger pumps air into the engine at two, three, four times atmospheric pressure; consequently, the air/fuel charge inside the cylinder is greatly increased and the potential power output from the resulting combustion is also greatly increased. Originally, turbos were an aid to the aviation industry, helping piston-powered aircraft to maintain manifold pressure the higher they climbed through the skies (there being less air at higher altitudes, and all that).

In the world of Formula 1 it was Renault Sport, back in the late 1970s, who were the first to experiment with turbos. For the race engineers, turbocharging was like a present from the gods, a gift of seemingly limitless power. Driven by waste exhaust gases, the faster the engine worked, the faster the turbo worked; the faster the turbo worked, the more power it produced; more and more power, on and on until . . . ka-blammo! Massive, cataclysmic engine failure. It may have seemed like a gift but there were many technical challenges to overcome before the benefits could be fully enjoyed; the secret was being able to keep the multitude of parts within the engine dancing in harmony for the duration of the Grand Prix.

The extra supply of fuel/air mixture resulted in more power but it also resulted in increased stress and strain within the engine too. And as the drive turbine of the turbocharger was powered by exhaust gases, it stands to reason that heat build-up within the unit was also extreme. Not only did this create problems with regard to effective lubrication of the internal shaft, linking the exhaust turbine and the intake impeller, but it also resulted in the undesirable heating of the air supply to the engine. The ideal is to keep the airflow as cool as possible (air is more dense at lower temperatures, hence there is more oxygen per unit of volume, and more oxygen equals more power). Those problems notwithstanding, perhaps the biggest hurdle for the race engineers to overcome was that of the dreaded 'throttle lag'.

As a consequence of the turbo being driven by exhaust gases (with no physical drive linkage to the engine), the rotational speed of the turbine/impeller shaft will begin to lose velocity the moment the driver lifts off the throttle, effectively removing the extra boost pressure. That's no problem during 'closed throttle' conditions, where no power is desired; but the slowing turbine becomes a big problem when the driver again demands full throttle. He stamps on the pedal, the throttle opens but the turbo has to regain its lost momentum before the boost pressure becomes fully effective. And the period of time between the driver hitting the throttle pedal and the turbo resuming boost pressure is called throttle lag. The effects of throttle lag on a racing engine can be extreme, felt as a sudden brutal *snap!* of power as the boost pressure cuts in, not nice for the drivers, especially at the start of a race.

I remember chatting with Michele Alboreto, back in early 1994, while I was making a seat for him at the Benetton factory. He was explaining how his turbo-era Ferrari used to sit on the grid at the start of the race, apparently going nowhere, when all of a sudden ... BANG! The car shot away as though someone had just lit the touchpaper of a solid rocket booster. 'Several times,' he said, 'the car simply turned a sharp left or right, it was impossible to hold on to it!' He made it sound absolutely frightening, but Michele was laughing about it, his eyes bright at the memory of it all. He was an interesting chap to talk with; intelligent and technically gifted as well as a competent driver – a rare breed, they don't come along very often.

Sad to say, Michele was killed in April, 2001. He suffered a terrible accident while testing the Audi R8 sports car at the Lausitzring circuit, near Dresden. He was forty-four. It was Mario Andretti who summed up such awful tragedy so succinctly when, on hearing of the death of his team-mate Ronnie Peterson, back in 1978, said: 'Unfortunately, motor racing is also this.' Six words that speak volumes.

All I can add is that I feel honoured to have had the opportunity to meet Michele, to have chatted with him, one on one. I shall cherish the memory of that day for ever. He was a good man, a gentle man. I treasure the book on Ferrari turbos he autographed for me too; it sits on a shelf amid my most valued mementoes.

As to the hassles of throttle lag – clearly a problem for Alboreto's Ferrari as well as the rest of the turbocharged cars – well, although the symptoms were reduced as research progressed, the engineers never did cure it completely. Perhaps the most productive idea was to fit two smaller turbos, one feeding each bank of cylinders, as opposed to one large turbo supplying the lot. This reduced the mass of the internal components and allowed the turbine/ impeller to accelerate quicker on initial throttle opening. But two small turbos weighed more than one big turbo, and now the designers had to house two units instead of one ... problems, problems.

Nevertheless, for the guys designing, building and bench-testing these engines it must have felt as though every day was Christmas. Very exciting work! ('Yes, dear, the dyno run is nearly over, you can put the dinner on, I'll be home in twenty minutes.' Ka-blammo! 'Er ... better make that three days ... hope the dog enjoys my chops and gravy. Oh ... and remember me to the kids.')

Fifteen years later, the sport's leading normally aspirated 3.0 litre engines are now nudging the 900bhp mark. Fifteen years of continual development to get back to where we once were. No question, fifteen years is a lifetime in terms of Formula 1 research and development programmes, but the fact that the engine manufacturers have managed to create engines – *reliable* engines – with a power output approaching those heady days of the mid-eighties is great testament to their skill and dedication. Sure, they're still well shy of the 1300bhp mark (I can't ever see that gap being

breached), but they are fast closing in on the race day power output
of the McLaren-Honda MP4-4.

Everyone wants more power; the engine manufacturers are always
working to improve the output of their engines, trying to squeeze
any last drops of energy from their designs; the most productive
method of gaining power is to increase the speed at which the
engine works, make it rev quicker.

As a rule of thumb, over the last couple of decades F1 engine
revs have increased at the rate of approximately 500 per year.
Contemporary engines are fast approaching 20,000rpm. Whether
or not that figure can be reached (and surpassed) will largely depend
on the FIA, I suspect. If the current technical regulations concerning engines remain in place then we're looking good, if not –
and it's looking increasingly like they won't – then I think we've
got a long wait on our hands.

Apparently, the FIA are keen on the idea of amending the regulations to force the teams to use just one engine per car throughout
the entire race weekend. The only way for the manufacturers to
comply with this would be to make their engines more robust –
less stressed, less powerful, more reliable. Not only that, there have
also been suggestions that this 'one engine per weekend' rule could
be expanded to become a 'one engine per six races' rule. Renault's
reaction to that particular proposal was very straightforward: If that
happens, we're off.

More work in less time equals increased output, the rules of any
efficient business. And an efficient engine works on the exact same
basis. The problem is that regardless of what speed the engine is
revving, for every two revolutions of its crankshaft, the engine still
has to induct, compress, burn, and exhaust its charge of fuel/air
mixture. Every advance in engine speed results in less time for the
necessary suck-squeeze-bang-blow chain of events to take place.
When running flat out, there are over 95,000 combustion events
occurring each minute within the cylinders of a current V10. More
than 1500 'bangs' every second.

Simply by lightening all the internal components to the absolute minimum, increasing bearing tolerances, leaning off the fuel mixture and greatly advancing the ignition timing, the engine manufacturers could easily increase their horsepower production. Built like this an engine would go like a bat out of hell. The only drawback is that it would go like a bat out of hell for approximately ten seconds, after which it would swiftly metamorphose into a scale model of an exploding star. Fun to observe, no doubt, but not much use in our quest for Grand Prix laurels.

And here lies the crux of the matter: any gain in power at the expense of unpredictable reliability is utterly pointless. The age-old racing adage 'To finish first, first you have to finish', remains as relevant today as always. The engineers do throw a certain amount of caution to the wind when building short-life qualifying engines, but even these highly strung units have to remain reliable for at least a few minutes. A blisteringly quick 'out-lap' followed by nine-tenths of a timed-lap is worth nothing; the car has to cross the timing line in order to qualify for the race.

In trying to extract more power, one of the biggest problems is that the basic design of a piston engine is inherently flawed. It sounds odd to suggest this but a piston engine will always be a relatively inefficient machine. The net requirement of an engine is to supply power to the gearbox, to drive the transmission's input shaft. This is achieved by coupling the crankshaft to the transmission's input shaft via a clutch assembly.

In order to get the crankshaft to rotate we use a series of connecting rods and pistons which go up and down in straight lines: reciprocal motion. This means accelerating the mass of a piston towards the top of its cylinder, then slowing it again until it comes to a complete stop. Next, we totally change the piston's direction of travel and accelerate it downwards, stop it at the bottom, change its direction ... and so on. Kind of like a boxer working out against a punchbag, when what we actually want is for his arms to spin in circles. The ideal solution would be to have everything rotating inside the engine, without any of that nonsensical reciprocal motion slowing things up and causing all kinds of unwanted vibrations.

Indeed, such an engine already exists; designed several decades ago by Dr Felix Wankel. The Wankel rotary engine is perhaps best known for powering some of Mazda's road cars, the RX7, for example. Wankel's engine contains neither pistons or con-rods, valves or camshafts. Instead it uses a three-sided rotor, each side of which forms a separate combustion chamber; the path of the rotor following a slightly eccentric path around a geared output shaft. Every moving part is travelling in the same direction as the fly-wheel, exactly what we want; consequently, power loss is kept to an absolute minimum.

Nothing's perfect, of course – people or machines – and, historically, the downside to the rotary engine has always been its relatively poor fuel consumption. Nevertheless, it is an extremely compact, very well-balanced unit. I think if a mere 10 per cent of the money that has been spent over the years in improving the flaws of the piston engine had been invested in developing the rotary engine, then the piston engine would be as long dead as the steam engine.

So, why don't the Grand Prix engine manufacturers scrap their antiquated piston engines and design their own rotary designs – or even more exciting, why don't they pin a new piece of paper to the drawing board and develop something completely new, something to take engine design into the twenty-first century? After all, the wheezing old piston engine has been with us for more than a hundred years, surely there must be other more ingenious alternatives? As a kid growing up in the 1970s, amid the oil crisis of the time, I recall hearing stories at school of people that had invented revolutionary power plants: light, incredibly fuel-efficient units 'no bigger than a cornflakes packet'. Remember those? Whatever happened to them? Rumour at the time suggested that the patents for any such engines had been 'procured' by the 'oil companies' and the blueprints had been secretly stashed ... can that really have happened?

Regardless of any personal desire to see some new engineering marvel take the world by storm, I guess the questions I've just posed are purely rhetorical. There are perhaps a thousand reasons why the piston engine remains the master of the automotive universe; primarily, though, it's because the thing is such a well-understood quantity. The road car industry has invested billions of dollars in it, they have refined and honed the piston engine to the point where it has become both fuel efficient and cheap to produce; is smooth, quiet and reliable in service, and equipping one with a turbo will supply more than ample power to satisfy the needs of any exotic sports car.

And the reason why we're not going to see any revolutionary engine designs bursting on to the Formula 1 scene is very simple: Article 5.1.1 of the F1 technical regulations states: 'Only four-stroke engines with reciprocating pistons are permitted.' That one small sentence lays waste to all of Dr Wankel's work, right there. Chop. Gone!

The regulations go on to say that the engine's capacity must not exceed three litres and that it *must* have ten cylinders. The regulations also state that the maximum number of valves per cylinder is limited to five – and although some teams once did use this many, I'm reasonably certain that no one actually bothers to use a five-valve system any longer. Everyone has arrived at the same conclusion: four valves – two inlets and two exhausts – is perfectly adequate. The small gain in fuel flow offered by using a fifth (inlet) valve per cylinder simply isn't worth the extra hassle of having to incorporate an additional ten valves into the engine. They are, after all, an extra ten components that have the possibility of failing, of killing the engine in a millisecond of malfunction.

Supercharging of the engine is also banned (this general engineering term also includes the use of turbos) which we've already discussed. There are several differences between a supercharger and a turbo but their basic principle of operation remains the same, namely, supplying a boosted flow of air to the induction manifold. In order to remain focused on F1, however, I propose we leave it at that but I'm sure you would find it interesting to pursue the subject of superchargers via another source. Have a look through some drag-racing books and you'll see what I mean; better still go to a drag race itself. Even if you're not an enthusiast of straight-line racing, I guarantee you'll be amazed by the sights, smells and sheer brute power of the engineering. Actually, it's always been a desire of mine to help strip and rebuild a top-fuel engine, then to see it fire up and blast down the raceway, it must be quite a thrill. One day ... maybe.

The rule stating that the engine must have ten cylinders only entered the technical regulations from 2000. Until then it had been possible to run any number of cylinders up to a maximum of twelve, and prior to that ruling there had been a vast array of different designs with any number of cylinders. For compactness of design, however, the 'vee' engine has always been the most popular choice. Arranging the cylinders in two offset banks allows for twice the number of pistons to be connected to a crankshaft that is only marginally longer than that of a 'straight' inline engine; for example a V12 is but slightly longer than a straight 6.

When one hears mention of a 75° vee engine, or 90°, or 110°, or any other figure for that matter, it refers to the angle, or degrees of offset between the two banks of cylinders. The bigger the angle – up to 180° – the wider apart the cylinders are. Should your appreciation of trigonometry be as pedestrian as mine, you might find it useful to rummage around in that drawerful of things you've never quite been able to throw away and dig out your old school protractor; it will certainly help you to visualise these angles. I bet you always knew that scratched and faded plastic semi-circle would come in useful again one day – well, today's the day. If, however, you haven't got a protractor because, just like mine, it was nicked out of your satchel by Dez Scoggins, back in the mid-seventies, then it might help to look at the hands of a watch. Ninety degrees is a right angle, and would look like three o'clock on a watch face; 180° is double that, so the hands of the watch would read nine-fifteen. A few simple sums and playing around with the hands-adjuster will show any angle you choose.

The ultimate offset of 180° is effectively a straight line: the two cylinder banks sitting geometrically opposite each other. Increasing the angle beyond 180° merely results in the cylinder banks beginning to move closer again (we just have to turn the engine upside down). In this 180° configuration there is no vee angle, of course, the two arms of the V are perfectly level and the engine is now called a 'flat' engine. Occasionally one might hear this configuration referred to as a 'boxer' engine.

Keeping the engine's crankshaft as short as possible has always been desirable, not merely for packaging and weight saving, although these are certainly major considerations, but also because a shorter crank is less susceptible to flex and the horrors of wind up, where one end of the shaft twists relative to the other (remember the example of our twisting baguette when we discussed the torsional rigidity of the chassis?). This is a similar deal and it's not good, as this will alter the delicate synchronisation between the piston and valves; disrupt ignition timing; and lead to all sorts of vibrations and general running problems.

Over the years, attempts to increase the number of cylinders without suffering the potential penalties of increased crank length have resulted in some ingenious, some quite surreal configurations. Back in the 1960s, BRM produced an amazing-looking H16 motor, little more than a V8 in length. Its curious design was basically two flat-eight units, one bolted atop the other, its two – yep, two – crankshafts connected by steel gears. It may have been something of an oddball but it did manage to win a race – just the one – the H16 powering Jimmy Clark's Lotus 43 to victory in the 1966 US GP. BRM scrapped the idea at the end of the following year, concentrating their efforts on a rather more conventional V12 unit.

A quarter of a century later and some engine builders were still at it, still fighting the tide of convention: desperate to keep both crankshaft and block length to a minimum, yet still allow for an increased number of cylinders. They wanted to build something radical, something that might eventually put the vee engine out of business. In 1990, a company called Life Racing Engines produced a W12, a frankly bizarre looking (and, as I recall, bizarre sounding) engine that – as the letter designation would suggest – was something akin to a V8 but with an additional four cylinders aligned between the two banks.

It was the heady days of pre-qualifying, a time when the sport had far more cars than there were available slots on the starting grid. The junior teams had to battle it out in their own Friday morning qualifying session merely to gain entry into the qualifying sessions for the actual race itself. The Life team fielded just one car, called a Life 190, driven by Bruno Giacomelli. I wanted them to succeed, too, I genuinely did; at least to make it through pre-qualifying. Well, to be perfectly honest, I really wanted to see that W12 take the start of a race, I had no personal attachment to the team itself. Sadly, though, it wasn't to be, I think Giacomelli was the last name on the time sheets each and every time the car took to the track. Oh, well, back to the drawing board. And the more one looks at the drawing board the more the idea of a vee engine makes the most logical sense.

While it's true that the regulations insist the teams must only use ten-cylinder engines, this rule was only introduced after every team participating in the sport at that time was already using a V10 engine; effectively, therefore, the new regulation was a way of freezing the level of technology. A year or so beforehand, by a natural process of evolution, research, and trial and error, all the engine builders had arrived at the same conclusion, that the optimum number of cylinders for a 3.0 litre normally aspirated engine should be ten.

Throughout much of the sport's history Ferrari had stayed loyal to their belief in the mighty twelve-cylinder engine, be it either a boxer or a vee; indeed the idea of the world famous Italian Scuderia using anything else seemed almost unnatural. Cosworth Engineering, on the other hand, the company responsible for Ford's Grand Prix racing engines, were seemingly always wedded to the idea of a V8; again, to use anything else just didn't seem ... well, *right* somehow.

When comparing Ferrari's V12 and Cosworth's V8, both configurations have advantages and disadvantages. A V12 produces good horsepower, but is not so tractable at lower revs; a V8's selling points are the other way around, producing less horsepower but more torque. The V12 is slightly longer; the V8 slightly bulkier. Two schools of thought.

Torque, by the way, is the term used to describe an engine's pulling power, its sheer grunt. (If one was to equate this to the attributes of athletes: a weightlifter or shot-putter has masses of torque, a sprinter has the horsepower.) Naturally, in our racing engine the ideal is to have lots of both. Torque allows the car to *pull* itself uphill and *drive* itself out of slow corners. And the engine's horsepower is the speed at which the car can work, not particularly its revs – though the two are certainly connected – but horsepower is the *pace* of the engine. These two properties, torque and horsepower, are inexorably linked and I know are always difficult to differentiate between. So here's another little analogy which might help: torque is the amount of load a dray horse can pull uphill; horsepower is how fast the poor old horse can pull it.

The following chart shows the relationship between torque and horsepower of a generic V10 Grand Prix engine. As the data is from the 1999 season, you'll notice that the engine's crankshaft speed peaks at 18,000rpm. The numbers are reliable, but continual progress by the manufacturers will have resulted in some improvements, most notably to revs and horsepower. Nevertheless, in the interest of preserving their accuracy I thought it preferable to leave the figures alone, rather than tinker with them to produce a mathematically adjusted version (based on hearsay and supposition) that would take into account the slightly higher revs of current engines.

RPM	FT/LB	BHP
12,500	249	591
13,500	277	708
14,500	268	736
15,500	255	758
16,500	252	796
17,500	231	783
18,000	224	776

A couple of years ago, after enduring a bitterly cold, three-day testing session in Barcelona, I enjoyed an enthralling few hours in the company of two Cosworth engineers while we all waited for a delayed flight back to England. Another tale of late planes, ah ... the joys of modern travel! However, to unashamedly misquote one of Marilyn Monroe's lines from *Some Like it Hot*: 'It's not how late you are, it's who you're waiting with.' I've always found the Cosworth chaps to be sound people, very down-to-earth. I knew these two pretty well from our mutual time together at Benetton, during Michael Schumacher's stint with the team.

We propped ourselves against the bar, and, chatting away, got on to the subject of how and why all the engine manufacturers had eventually opted for the V10 solution. Ferrari had finally pulled the dust sheets over their beloved V12 engines at the end of 1995 – just as our former driver joined them – while Cosworth themselves had moved away from their illustrious V8 in 1997 and concentrated on an all-new engine, the Zetec – RV10.

Although Michael has never actually raced a V12 Ferrari, he did test drive their 1995 chassis, the 412T2, as soon as he'd pulled on his scarlet overalls. His post-test remarks merely served to confirm what are the generally accepted properties of a V12 engine: the low-speed drivability was no match for his V10 Renault-powered Benetton, but the horsepower was superior to that of his old car. As I say, no real surprise in those comments, but it's always reassuring to know things are as they should be. Certainly it would have unnerved a lot of engineers if he'd said anything to the contrary.

The reason the V10 has become the universal choice of the moment and for the foreseeable future, no doubt, is because it's a *compromise*. Surprise, surprise ... impossible to escape that word, isn't it? The V10 strikes the happy medium between eight cylinders and twelve; primarily that compromise is one between mass and friction.

It's clear that an eight-cylinder engine will have fewer moving parts than its twelve-cylinder counterpart – four fewer pistons, four fewer connecting rods; perhaps as many as twenty fewer valves, not forgetting the extra bearings, springs, and cam-lobes too. In contrast to a twelve-cylinder design, the fact that all of those extra components are unneeded in an eight-cylinder engine results in a significant saving in frictional power loss. So far so good, but the downside of an eight-cylinder engine is that the size and weight of each piston will be unavoidably greater than those of a twelve-cylinder engine (for the same swept volume, of course).

Exactly the same pros and cons apply conversely to a twelve-cylinder engine; more moving parts results in more frictional power loss, but the reduced mass of the pistons allows the engine to respond quicker and rev higher. The average weight of a piston from a contemporary V10 is somewhere in the region of 250 grams; when we remember all of that awful reciprocal movement the engine must endure: up, down, up, down, up, down ... the weight of each piston becomes extremely important, the lighter the piston the quicker it can accelerate and decelerate.

Other than helping to reduce the overall length of the engine, there is another significant advantage of using a vee configuration over an 'inline' engine, namely that of lowering the mass of the engine in the car (lowering by positioning, I mean, not of reducing its actual weight). And increasing the degree of offset between the cylinder banks allows the mass of the engine to be positioned even lower in the car. Okay, following this train of thought to its logical conclusion would suggest that a boxer engine will give the optimum weight distribution, and, yes, that is certainly true;

unfortunately, however, a boxer engine is also very wide and this creates its own problems.

The engine's radiators sit one each side of the cylinder block; and the cooling air passing through them has to be channelled underneath the bodywork, around the engine bay and out through carefully designed exit ducts, either at the very rear of the car or along its flanks. Some teams have now designed periscope style air ducts, too, that sit atop the bodywork, immediately behind the radiators. The cooling air exiting the radiators and flowing rearward is also used to help dissipate the latent heat of the engine's block and its twin exhaust systems. Great consideration is given to controlling the characteristics of the airflow beneath the engine cover; merely because this flow is all happening 'out of sight' it doesn't mean it's of no importance and can be overlooked.

The maximum width of an F1 car must not exceed 1.8 metres, and 'building land' within that 1.8 metres is at an absolute premium. Unfortunately, this is where the width of a boxer engine lets us down; the cylinder heads sit too low in the car to allow for the inclusion of the exhausts, remembering that unlike the cars of the sixties and seventies, current cars have a flat floor, sometimes called an under-tray. The engine is enclosed twixt this and the bodywork, using a boxer engine there really wouldn't be sufficient clearance between the exhaust ports of the cylinder heads and the floor to allow for the inclusion of the exhaust pipes.

Okay, one might suggest a possible solution to this would be to design an engine transposing the inlet and exhaust ports, allowing the exhaustion system to connect above the cylinder heads rather than below, but this merely creates a catch-22 situation. We're stuck with the same conundrum: there would still be insufficient clearance for us to mount the throttle butterflies and inlet system between the cylinder heads and the floor of the car. Yes, I guess it *could* be done, nearly anything's possible, but it isn't done because there's a better overall solution.

Exhaust location is just one problem to take into consideration, there is also the positioning of the radiators and oil coolers to think about, and we mustn't overlook the vast array of oil pipes, hydraulic lines and wiring harnesses too. Notwithstanding the need to locate all of these things, the designers then have to create sufficient space to channel the air passing through the radiators and inside the engine cover. In conclusion, then, an inline engine is both too long and too tall, and a flat, boxer engine is too wide. Once again, all roads are leading us to the inevitable – we're back to using the services of the good old vee engine.

The engine of a contemporary Formula 1 car is bolted directly to the rear face of the chassis. Unlike the fifties and sixties, there is no longer any supporting space-frame to cradle the engine, nor any rubber mountings similar to those used for road cars. In point of fact the installation of a Grand Prix engine is the height of simplicity. (In essence, each individual stage of a race car is simple, it merely appears complex when one stumbles across the whole ensemble. The untrained eye tends not to see a series of united subassemblies, instead it becomes overwhelmed and informs the brain of an encounter with a rather angry fire-spitting dragon.)

Depending on the design of a particular engine, there will be four or six location studs protruding from the chassis: always two at the bottom to hold the cylinder block, then either one or two for each cylinder head. Unlike a road car, the engine isn't lowered into position with a hoist, rather the chassis and the engine are pushed – or mated – together.

With the chassis sitting on two high-stands, and the engine resting atop a small, height-adjustable trolley, the engine's location holes are carefully aligned with the studs and the engine is pushed home. Specially machined titanium washers-cum-load spreaders slip over the studs, and a dab of (blue, 242 'nutloc') Loctite is added to the threads before the self-locking K-nuts are tightened to the correct torque (usually around 55 ft/lb, depending on the actual size and pitch of the nut), and that's that: the engine and chassis are united.

I should add that although Loctite is a brand name, I'm not using this opportunity to endorse the product, but I think it's fair to suggest that Loctite is generally considered an industry standard; in exactly the same way that Coke seems to be the most frequently used word in the language of soft drinks. And 'K-nut' is common motor racing parlance to describe any superior quality, aircraft specification nut, regardless of its manufacture.

These high-carbon content steel nuts are delicately crimped at manufacture, resulting in their top becoming slightly oval; it is this feature that grips the thread of the mating stud, or bolt, so effectively. They are lightweight, very hard and ideally should be used only once to ensure their integrity; each time a nut is removed, drop it in the bin and fit new. These fasteners are also terribly expensive, but this *is* Formula 1 we're talking about so that's perfectly okay. We'll just add another sponsor's sticker to the car to cover the invoice. We don't need distractions such as 'where's the money coming from?'; our job is to build the car, not to pay for it, that's why we have accountants on the books. We have to remain focused on the racing.

One might question why Loctite is used in conjunction with these self-locking nuts; and it's true, it might seem a tad belt-and-braces. The problem, or at least the potential problem, of a nut working loose stems from the high-frequency vibrations emitting from an engine designed to work in excess of 18,900rpm; an engine that isn't equipped with rubber mountings to help dampen those vibrations before they course through the rest of the car.

At specific points throughout its rev range an F1 engine will make the entire car buzz. Experienced drivers will often complain about it, new arrivals to Formula 1 will occasionally even vomit as a result of it. When the car is fired up in the pit garage, merely placing one's fingertips on the rear wing is sufficient to feel the effects, similar to the numbing sensation produced by an orbital sander or an electric jigsaw. At this point the engine is running at a reasonably sedate 5000rpm. Throughout the race the drivers are subjected to close on four times that number for ninety-plus minutes. These vibrations will penetrate his spine, legs, arms and hands; sufficient

TOP Jose Froilan Gonzalez – a big man, a charioteer from a different era . . . (LAT) An era of brute strength, outstanding bravery and spectacular accidents. **BOTTOM** Hans Hermann is thrown clear of his airborne BRM, a result of brake failure during the 1959 German Grand Prix (Popperfoto).

TOP Working on the front of a Cooper in 1966, a young mechanic learns the importance of fine detailing. His meticulous approach to the job would later form the philosophy for the whole of the McLaren International empire. The mechanic's name is Ron Dennis.

BOTTOM A Tipo 60 Maserati from 1960, revealing the car's splendidly complex 'birdcage' space frame chassis (both LAT).

Two of Einstein's giants. With Jim Clark inside the car,
Colin Chapman squats beside the aluminium monocoque
of his beautiful Lotus 25 of 1962 (Phipps Photographic).
The inset shows John Barnard's original carbon fibre
monocoque of 1981. This simple black tub was destined to
reshape the entire future of Grand Prix car design (LAT).

The pursuit of excellence: **TOP** McLaren's cramped and grubby pits at the 1973 German Grand Prix. **BOTTOM** Under the strict, authoritarian control of Ron Dennis, the McLaren pits have become the industry's state-of-the-art (both LAT).

TOP The wonderful swirls and colours of a contemporary Inconal exhaust system.
BOTTOM A desire for more cylinders without any appreciable increase in crankshaft length led BRM to produce this H16 engine in 1966 (both LAT).

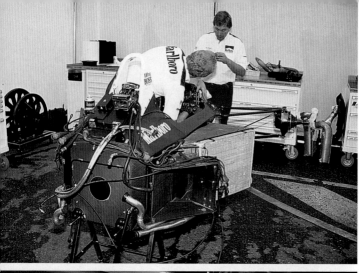

The three fully stressed members:

TOP The monocoque, with its flat rear face to which the engine is mounted. **CENTRE** The engine, seen here atop a trolley and ready for installation. **BOTTOM** The car's rear end – the transmission, suspension and rear wing (all LAT).

TOP Mated together, the chassis, engine and transmission assembly form the basis of our modern, modular Formula 1 car, in this instance a Ferrari-powered Sauber (LAT). **BOTTOM** The rear suspension sitting on top of the transmission casing, revealing the dampers, springs and the delicate roll bar assembly (LAT).

TOP A 1969 Matra, the sport's finest offering in what was Concorde's maiden year.
BOTTOM The 2003 Ferrari chassis, raced during the supersonic aircraft's final year of operation. It took Formula 1 a long time to attain anything close to Concorde's level of aerodynamic finesse (both LAT).

even to make his teeth chatter. Unpleasant, no doubt, and we certainly want the driver to feel as comfortable as possible in the car; it's difficult for him to give of his best if he's turning green and preoccupied with nagging toothache. At times like this, however, he should be able to draw solace from the knowledge that he is being compensated with unfeasibly vast sums of money for his discomfort, his loyalty and commitment to the team.

Of course, no one is in favour of these vibrations; they help nothing, cause only problems, and the engine manufacturers try their utmost to alleviate them as much as possible. Naturally, some engines are more prone to this problem than others (much depends on the precise angle between the two cylinder banks and the result that has on the engine's internal balancing), but no manufacturer is immune. It is the nature of the beast; and it is for this reason that the teams elect to play doubly safe with the security of their fasteners. And this is not just limited to engine location either. The transmission and differential assembly; the rear wing pylons; suspension pick-ups, damper mountings, pretty much anything held fast by nut and bolt is susceptible to the perils of vibration.

In this type of racing application the engine is not merely a producer of propulsive power, it is in every sense an extension of the carbon fibre monocoque, known as a fully-stressed member. Rigidly fixed to the chassis, the engine is the next link in the chain, the cylinder block and heads are designed to carry the same suspension loadings as the chassis itself. Consequently, the engine must be designed to resist as much torsional flex as possible, and this is the reason why it cannot be equipped with rubber mountings; they would allow the engine to move relative to the chassis, and we absolutely cannot allow that to happen.

A Grand Prix engine is lubricated by a 'dry sump' system, meaning that the oil is not stored in a pan beneath the crankshaft, as is the case with the majority of road car engines (this basic system is called 'wet sump' lubrication). Instead the oil for our racing engine is held in an externally mounted reservoir, and without need of an oil pan sitting beneath the crank, the engine can sit lower in the car. (Remember our two golden rules for any car component: make it light and mount it as close to the track as possible.)

The underside of an F1 engine is sealed by a flat aluminium plate; actually this is more usually a casting but 'flat' and 'plate' are the words to concentrate on, they give a more descriptive image. And when the engine is mated to the chassis, this plate – the bottom face of the engine – will sit absolutely flush with the bottom face of the chassis. Any slight height irregularities on this casting will have been milled away by the engine manufacturer beforehand; troughs can stay but any high-spots *must* go.

To help visualise this, imagine a house brick (our chassis) and a box of matches (our engine) sitting on a tabletop. We butt the matchbox up against the brick, our engine is installed. The brick and the matchbox are different sizes but the bottom face of each sits on the same plane, the top of the table.

This absolutely flat underside of the car, known as the reference plane, is extremely important. With the sole exception of the FIA's legality skid-block (which we'll discuss later) no 'sprung' part of the car – everything but the wheels and tyres – is allowed to sit or hang below this point.

The reference plane is a zero point; using this as the baseline for their measurements the FIA carry out their legality checks to ensure the car complies with the technical regulations governing its permissible dimensions. For example, when the scrutineers check the legality of the front wing, the bottom face of the wing's endplates – the small vertical plates attached to each end of the wing – must be no less than 100mm above the reference plane.

Ideally, the teams would like the front wing endplates to be as close to the surface of the track as possible, it aids the car's aerodynamic efficiency. However, the reason the FIA use the reference plane as their baseline – never the surface of the track, concrete floor, or anything else – is to prevent teams circumnavigating any dimension regulation by raising or lowering the ride-height of their cars. Irrespective of any suspension movement, the distance between the underside of the chassis and the underside of the wings remains static.

As for the engine in our dream team car, do we manufacture our own or do we form a partnership with an existing manufacturer? I have to admit it would be wonderful to create an engine from scratch. Imagine the thrill, the tingle down the spine when the first prototype barked into life. Nevertheless, we have to remember the need for competitiveness, for reliability; and we have to remember the pressures of the racing calendar, how quickly those races arrive one after another. I don't think we can risk the heartache and headaches associated with building our own engine. We don't want to end up chugging around at the back of the pack with some completely useless smoke-bomb of a contraption, splurging oil over the track and firing its pistons airborne like some frenzied Soviet rocket launcher.

So, it's an experienced partner we're after, and if we're going to form an alliance with a manufacturer then it's obvious what we're looking for: power, dependability, and the technical support and funding to ensure the engines will remain at the cutting edge throughout the season. There are a lot of famous names out there to choose from, it's a difficult decision, but some manufacturers do seem to have taken their eye off the ball somewhat. Some engines are down on power, some lack durability, and others are sadly short of both. We don't want our dream team to form an alliance based on after-dinner reminiscences of times past, yarns of the good old days and promises of how rosy the future will be. That isn't good enough, not for us. The races fall every fourteen days, we need results *now*, not next year.

I find myself caught between the merits of two companies: BMW and Ferrari. It's true that I've worked with both of these organisations, but my role was as a mechanic with their road car divisions, I was never a part of their racing programmes. I point this out merely to dismiss my past relationship with them as the reason I have chosen them here. Both of these distinguished companies are producing fine Grand Prix engines. They stand out from the crowd. In BMW's case it's their phenomenal rate of technical progress.

After bowing out of Grand Prix racing in the turbo era, the company returned to the Formula 1 arena in 2000; but their commitment to making their all-new V10 engine the best in the pit lane has been quite outstanding. Back in 2001, in the paddock of the Indianapolis Motor Speedway, I had a long chat with BMW's chief mechanic, Max Fluckiger. Max and I used to work together, both race mechanics with Benetton. A lifelong enthusiast of the BMW marque, as soon as the possibility arose to join their rejuvenated F1 operation Max quit our old paymasters and headed off to Munich. He hasn't looked back since; clearly loving his new position, the fresh challenge.

I asked if he could throw some light on exactly how he and his colleagues had managed to make such exceptional progress in so short a time. He explained that (as ever) it was all down to effort and commitment. Well, yes, I don't think anyone would dispute that explanation, but there's much more to BMW's success than just that: effort and commitment are standard requirements of every team. Max also said that almost every week – and nearly always for every race – something new is coming online. The company's research and development never stands still; no sooner has one test piece been drawn, manufactured and dyno-tested than the next development piece is already in the pipeline.

By the end of their first season the Williams-BMW partnership had produced a handful of podium finishes and (of far greater significance to those within the industry) they had taken third place in the constructors' championship. Back in Munich, at the same time as the 2000 season was winding down, BMW's 2001 engine, the P81, was already well into its initial dyno runs. It wouldn't be long before it was revving higher and producing more power than its predecessor – as one would hope – but word in the paddock suggested their new unit was somewhere in the region of twenty kilograms lighter too. Now we're talking! The 2001 season yielded no less than four wins for Williams-BMW, and by end of play in 2002 the partnership had secured second place in the constructors' championship. The 2003 season was no less impressive: another four race wins, another second-place finish in the constructors' championship – and this time they were fighting for outright victory throughout the final round of the season, in Suzuka, Japan – the honours finally falling to Ferrari.

The results of BMW's intensive development programme have been clear for all to see. My personal highlight, however, was watching the qualifying session in Monza, for the 2002 Italian Grand Prix. It was there that the BMW V10 broke the world record for the fastest revving engine in the history of the sport (perhaps in history, period). When Juan Pablo Montoya's FW24 Williams tripped the timing beam, securing pole position on the way, the onboard telemetry revealed his engine had been running at 19,050rpm. I don't want us to become embroiled in analysing meaningless lists of numbers, but here's just a few that I think are worth a second look. The peak crank speed seen on Montoya's qualifying engine that afternoon equated to a staggering 317.5 revs per second; a click of the fingers and a piston has travelled up and down its bore 635 times, en route producing more than 158 individual combustions.

If you can get your mind round that concept then you've got the advantage over me, I can tell you. I really struggle with the blistering speed of it all; I look at my watch as it ticks the passing of a single second and find it hard to comprehend that such feats of mechanical engineering can ever happen: at those crank speeds the expanding fuel/air mixture has just six milliseconds (0.006 mS) to transfer its energy load to the piston's crown before the exhaust valve opens and the piston – already on its next stroke – is forcefully ejecting the spent gases into the exhaust system.

There's no question that BMW are right at the fore in the battle for extra horsepower. However, some might suggest that (in what are still relatively early days of the company's return to F1) they are living just a mite too close to the edge. If BMW have a weakness then it's their sporadic reliability problems – not terrible, but neither is their copybook blot free. In 2002 I can recall at least four race retirements for the two Williams cars were due to engine failure. And in Monza that year (the very day after Montoya's engine had performed so heroically in qualifying), Ralf Schumacher, Montoya's team-mate, had to jump into the spare car just prior to the start of the Grand Prix due to fuel pressure problems with the engine in his race car. Then, a mere two laps into the race itself, the engine in the spare car let go amid a cloud of smoke.

Reliability problems also hit them in 2003, when Montoya's engine destroyed itself while the Colombian was leading the Austrian Grand Prix. Okay, we know that ifs and buts can be used to produce all manner of statistics but here's one worth considering: If Juan had won that race he would have scored ten points, Michael Schumacher would have scored two less, and Montoya would have been leading the drivers' championship going into the final round of the season. And he was running away with that race ... when hydraulics failure forced his retirement from the event. Ouch!

All of which brings us back to the point I made earlier: to finish first, first you have to finish; and, within the bounds of reason, an increase in an engine's performance at the expense of its longevity is really not much use to anyone but the opposition. If during a Grand Prix the driver is forced to retire from the race, the downcast mechanics wheeling the car into the garage – or, worse still, the driver pulls directly off the circuit and stops the car at the side of the track – then his team has failed, has failed in its very reason for being. A race retirement is a terrible thing, to suffer the ignominy of such humiliation in front of one's peers ... not to mention the watching millions around the world.

That isn't to suggest that the specifications of BMW's qualifying engines at Monza were the same as those intended for the race, that certainly wasn't the case. Neither am I suggesting the team are building engines knowing them to be fast but flawed – if the engineers were aware of a problem, naturally they'd fix it and move on. All I am suggesting is that manufacturing super-competitive engines is exceedingly complex, and compared to their time-served rivals BMW are still scampering up a very steep learning curve. Sure, BMW have been involved in F1 before; but that was then and this is now; and in this contemporary period – the days of the normally aspirated 3.0 litre V10 – they are the new kids on the block. Nevertheless, the current gang leaders had better watch out; over the coming seasons, if BMW remain committed to Formula 1, there could be a dramatic shift in power. Right now, however, my gut feeling is that we should leave BMW to further develop their engines. We, on the other hand, should open up negotiations with Scuderia Ferrari.

Have you noticed how little media attention is generated by Ferrari's engine department? As for the other manufacturers, stories abound. Renault are working on curing their lack of pace with plans to ditch their seemingly problematic super-wide 110° engine; Mercedes are considering a twin sparkplug ignition system to help improve the efficiency of their engine's combustion; Honda have redesigned their cylinder block to try and cure its tendency to flex under extreme loads and pinch the crank bearings (remember Giancarlo Fisichella's spectacular engine failure at Spa in 2002, where his Jordan resembled more the launch of a NASA space shuttle than an F1 car driving out of Eau Rouge).

But with Ferrari's V10 engines the news is always subdued. I think this is an instance of no news is good news; it suggests to me that they have no great problems, nothing to report. Unflustered and unfazed, Ferrari's two engine gurus, Paolo Martinelli and Gilles Simon, with their talented team of engineers go about their business in a calm, methodical manner. And the results of their combined efforts are a series of great Grand Prix engines – race-winning, championship-winning engines. And that's exactly what we need in the back of our car.

The 051 Ferrari engine, the motor that powered the team to fifteen race victories and both world championships in 2002, didn't rev as high as the P82 BMW, around 18,500rpm. As a result it was marginally down on horsepower, pumping out somewhere between

880–890bhp, as opposed to 890–900 for the BMW. But unlike the P82 the Ferrari engine proved virtually indestructible.

Ross Brawn and Nigel Stepney invited me into the Ferrari pits at Indianapolis to look over the F2002. Displaying a little nervous reticence, the mechanics tending Schumacher's chassis tentatively removed the bodywork to allow me to see the installation of the engine and transmission. And, I should add, this would never have happened if it wasn't for the exceptionally kind indulgence of Ross and Nigel, both former Benetton colleagues. I shall remember that sight forever. I was amazed at how compact the 051 engine was – it seemed too small to be a V10 engine (I had to count the exhaust pipes to satisfy myself); there didn't seem to be sufficient volume to the engine for it to contain everything necessary to make it work. The precision, the engineering detail to every component was, quite simply, breathtaking. The car was staggeringly beautiful.

The last F1 engine that I installed was in 1998, attached to the rear face of a Benetton chassis. The engine was a V10 but I can't remember what we were supposed to call the thing. Depending on politics or money or both, the engine was either a Renault, a Mecachrome, a Supertec or a Playlife: basically just different badges for the same thing. It was a nice, tidy, compact unit, but it *looked* like a V10, the dimensions of the block suggested as much. Sizing up the 051 Ferrari engine in the back of the F2002, however, I'd say it was at least 25 per cent smaller. A whole *quarter* ... gone! The 051 looked no bigger than a V6 – a very small V6 – so much progress in just a few seasons. Nigel Stepney could sense what I was thinking. 'Small, isn't it?' he said, beaming at me like a proud father.

To top off the occasion, Ross consented to my interviewing him, there and then, and to allow our Speed Channel cameras to film the car just as it was, bodywork removed, engine and gearbox exposed! The finished segment would be a world exclusive, never before had the F2002 been filmed in such a vulnerable condition. Ross explained that Ferrari were quite aware of the tremendous support the team enjoys across America, and if showing the car like this would help their fans to better understand how it worked, then he was more than happy to help. It was an admirable gesture, and the letters and e-mails of praise that followed the segment's airing confirmed just how much it was appreciated.

'Wingrave, you're the banker among us,' I said, 'so you'll be used to dealing with money. I'm going to give you the honour of buying the engines for us; get your chequebook out. I hope they pay you well in that bank of yours, George, because my best guess is that Ferrari are going to ask for something close on twenty million quid for a year's supply of engines ... but they might insist on a two-year deal, so better make out the cheque for a round forty mil'. Do you need to borrow a pen?'

'Hell's bells!' he laughed. 'Forty biggies, purely on engines! Well, you're the boss, old man, if you think we need them then we're going to have to buy them. I say, does Jean Todt treat us all to a good lunch at the Cavalino for that?'

Paul Kelver came trotting back to the table, and for a man who'd just had his flight to Paris cancelled, he was looking pretty chipper. 'Chaps, I've got some good news and some not so good news,' he said.

'Hang on, Kelver, that's my line!' said Hentschel, but his friend waved the protest aside and quickly carried on; he wasn't to be interrupted.

'Quiet, Carl, and listen won't you? Now, I've just been in negotiation with one of the Air France girls, back there and...'

' "Negotiation"? What on earth do you mean by that? You've been trying to charm her, Paul, we've been watching you! All that casual leaning on the desk and constant fiddling with your hair – it's pathetic! She's not interested in a grizzly old sod like you, mate. And, more to the point, we've been waiting for over an hour for our drinks. We could have died of thirst!'

'Carl, do shut up ... just for one minute! This is the deal: Air France have given us two options; first, we can reclaim our bags, go to a hotel and catch the flight tomorrow night; or second, if we're prepared to stick it out here a few more hours, they'll put us on the first flight in the morning, out of here at eight o'clock. They say the fog will have gone by then, all being well.'

Instinctively we all turned and looked out of the windows. Difficult to see much because of the reflected lights from inside but there were definitely more orange glows than earlier; sodium lamps that had been invisible an hour before. It certainly looked as though the mist was finally heading out to sea.

'What time is it?' asked Wingrave. It was already three o'clock. 'Well, look, chaps, we only have to bunk down here for another three or four hours and they'll be calling us for the morning flight. I'm for staying here, what say you?'

'Oh, there's something else, ...' said Kelver, a schoolboy grin spreading across his face. 'The morning plane to Paris is flight number AF001.' The grin broke into a broad smile. We looked at him blankly. 'AF001 ... come on chaps ... AF001 is a Concorde flight – they're offering to upgrade us! So, what do I tell her ... do we stay or do we go?'

For me the decision was easy. I'd never flown Concorde, something that had been on my list of things to do and make for as long as I can remember. I thought I'd lost the chance after that awful crash in Paris, when they'd grounded all Concorde aircraft. In fact, the green light putting the fleet back in service had happened only a matter of a week or two before. The vote to stay put was swift and unanimous.

We handed Paul Kelver our now useless boarding passes and he took them down to the reception desk. And, I noticed, Hentschel had been spot on. As soon as Paul left us he did start to push his hair around. Minutes later he was back, this time his arms full of plastic packets containing Air France travel blankets, a rich deep blue colour. He had our new boarding passes too: Flight AF001 New York–Paris. Boarding time 07:30. George was right, we had to while away only another four hours and then we'd be soaring into the morning sky aboard the world's most prestigious commercial aircraft. All things considered, this really was turning into a most extraordinary trip home.

6

Ah, Yes ... But is it Art?

'As Grand Prix fabricators, what we're attempting to achieve
is the perfection of eighteenth century skills using twenty-
first century materials.'
Robin Grant – Renault Sport

Okay, we have our spanking new chassis sitting comfortably upon
its two high-stands, and we already have the fuel tank, pumps and
pipes installed (and we've double-checked that the mechanical fuel
pump drive is in position, too). Sitting atop its trolley, we have
wheeled our shiny new Ferrari engine into place and now have it
securely fixed to the rear bulkhead of the chassis; the nuts felt
'right' as we tightened them along the threads of the studs, and the
torque wrench clicked off exactly as we expected; our hands and
our tools are both in agreement, both sending confident signals to
the brain. All is well.

A quick visual check confirms that nothing, such as a stray cable
or section of wiring has been accidentally trapped between the
engine and the bulkhead, not that we expected to find anything
because it would have shown itself when we tightened the nuts.
Anything trapped would have been felt through our fingers. (It
sounds odd but it's true: nine times out of ten a mechanic can
sense, just *sense* when something is not as it should be.)

Chassis, bag-tank, lump; as far as our car build is concerned,
things are going good. However, to ensure that things continue in
this vein we need to be *extremely* careful right about now. Before
we lower the bed of the trolley and pull the thing out from underneath the engine, it is absolutely imperative that we ask one of our

mechanics to hold on to the front end of the chassis. Forgetting to do this would be a bad thing – very, very bad.

We have just bolted an engine weighing somewhere between 95– 100 kilos to a chassis which weighs approximately only half as much. When we pull out the trolley, if somebody isn't hanging on to the front of the chassis to help counterbalance the weight of the engine at the rear, we will quickly see our chassis/engine combination do an impromptu impression of Thunderbird Two – sitting on its launch ramp, tilting skyward at a jaunty forty-five degrees in preparation for take-off. Unbalanced by the mass of the newly installed engine, our chassis will pivot on its rear high-stand, slip rearward and the back of the engine will drop to the floor with an almighty, heart-stopping SMACK!

If this happens we might be extremely fortunate, managing to escape the incident with just a couple of bent gearbox mounting studs … at worst we will have cracked the cylinder block casting, effectively scrapping a £300,000 engine before getting as far as turning the ignition on. It doesn't bear thinking about. Have I ever done it? Thankfully, no. Have I ever seen it done? Oh, yes. After a series of very late nights, experienced, but tired, people are capable of any number of rookie mistakes.

In the seconds immediately after such an experience, those responsible always seem stuck in a quandary: whether to simply fall to their knees and sob themselves to sleep; whether to swallow that strychnine tablet they've been saving for just such an occasion; or whether to drop tools, sprint down the pit lane to freedom and try for a new life, perhaps rum-running between the islands of the Caribbean.

At this point of the engine installation, the preferred technique is to have someone hold the front of the chassis, as we said, then lower the bed of the trolley a tad, merely sufficient to pull it backward and relocate it at the very rear of the engine. Next, jack the trolley back up, only a little, just enough to lift the engine/chassis clear of the rear high-stand. Now, pull the rear high-stand clear of the chassis and reposition it beneath the engine, let the trolley down and pull it clear ... and *voilà*! Using the same two high-stands, the weight of the whole engine/chassis assembly is now safely supported; no wrecked engine, no ashen-faced mechanics looking for alternative careers.

Next come the exhausts. Theoretically, I suppose, they form part of the engine but I think this often overlooked section of the car deserves its own chapter. Exhaust systems are fun. Remember that when you next burn your hand on one.

A correctly 'tuned' exhaust system will add power and drivability to a Grand Prix engine; consequently, the diameter, length and precise layout of the pipework is of crucial importance.

It would be pointless to tell you that the work involved in fabricating and welding the exhausts is both detailed and highly skilled. Even if you're a total novice to the technical side of this business, I'm sure you realise by now that everything about Formula 1 car production is highly skilled; I mean, nothing's going to be done slapdash, is it? Nevertheless, I would like to emphasise that exhaust fabrication requires more than just technical ability, it also requires artistic insight. When complete and ready for installation on the cylinder heads, the finished exhausts are truly beautiful; intricate swirls of interlaced tubes, sculptures worthy of exhibition. Put it this way, I'd far rather pause in a gallery to admire some perfectly formed Grand Prix exhausts as opposed to a dishevelled array of seedy bed linen, or a hunk of mutton floating in a tank; or, while we're on the subject, that awful, soul-sapping collage that Dez Scoggins glued together, consisting of nothing more than an array of randomly placed geometry equipment.

Back in 1990 in my early days with Benetton, a time when the team was based in Witney (with a total workforce of less than fifty, if you can believe that!), one of our exhaust fabricators, a chap by the name of Malcolm Green, was himself a former silversmith by trade. His work was astonishing. And as with any master craftsman he made it all look so easy too. Much time was spent circling and moving around the pipes, pondering them from different vantage points, one eye closed, then the other, sizing things up, deciding exactly which pipe needed just a fraction more tapping to make everything fit perfectly. There was also much bouncing of one of those rubber super-balls off the factory walls, though I suspect that wasn't quite such a vital part of the fabrication process. Perhaps it was; maybe I was merely too wet behind the ears to appreciate the process. Whatever. I do know that his finished exhaust systems were very spectacular.

Formula 1 fabricators are true artisans, in my opinion gifted beyond compare. They are jacks of all trades, masters of all trades, too. They have to be, the skill of fabrication is the skill of total versatility; they possess the enviable ability of being able to look at a drawing once, then set to and produce the most intricate pieces using nothing but a guillotine, a few basic hand tools and a TIG welder.

In the fifties, sixties and seventies – the days of yore – the fabricators were responsible for manufacturing nearly all of the car: the space-frame chassis, body panels, wings, suspension, pedals. Lamentably, however, with the advent of composite materials, their demand has been in constant decline ever since. The chassis, suspension bodywork and wings are all now manufactured from composites.

Only a few seasons ago the very notion of producing suspension components from carbon fibre was unthinkable, now it is the norm. The suspension 'upright', the bearing carriers for the stub axles, used to be hand-built by the fabricators, each tiny cooling fin cut and welded into place, a long and complex job. Now, however, the latest state-of-the-art milling machines and 'wire-cutters' can produce an upright from a single billet of titanium – just dial in the coordinates, press go, stand back and watch it happen. The finished upright is a wondrous piece of engineering: strong, light-weight, durable. But computer-generated artwork will never be a substitute for true artistry, will it?

Nevertheless, it also remains true that while every other depart-ment within a team constantly grows, the industry's payroll of fabricators seems only to diminish. I doubt very much their skills will disappear completely, they are always being called upon to save the day, to knock up a last minute solution: a bracket here, a bracket there; something to hold a what-not in place; a midnight rework of a radiator that refuses to stay put, or something to make the bodywork fit together. And there's always the exhausts, of course.

The exhaust pipes themselves are fabricated from a special material, Inconal, an alloy consisting mainly of nickel and chromium, although there's even a bit of iron in there somewhere, basically it's an exceptionally high grade of stainless steel. In the pit garages late at night, when the mechanics are running the engines (with no cooling air blowing over the pipes) the Inconal quickly changes through a rainbow of colours: red to orange to yellow in the blinking of an eye, then to white; finally the sections bolted directly to the cylinder heads become near translucent, the pipes take on a gaseous shimmer, caused by the searing, blasting heat inside. Really very pretty but, sadly, a sight which few people will ever have the opportunity to experience.

The twin, left and right exhaust systems of a Formula 1 car are nearly identical. Perhaps it would be better to describe them as mirror images of one another. The reason I say nearly identical is because there is a slight side-to-side difference between the two, a consequence of the relative positioning of the cylinder bores cast within the block. The two opposing cylinder banks of a vee engine may appear symmetrical but they have to be slightly offset (front to rear) in order for the connecting rods of both banks to attach to the centrally located crankshaft, something we touched on in the last chapter. The cylinders are offset by approximately fifteen millimetres, on some engines a little more; it entirely depends on the design specifications of the individual manufacturers.

Per bank of cylinders, an exhaust system consist of three sections. The Primary is first. Each of the engine's cylinders is equipped with one of these, a pipe measuring anywhere between 35–45mm in diameter, bolted directly to the cylinder head. From here the five

Primary pipes converge into a larger (80–100mm diameter) tube known as a Collector. Designed with five inlets but only one outlet, the purpose of the Collector is to reduce the five pipes down to just one. However, the 'tuned length' of the Primaries is very important, each pipe, regardless of whether it's mated to a cylinder at the front or rear of the engine, has to be exactly the same length. This is the reason why the Primary pipes spiral around one another like strands of spaghetti; the five pipes have to converge with the Collector, but with no compromise to the preset length of the individual pipes.

But there's even more to take into consideration. The car's two Collectors sit on the same lateral plane, normally a line just to the rear of the engine block. It is at this stage that the slight offset between the left and right banks of cylinders has to be allowed for. It isn't desirable merely to lengthen the pipes on one side of the engine to compensate for the discrepancy, the engineers must keep all the Primary pipes an equal length. In order to achieve this the fabricators have to carefully manipulate the Primaries of both sides (effectively pulling and pushing the two sets of pipes), to allow all of them to terminate in line with the fixed position of the Collectors.

On leaving the Collectors the gases flow into the next stage – the system's exit or outlet – known as the Secondary. Not so long ago the desired location for the exhaust outlets was either flush with the car's diffuser (the finned, tunnel-shaped section of the floor sitting between the rear wheels), or just above the diffuser. Mounted here the pipes were trapped between the floor and the rear part of the engine cover. Contemporary practice, however, is to exit the exhausts through the bodywork itself, the twin outlets sited just ahead of the lower element of the rear wing assembly.

The theory behind the original concept, of having the outlets sitting flush with the underside of the diffuser, was that the blasting flow of the escaping gases would help to speed the airflow travelling beneath the car, front to rear across the diffuser. Increasing the velocity of the under-car airflow (relative to that flowing over the top of the chassis) helped to lower the air pressure beneath the chassis, which in turn helped to produce downforce. The idea gained popularity at the end of the turbo era, towards the end of the 1980s, when the detailing of exhaust systems took on a greater significance.

It worked in practice, too; no question about that. Unfortunately, however, the gains came with an unavoidable downside. Additional downforce was only gained when the car was running on full throttle, hammering along the straights or negotiating high-speed corners. The extra assistance melted away in the mid- to slow-speed corners. Naturally, the volume and velocity of the exhaust gases reduced the moment the driver backed off the throttle; this also affected the downforce being produced and the rear of the car could begin to feel somewhat unsettled; not by much but enough to unnerve the drivers.

What we must remember here is that one of the most important requirements of a Grand Prix race car, of any race car, is that its handling should always be predictable, that it should always inspire confidence in the driver. When a driver feels confident in the machine he is strapped into, he will (at least, he should) be prepared to commit himself one hundred per cent, be prepared to drive to the absolute limit of the car's potential. The moment he loses confidence his team are on a hiding to nowhere.

In light of that we can perhaps begin to see why the diffuser exit exhaust lost popularity. Great idea on paper but if the driver isn't happy, then the designers need to come up with an alternative. Their solution was to move the outlets higher up, above the working surface of the diffuser, so negating their assistance and/or hindrance to the car's aerodynamics; and this somewhat conservative approach remained the norm throughout much of the 1990s.

The next evolution arrived in 1998, at the Spanish Grand Prix. It was at that race where Ferrari revealed a slight redesign to their F300 – the car now sporting its exhaust outlets sitting atop the bodywork. Instigated by the team's chief designer, Rory Byrne, certainly the idea looked a touch outlandish but within hours of its unveiling at Barcelona, Ferrari's rivals were busy investigating the concept for themselves. Within no time at all the system had been widely adopted, and now there isn't a car in the F1 pit lane that doesn't make use of Rory's original idea. McLaren were the last to hold out, but even the great Adrian Newey finally capitulated, fitting the same-styled exhausts to his MP4-17, the team's 2002 chassis. Actually, this car proved so successful that they retained it throughout the following season too, albeit with a significant number of upgrades.

There is certainly a degree of aero assistance to be had by these over-the-top exhaust exits. Blowing the gases past the underside of the lower element of the rear wing may help to produce a little extra push from the wing – effectively using the same aerodynamic principle as when the exhausts exited under the diffuser – but their primary advantage is really one of 'packaging' (a horrible word but sometimes there's no avoiding it).

Pulling the Secondary pipes upwards and shoving them through the bodywork frees up a significant amount of space at the rear of the car, allowing the body panels adjacent to the inside face of the rear wheels to be pulled tighter to the transmission's casing, enhancing its 'Coke bottle' styling. This narrow waistline at the rear of the car is very desirable as it allows the air flowing rearward along the outside of the side pods to be channelled around and away from the rear tyres, helping to reduce turbulence and drag as far as possible.

I believe it's no coincidence that Rory chose to introduce these over-the-top exhausts back in 1998. It was then that the technical regulations were amended, insisting that the overall width of the cars should be reduced by 200mm, from 2.0 metres down to 1.8 metres.

The rule change resulted in each wheel having to be positioned 100mm closer to the bodywork than before. This made it all the more important for the designers to squeeze the body panels as tight as possible to the transmission in order to help channel the airflow around the rear tyres. The easiest way to pull those panels closer to the transmission was to move the exhausts out of the way, and the only way to do that was to move them upward, exiting the pipes above the bodywork.

When the engine is initially fired into life, the exhausts sound distinctly off-tune, rough, something akin to a strangulated, drawn-out gargle. Once the engine has been brought up to temperature and the internal tolerances have settled down, the throttles are gradually opened a little further via a plug-in hand control – a simple handgrip equipped with a thumb-operated button, looking something like the handle of a walking cane. The revs begin to climb and the exhaust note instantly changes ... Rrrrrrraaaasssssp! Rrrrrrraaaasssssp! Rrrrrrraaaasssssp! The note starts low, rising to a bright, clear exclamation.

The pitch and clarity of the song depends on engine design, of course; as a general rule of thumb, the more cylinders the engine has, the prettier the song. It's perhaps no surprise then that the once undisputed diva of the F1 pit lane was the Ferrari engine – not their contemporary V10 – no, it was the song of their glorious twelve-cylinder power plants. I remember standing in the Monaco pit lane, listening entranced as the Ferrari mechanics ran the engines of their three 641 cars, bringing the motors up to operating temperature before they were taken on to the track. In Monaco, remember, the teams have to work in the open as there aren't any proper garages; they are merely allocated small 'boxes', barely sufficient to store their tools and tyres, let alone the multitude of other essentials needed to run an F1 car. This means that it is impossible to keep things private; the teams are exposed to the world – and its millions of prying cameras.

The V12 Ferraris sounded crisp, the throttle blips produced rifle cracks and the rear of the car spat forks of flame. Crack! Crack! Crack! Droves of mechanics fussed over the machines, while others desperately tried to keep the throng of photographers at bay. Colourful, loud and passionate: the frantic scene perfectly captured the reason why Ferrari command such a unique place in Grand Prix racing.

As the hot gases race through the exhausts, they create an internal resonance, a series of positive (travelling towards the engine) and negative (away from the engine) pressure waves. These pressure waves are a well understood science, and this is the reason why the pipes are manufactured to a specific, tuned length; these negative pressure waves are of significant advantage in helping to empty the cylinders of their spent charge.

As the positive and negative pressure waves flow back and forth within the exhaust pipes, the ideal situation is to have the negative wave flowing when the exhaust valve opens, thus helping to draw or scavenge the spent gases away from the cylinders. During 'valve overlap' (the period when the intake and the exhaust valves are open at the same time) the action also helps to start the flow of the fresh charge of air/fuel mixture.

Conversely, the worst situation is to have the positive wave acting when the exhaust valve opens, this will actually hamper performance, trying to push the spent gases back inside the engine. The frequency and flow characteristics of these internal harmonics and the pros and cons over exhaust performance are sensitive to specific engine revs; sometimes they work for you, sometimes against you.

There's always a lot of pit lane mutterings in Formula 1, mechanics and engineers from different teams are forever swapping snippets of information (or blatant rumour) with one another in the paddock. The intense security surrounding the industry breeds a desire for rivals to talk, to learn as much as possible about a third party: A talks to B to discover what he knows of C; B talks to C of A's latest technical breakthrough; and, naturally, to complete the circle, A then talks to C. It's the way of things, always has been.

A little earlier I mentioned that McLaren were the last team to hold out against periscope exhausts, and here's a possible reason for their apparent reluctance to switch – all speculative I should add, but worth sharing.

Throughout the winter testing sessions preceding the start of the 2000 season, while most aerodynamicists and engine manufacturers were busy investigating the merits of fitting Ferrari-esque exhausts to their own machines, McLaren's engineers preferred to concentrate on perfecting their original exhaust system. There was talk in the paddock that McLaren were busy developing a system designed to optimise the characteristics of their exhaust harmonics; a device to negate the detrimental effects of the positive pressure wave, allowing only the useful, negative pressure wave to work its magic.

There's no suggestion that McLaren were working on something contrary to the regulations. Before any newly developed technology can be used at a race meeting it must first be endorsed by the sport's governing body. Certainly, McLaren would have approached the FIA's technical delegate for approval of any new device. Let's face it, there's absolutely no point in testing and developing something in private, only to have it banned by the FIA come the first race of the season because it doesn't comply to the rules. Nevertheless, the bond of discretion between the technical delegate and the different teams is sacrosanct, for obvious reasons it must be so. In the normal course of events, the details of any newly approved technology are kept strictly between the team in question and the FIA.

As far as McLaren's research and development programme was concerned, one thing was certain, the exhaust note of their MP4-15 was quite unique: slightly muffled at idle, yet screaming a distinctive howling wail at high revs. Not only that but the engine note underwent a sudden frequency change as the cars blasted along the straights; not due to a gear upshift, or the usual Doppler effect caused by the compression and expansion of sound waves as a car travels towards, then past an observer. No, this was something else. It was intriguing and I followed the winter testing in Jerez with great interest that year.

The garage doors went up, David Coulthard drove a five-lap run, the exhausts emitting a conventional note, and he returned to the pits. Doors firmly closed. Fifteen minutes later, doors up and off went DC for another five-lap run. This time, however, the exhaust note sounded distinctly different. Back into the pits; doors closed.

The mechanics worked on the car for a further fifteen minutes and sent DC out once more; engine note back to as it was.

McLaren were conducting back-to-back tests; it's a standard procedure. Carry out a control run to establish a baseline, followed by another run with the new, experimental parts fitted. Then go back to how the car was originally prepared and carry out another control run. This allows the engineers to study the data, knowing that the new components have been tested (and compared to the car's original configuration) at the same time of day and under exactly the same track conditions. Working in this methodical fashion greatly reduces the possibility of acquiring misleading data, the team led astray by subtle changes to the ambient temperature or wind speed.

Always fifteen minutes of covert spanner work, sometimes a little less; seldom, if ever, would the mechanics take any longer to make their changes. Fifteen minutes isn't sufficient time to change the engine, that would take at least three times as long – and that would be working flat out. Testing is very rarely conducted at that pace, such stress is the reserve of race weekends. But fifteen minutes would have allowed the mechanics ample time to change the exhaust pipes, at least a particular section of the exhaust pipes.

I often talk to the McLaren mechanics (well, mechanics from pretty much every team, I guess), I know a few of them reasonably well, but I could never get them to open up on the subject of their car's unique exhaust note. They were happy to chat about non-specifics; but, whenever I broached the subject of exhaust harmonics, they would become incredibly interested in a spot on the ground, or enquire how my house restoration was progressing. Mind you, they were more than happy to discuss the antics of every other team in the pit lane. I knew better than to force the issue, they were working, and whatever they were developing was strictly their business. And that's fair enough, it was exactly the same when I worked with Benetton, 'tis the nature of the business.

For optimum performance, specific points of the engine's rev range require the exhausts to have a different tuned length. The ideal way of assisting the harmonics would be to design a system incorporating a method of varying the length of the pipes to suit the differing engine speeds – not unlike a musician adjusting the length of his trombone. The principle is well understood but unfortunately (just as with turbocharging) any such device would fall foul of the technical regulations. Indeed, Article 5.4 is most unambiguous on the subject: 'Variable geometric length exhaust systems are forbidden.' Tricky. The teams know that altering the characteristics of their car's exhaust system will give a potential power advantage, but the rules are the rules are the rules. How, then, are the engineers to find room for a little creative manoeuvring within the tight confines of the rule's wording? How about if they attempted to alter not the *length* of the exhaust pipes but, instead, tried to orchestrate some influence over the system's *internal* characteristics?

It's certainly plausible that careful manipulation of an hydraulically activated butterfly valve could minimise harmonics-induced flat-spots. Such an assembly (one mounted in each of the Collectors?) could be controlled by microprocessor, precision-phased to open and close in conjunction with the direction changes of the internal pressure waves; effectively throttling the internal diameter of the pipes for an instant and disrupting the resonance of the exhaust. The idea of such an exhaust butterfly is by no means new; more than a decade ago the motorcycle industry were experimenting with exactly this technology.

McLaren's car for the following season, the MP4-16, carried an identical signature tune, too, and again Neil Oatley (at that time the team's chief designer) and technical director, Adrian Newey, opted to keep their car's exhaust exits in the same position. As we touched on earlier, it wasn't until the launch of the MP4-17, their 2002/2003 car, that McLaren finally elected to go with the flow (excuse the unintentional pun) and exit their exhausts through the engine cover. And that unique engine note has never been there since. If McLaren were developing something along these lines, it may well be that the idea was eventually discarded because any potential gain in engine power was outweighed by the aerodynamic advantages of relocating the exit pipes through the bodywork and narrowing the waistline of the rear end of the car.

Okay, some might view these ponderings as inconclusive, I don't argue that. Nothing I've shared with you here either confirms or refutes the possibility that McLaren (or any other team for that matter) had managed to develop any exciting harmonic damping valve. But don't you find that the mystery, the intrigue of what *might* be going on behind those garage doors, plays a major role in the allure of Formula 1? I do ... and I love it! Providing the demarcation between fact and speculation is clearly defined, I find these pit lane stories fascinating.

Here's another little reminiscence I'd like to share with you. Although it does kind of lead on from the story above, there's no pit lane speculation attached to this one. It concerns something that actually happened to me, something very memorable.

In the summer of 2001, a film crew and I were invited along to McLaren's ageing headquarters, in Woking. Speedvision were doing some filming there and we spent much of the day encamped at the factory. It soon became obvious that the McLaren empire had outgrown the old facilities. Over the years the team had slowly occupied much of the local, rather jaded-looking industrial estate but were clearly still short of elbow room.

Actually, they are in the process of building a new facility – Paragon – a colossal project designed to house all the elements of their now vast operation under one roof. According to the *Oxford English Dictionary*, paragon is 'a model of excellence, or an excellent person or thing'. I like the name, it suits McLaren's philosophy: an organisation that gives careful consideration to the tiniest of details.

When working with Benetton as a race mechanic, I felt more nervous with Ron Dennis watching us from the pit lane during one of his nightly promenades past the garages, than when Flavio Briatore was standing right next to me. Ron knew exactly what I was doing, knew exactly the correct procedure my work should follow. Flavio didn't. Flavio is a marketing man, where Ron is himself a former mechanic.

It's a long-standing habit of Ron's to walk along the pit lane in the evening, when things are quiet, when the stands are empty and his corporate guests have long since drifted off to their hotels. He scrutinises each team in turn, stands at the front of their garage and quietly ponders things; making a mental note of everything, picking up on any novel procedure, anything that could be improved upon and used by his own team. He notes the work of the efficient mechanics ... and remembers the faces of the rest.

However, I digress. A section of the building in which Speedvision were filming had been set aside as a storage area; many of McLaren's old cars sat in racks, one atop the other: several high, several deep, each housed in its own tiny cell, all draped in polythene dust sheets. Naturally, every corner of the room was spotless, there seemed little need for protective coverings, perhaps they were intended to catch the occasional drip of engine oil or hydraulic fluid? It goes without saying, however, that the sheets were also spotless.

A few people walked to and fro, busying themselves with daily tasks, yet there was a distinct stillness to the place, an air of calm prevailed. The area round the racks was quiet and softly lit; there was a low murmur, more a resonance of conversation that carried through the gloom. Mechanics padded silently past the rows and columns of silent, gleaming race machines. They created a wonderful image: guardians protecting a legendary dormitory; the cars sleeping, removed from the passing of time, like ranks of mythical knights, now resting, forever safe after their heroic battles.

All the cars I could see were preserved in their correct Marlboro livery: vivid red and white, the striking colours of a classic era. A sharp tingle spiked the back of my neck. I walked closer towards the cars on the lower racks, peering through the plastic quilts to see if I could make out the drivers' name stickers ... and there they were: SENNA. SENNA. PROST. PROST. SENNA. Cars from 1988, from 1989 and 1990, 1991, and more ... many more. Here were the turbo cars that Ayrton and Alain had driven to those remarkable fifteen victories; the very ones that had streaked past me, lap after lap as I watched atop the sodden spectator-banking at Silverstone. I remember standing on tiptoe, mesmerised, each time they roared into view and zoomed along the pit straight. I had seen these cars in action, had smelt them, heard them, even felt the air vibrate. I had been a part of the event, experienced it first-hand; that's what 'going to the races' is all about. It's something that television coverage can never quite capture, no matter how good the pictures or insightful the commentary.

That race weekend had inspired me, I wanted to be on the opposite side of the track, working in the pits as opposed to watching the flurry of activity through the catch fencing. Well, that had happened, of course, and now, years later, I was standing in McLaren's own factory, again looking at those same wonderful cars. Talk about standing on hallowed ground! I closed my mouth, realising my jaw had dropped and took a deep breath. Lost in reverie I'd stopped breathing! I was well aware I was enjoying a privileged position, honoured to be left alone in such an intimate setting. This part of the factory wasn't a museum, nothing was intended to be on display, this was more like browsing through an artist's studio, leafing through great works of art as they stood propped against the walls.

I'd forgotten just how big these cars were; the width of them – the height of the rear wings, the size of the tyres – everything was enormous ... and magnificent! I turned and asked one of the mechanics if I could lift the cover and peek inside the cockpit. 'Yeah, go on, Steve,' he said, 'you know the drill.' His response took me by surprise, although we hadn't been introduced clearly he knew me ... then the penny dropped. This was a mechanic I used to chat with in the pit lane over a decade ago, he'd given up racing and now remained here, in Woking.

I turned my attention back to the cars reclining beneath the covers, slowly raising one to peek inside at Ayrton's MP4-5B from 1990. I allowed my fingers to slide over the immaculate paintwork, cold to the touch. My inaugural season in Formula 1 was spent preparing cars that would race against this very McLaren. Benetton versus McLaren ... To be honest it wasn't much of a contest, McLaren were at the height of their prowess, we were still finding our feet; nevertheless, we did manage to win the last two races of the season, not bad by any means. By the end of the year, however, Ayrton Senna had taken six race victories and claimed his second world crown, and McLaren had won their sixth Constructors' trophy. It would be another four years before Benetton could produce that sort of form, and as for claiming six Constructors' trophies – forget it. Flocks of aerodynamically efficient, genetically engineered pigs would be winging their way to Africa for the winter before Benetton would ever win more than a single team cup.

I thoroughly enjoyed my day filming at McLaren, but as we were preparing to wind up and head off home there was one more treat in store. A couple of days before we arrived, one of these sleeping cars had been carefully removed from its den, and the mechanics had been fussing over it all day. The McLaren-Honda MP4-7, chassis number 10 (Gerhard Berger's race car for the final four races of 1992) was to be coaxed out of hibernation. A couple of Honda's engineers arrived to oversee the car's first 'fire-up' for more than eight years.

The car's engine was the last V12, 3.5 litre power plant to be produced by Honda. Not unsurprisingly, after such a long sleep the engine was somewhat reluctant to wake up. On the engineers' first attempt to coax it back to life it merely coughed, sneezed, then belched a rather ominous looking cloud of black exhaust smoke. The engineers looked a tad perturbed, studied their laptops for a time, then massaged some software. Thumbs up. On the second attempt the car growled, then barked – very loudly – then it seemed to choke on something, like a piece of bread caught in the windpipe, whereon it stopped again. Apparently one bank of cylinders wasn't listening to instructions, only the throttle butterflies on the right-hand side were paying attention.

Teeth were sucked and more laptop keys were tapped. Thumbs up. The starter was engaged, the crank turned, all throttles opened in unison and with a series of bright retorts the engine burst into life: crisp, alert, desperate to rev! The Honda engineer squeezed his remote hand-throttle a little more and the twelve pistons leapt with enthusiasm, the exhausts howled their encouragement! After five minutes, with everyone satisfied that all was well, the engine was cut and a circle of satisfied mechanics beamed at one another. A piece of racing history had been brought back to life.

While the mechanics were working on their 1992 chassis, eventually I had to turn away to escape the noise of the exhausts. Doing so my attention was caught by another car, not one in a storage rack, this was on the ground, sitting by itself in a corner of the building. It was a silver and black car, a West liveried MP4-15 McLaren, one of the team's 2000 cars. This later-generation car was one that may have been fitted with an exhaust harmonics control valve! And there it was, unchaperoned, with no one giving it the slightest attention. Not only that, but the bodywork wasn't secured down, merely resting on top of the airbox and engine. All I needed to do would be to sidle over, lift the bodywork just enough to peek inside and all would be revealed.

With hindsight perhaps the question is: Do I now regret walking away from the car and not looking? As it happened, as soon as the mechanics had killed the engine, I thanked them for their help and hospitality and drove back to the hotel. Well, I didn't regret it, not that day. McLaren's secrets remained McLaren's secrets. I'd done the right thing, I felt sure of that. But now, tonight, this very evening as we sit here in fogbound JFK airport debating the issue...

The Air France people were wonderfully organised. Within a couple of minutes of Paul Kelver dropping off his load of blankets, an assistant arrived with pillows. 'Okay guys?' she asked. 'I'm really sorry about this,' she said, nodding at the weather, 'but I think you've made the right decision to stay here ... I mean ... you get to go home on Concorde, that's pretty cool, isn't it? Have any of you guys flown Concorde before?' We all shook our heads, all except Wingrave; he'd returned to the bathroom.

'Well, I suggest you try and get some rest, we'll be right over there at the desk if you need anything,' she said, this time nodding at her colleagues. She placed the pillows on Wingrave's empty chair. 'Pull up some more seats guys, if you rest your feet on one you can make a kind of lounger.' She and her team were well drilled, clearly this wasn't the first time they'd had to convert their lounge into a makeshift hotel. Then, as if by magic, the lighting dimmed and the lounge was bathed in a subdued glow, throwing the lights of the bar's cooling cabinets into stark relief. 'Oh, and just so we know where everyone is, airport security asks that you stay in the club lounge, okay? It's all closed out there anyway, so there's really very little point in going anywhere – everything you need should be right here ... we have wash kits by the desk, too – just ask if you need anything.'

Carl Hentschel dragged two more leather seats towards our camp, I followed suit and we soon had four beds in a line, we set them facing away from the brightness of the bar.

'Ah, well done chaps,' said Wingrave, smiling as he returned. Low snoring noises began drifting from Paul and Carl's direction less than five minutes after they'd kicked off their shoes and draped themselves in blue blankets.

'Tired, Steve?' asked Wingrave from his makeshift bunk; unlike his friends he was still upright, a blanket slung cloak-like around his shoulders.

'I should be, it's certainly very late ... but, no, not really. My legs and feet are aching a bit, from all the walking I did this morning, but I don't feel at all sleepy. I think it's all this Grand Prix talk – it's set my mind racing.'

Oblivious to my pun, Wingrave smiled encouragingly. 'Well, let's carry on then ... if you'd like to, that is? I hardly ever sleep these days, an hour or two at most seems enough.'

I told him I'd be happy to continue. I unwrapped a blanket and threw it over my outstretched legs.

'Now, where were we up to? Ah, yes ...'

7

Shifting Times

'It just sort of span out of control, threw me out on the
circuit and did the only decent thing it could do, which was
to set itself on fire.'
Tony Brooks – talking of the ill-handling 1956 BRM

Before we were sidetracked investigating the exhaust system, we were about to manufacture and install our car's transmission. No mean feat. Like the engine, the gearbox forms a vital link in the car's overall rigidity, it too is a fully stressed member. There is no separate space-frame or cradle into which the gearbox housing safely nestles; no rubber mountings to support the housing and dampen any vibrations. Along with the monocoque and engine, the gearbox has to carry and withstand every load the car is subjected to.

The torsional strength of our finished car (and consequently much of its on-track handling) stands or falls on the sum of three individual elements: the monocoque and engine we've already discussed – the transmission is the third. Just as the monocoque contains the mounting pick-ups for the front suspension and steering system, the gearbox contains the pick-ups for the rear suspension and drive train: the driveshafts, stub-axles and uprights; the bearing carriers for the stub-axles, fixed between the upper and lower wishbones. Several additional parts are bolted ahead and behind these three major components but they do not form part of the core of the car, they can be added or removed at will. For example, the car's rear wing assembly and the rear crash structure are both fixed to the back of the gearbox housing, but they do not affect the car's inherent torsional rigidity.

It might help to explain that the rear crash structure is a safety feature required by the technical regulations. Basically it is a block of carbon fibre and aluminium honeycomb, looking not entirely unlike a witch's pointed hat. It is specifically designed to crush in on itself, concertina fashion, during an impact, so helping to dissipate some of the colossal energy released in the event of an accident. (Actually, the nose of the car, the aerodynamically shaped section extending ahead of the front wing is designed to work in exactly the same way.)

The crash structure is connected to the rear of the car by one of two methods; either it fits directly over the stunted tail of the gearbox (where the differential is housed) and is bolted into place, or – and this is a far more elegant solution – the crash structure is moulded in such a way so as its forward section forms the rearmost part of the gearbox, commonly known as the 'diff cap'.

Once bolted into place, the rear wing's mounting pylons are then fixed to the crash structure. To aid clarification, beginning at the front and moving towards the rear of the car, the sequence of parts is: the front wing and nose assembly, the monocoque, the engine, the gearbox, the rear crash structure, and finally the rear wing assembly.

In light of the fact that the gearbox plays such an important part of the whole, basically forming a third of the entire chassis, one will often hear it referred to as the 'rear end' of the car. During practice and qualifying sessions, when the pit lane tom-toms are reporting that team X are frantically renewing the rear end of one of their cars, it refers to the entire gearbox/suspension/wing assembly. Because contemporary F1 cars are designed on this modular, three-section (monocoque-engine-transmission) principle, it's often quicker for the mechanics to swap the entire rear end of their car, rather than attempt a potentially time-consuming repair to a problematic driveshaft, seized suspension bearing, what have you. All of that infinitely more long-winded rectification work can be undertaken in the evening, after the sessions have finished and the immediate urgency to have the car on-track has passed.

As with every component we've discussed, in order to optimise the car's handling we want the mass of the gearbox to be as close to the ground as possible. Not only that, we also want the gearbox to be as far forward as possible. Ideally, if only in theory, we'd like to concentrate the combined mass of all the components at the exact centre of the car, an intersection point midway between the lateral and longitudinal centrelines, somewhere just to the rear of the driver.

In practice, lamentably, we're unable to do this. We can't, for example, move the hundred kilogram mass of the engine further to the centre of the car but leave the engine itself in its original position; sadly, the unalterable laws of physics won't allow it. In which case we simply have to do the best we can, we can't relocate the weight of the engine by magic, so we must mount the engine and transmission as close to the centre of the car as we can.

It is for this very reason that front-engined Grand Prix cars became utterly redundant within three years of John Cooper introducing his diminutive Cooper Climax. Cooper's race cars were designed with their engines positioned *behind* the driver, not sticking out ahead of him. The car made its first appearance in 1959, winning back-to-back championships – both drivers' and constructors' – in its first two seasons of competition.

The Cooper's layout proved an instant success, producing a light, agile, 'forgiving' race car. It left the rest of the industry scratching their heads and thinking, 'Now, why didn't we think of doing that!' However, in actual fact, the concept was far from new, it was more than a quarter-century old and had already been tested and raced with great aplomb. Designed by Ferdinand Porsche (yep, same chap), the magnificent Auto Unions of the 1930s had used exactly this layout: their mighty 4.4 litre, V16 engines positioned just as John Cooper would fit his compact 2.5 litre, four-cylinder Coventry Climax engines some twenty-five years down the road.

It took a while; but what goes around comes around, I guess, though I've never really understood why it had to take quite so long. I'm with Cooper's rival constructors on this one, why didn't they think of doing that? Cooper's theories of weight distribution and engine positioning kick-started a revolution in F1 design – principles which remain in use to this very day – and just like John Barnard's carbon monocoque, I can't envisage anything better coming along.

The area of physics associated with a desire to position the weight of the engine and gearbox closer to the centre of the car is called Moments. Moments deal with the turning effects produced on objects set in motion by the forces of mass and acceleration acting on them. In our particular case, the Moment that concerns us is called the 'polar moment of inertia'. It's a great name, full of tension, it sounds like a planet poised on the very brink of inter-stellar collision with a fire-filled star. In my experience, however, it's also a sure-fire conversation queller, a topic guaranteed to clear even the most crowded of Sunday lunchtime pubs.

Nevertheless, to condense the contents of several leather-bound volumes into one extremely small nutshell, the following little demo might help to throw some light on what it all means. Imagine the bar of a dumb-bell, each end laden with a weight. If one of us were to grip the bar in the middle and pivot our wrist to the left and right, we'd notice how reluctant the bar is to change direction. Once set in motion the weights want to keep moving in that direction – a consequence of the mass of the weights, their distance from the middle of the bar and the subsequent force of inertia acting on them.

However, if we move the two weights to the middle of the bar and again try to pivot the dumb-bell, we'll notice how much easier and quicker the bar changes direction. If we think of our dumb-bell and weights in terms of a racing car, it means that the further from the centre of the car the mass of the engine and transmission is, the more reluctant the car will be to change direction.

We want to concentrate the combined masses close to the centre because, once again, it's something that will greatly encourage the car's nimble handling. It will respond more predictably and react quicker to changes in direction if the weight at the front and rear is kept to a minimum and contained, as far as is practicable, within the confines of the wheelbase. This isn't to suggest that the ideal weight distribution between the front and rear axles is an even 50–50 split. Generally, the engineers will ask the mechanics to set the car with the weight distribution slightly offset towards the rear. (For example, 45 per cent on the front axle, 55 per cent on the rear; achieved by moving the on-board ballast fore and aft along the longitudinal centreline of the chassis.) However, trying to move the weight to the theoretically perfect position is a doctrine of design, just as making everything as light as possible is also a doctrine. Working towards both of these ideals will result in a superior car, one with a far greater range of potential adjustments.

All of which reminds me of an interesting episode that happened a few years ago while I was working with Benetton; a little vignette that will perfectly illustrate a team's constant pursuit of design ideals. Back in 1995, during a mid-season testing session, Ross Brawn asked me to remove two bodywork screws from the side panels of our B195 car – these are the vertical sections of the body that sit adjacent the exhausts. He also asked me to tape over the uncovered holes, presumably so as not to upset the aerodynamic flow of the bodywork. (Actually, it seemed unlikely that leaving such tiny holes exposed to the elements would have had *any* significant effect on the airflow, but I was happy to oblige; perhaps Ross wanted the holes taped more so as not to upset Rory Byrne, the team's chief aero specialist at that time. Rory wasn't at the track but he would have been most unhappy to think his car was running around the track with *holes* in it, and Ross has always been a considerate chap. Anyway, that bit of the story's all by the by, it's the screws we're interested in, not their holes.)

Ross had studied the number and location of the bodywork fasteners, had convinced himself that there was an excessive number of screws holding the panels in place and that removing two of them would in no way jeopardise the panels' security. I agreed with him (I think all the mechanics would have), considering how often we used to take them in and out during the course of a race weekend; it was a classic belt-and-braces job. Ross wanted to remove the screws, carry out a five-lap test run, and if all went well he wanted to bin the screws for good, so shaving their weight from the car's total mass.

The collective weight of those two screws was less than one gram, and, again, I was sure that doing away with them wouldn't make any noticeable difference to the performance of the car. Okay, in theory, yes, logic says it must make a difference, but an advantage in lap time so small it would be impossible to measure. I pointed this out to Ross. 'It's a philosophy, Steve,' came his reply, 'I thought we should give it a go, that's all; try to make the car as light as we can, that's what we're here for.'

Throughout the rest of the year's Grands Prix we ran the cars without those two bodywork screws. Actually, I seem to recall the production drawing of the body panels was altered, removing the surplus holes. I remain unconvinced that such a minute modification made a difference to our race cars, but I do know we secured both the drivers' and the constructors' world championships that year. Detail. It's all in the detail.

All Formula 1 transmissions are designed by the teams, in-house, but much of the actual manufacturing work is undertaken by outside companies. The casting process used to produce the housings and the complex machining and grinding of the shafts and gear ratios is not something the teams themselves are equipped for. It simply isn't cost-effective for them to invest in the horrifically expensive plant and machinery to produce what will inevitably be relatively small batches.

Irrespective that many of the teams are in partnership with or owned by major road car manufacturers, I'm unaware of any that use their parent company's production facilities to produce their transmission internals. Perhaps the most likely candidate to do so would be Scuderia Ferrari (where the road car and racing divisions share the same campus), but even they prefer to use local specialist gear grinders. The teams draw the components to their own specification and call on people such as Hewland, Xtrac, and Gemini to supply the finished pieces.

The gearbox is not as heavy as the engine, weighing only about a third as much; meaning that a contemporary generic transmission assembly (just the housing and its internals) would tip the scales at approximately 37.4kg. Okay, for a 'generic' figure you might suppose that number seems a tad specific, and you'd be right – it's absolutely spot on for a certain midfield runner of 2002 vintage. Also, the fact that the transmission is lighter than the engine means that we don't have the potential drama of the car pitching itself off the high-stands after we've bolted the clutch and gearbox housing to the back of the engine. The gearbox is mounted to the engine via a series of six or eight studs, the operation itself is similar to installing the engine to the back of the chassis.

Many different designs of transmission, materials and methods of housing construction have been tried over the years, some more successful than others, but the basic criteria – the engineers' wish list – remain the same as for everything else on the car: it must be lightweight, compact and reliable.

Nowadays, every team without exception uses a longitudinal transmission, sometimes known as an inline 'box, designed with their gear shafts following the line of the crankshaft. However, at the very end of the 1980s and leading on into the start of the next decade, a few teams – Onyx, Ferrari and Benetton amongst them – developed transverse gearboxes; their shafts running at right angles to the crankshaft.

Although this system was a little more complex as a result, requiring the use of two 45° bevel gears to transmit the drive from the engine to the gearbox, these transverse units weren't especially any less reliable. The reason for their introduction was, once again, to help improve the car's weight distribution. Turning the gear shafts through 90° made the gearbox considerably wider but it also moved the weight of the whole transmission assembly closer to the centre of the car.

Another significant advantage was that it was no longer necessary to separate the gearbox from the engine in order to change the ratios, removing a simple side cover was all that was required to gain access to the internals. Naturally, they proved an instant hit with the gearbox mechanics.

From a purely selfish perspective, the only pain with them was the struggle caused by having to feed the external starter between the diffuser and the bodywork, and then to locate its splined drive into the gearbox. On an inline 'box the starter shaft is located at the extreme rear of the car, easy to see and to deal with. But the layout of the transverse system resulted in the starter/gearbox coupling being completely hidden from view. A bit of a nightmare, frankly, especially if the car was hot, and even more so if the car had stalled during a pit stop.

John Barnard (Benetton) and Alan Jenkins (Onyx) were the two leading lights behind the transverse designs. Although they worked for rival organisations and had studied the problems associated with weight distribution quite independently, each had arrived at the same potential solution at pretty much exactly the same time.

Their transverse gearboxes only lost popularity within the industry because of the added width of the housings. The ever growing influence of aerodynamics over a car's final design, and the designer's wish to keep the rear of the car as narrow as possible (especially that sensitive area inboard of the rear wheels), resulted in the transverse 'box being consigned to history and a return of the inline, longitudinal transmission.

In the unending quest to reduce size and mass, one of the biggest advancements over the last five years concerns the engine oil reservoir. During our discussion on engines, I mentioned that Formula 1 motors use dry sump lubrication, meaning that the oil is not stored in a pan directly below the crankshaft but is instead stored in a remote reservoir. From this tank the oil is supplied to the crankshaft (and everything else) through a series of pipes and galleries, pressure-fed via an engine-driven pump. As the oil is spent and falls to the bottom of the cylinder block it is immediately scavenged by another pump (known, somewhat predictably, as the scavenge pump) and travels through a cooler before arriving back at the remote reservoir.

For many years it was standard practice to store the engine oil, a quantity of between nine and twelve litres, within an isolated chamber, cast as part of the transmission housing. Naturally, this resulted in the housing having to be made significantly larger than what would be necessary to house purely the gearbox internals. The machinery within the gearbox – the bearings and gear shafts, ratios and selectors – also need lubricating, of course, and rely on a different specification of oil (a far more viscous concoction than engine oil) known as a hypoid or 'extreme pressure' lubricant, designed specifically to cope with the demands of the intermeshing gear trains. Pressure-fed to the internals by its own pump, the gear oil (between two and three litres) in these boxes was stored in the space beneath the rotating shafts. The mechanics of the system worked fine, but the necessary size of the housing resulted in a less than ideal design.

Towards the close of the 1990s, both Stewart Grand Prix and Benetton Formula (and perhaps others that I'm not aware of) tried to do away with the need of specialised gear oil, designing their transmissions to make use of a supply of engine oil 'borrowed' from the reservoir conveniently located in the housing. This shaved a little size and weight from the 'box itself but most significantly it did away with carrying the weight of the gear oil. The net result was an overall saving of between 1.8–2.5kg. Not bad, not bad at all. However, the problem was that the gearbox was having to use an oil not designed for the purpose. Nothing too radical in that per se, the road car industry has been dabbling with the idea on and off since the summer of 1959, when Alec Issigonis introduced the Mini to the world. Nevertheless, dealing with 850-plus horsepower means that a Formula 1 transmission is subjected to far greater stresses and power loads than any road car (the 850cc engine that powered that original '59 Mini generated a modest 34bhp).

The concept soon lost favour; pretty quickly both Stewart and

Benetton had resorted to using gear oil. Interestingly, though, their decision to do so wasn't based so much on the engine oil's inability to cope with the pressures of the transmission, it was more a problem of reliable filtration of the lubricant as it circulated between its reservoir, the engine and transmission. In the event of a reasonably significant mechanical failure to an engine (and let's face it, at crank speeds in excess of 18,000rpm most of them are pretty significant) the teams would often suffer with transmission problems too, a result of particles of engine debris finding their way inside the gearbox. Most annoying of all, however, was that these transmission troubles would, more often than not, only show themselves *after* the car had been fitted with a replacement engine and sent back to the track. Irritating beyond belief. This was not through any lack of careful cleaning and rebuilding work by the mechanics, they did the best they could; but trying to find every last piece of shrapnel proved exceptionally difficult.

The next major advance was to relocate the engine-oil reservoir, to remove the storage chamber from the transmission housing altogether. This was a big step forward. What the teams did was to ask their fabricators to make aluminium tanks to take the place of the reservoir, and to sandwich this tank between the chassis and the engine. The monocoques were designed with a concave section moulded into their back face, a perfect shape to accept the remote oil tank. Once the engine was bolted in position the reservoir was enclosed between the two and hidden from sight. This new location was perfect, just as we've discussed – as close to the centre of the car as possible. The transmission engineers were free to design their latest gearboxes without an integral chamber. Gearboxes visibly shrank as a result, and in most cases housings are now 30 per cent smaller. Parties all round. From Ferrari to Minardi, the idea has been universally adopted.

Could things ever get any better? Well, Formula 1 isn't the pinnacle of automotive engineering for nothing – the industry never takes a day off. If a team isn't advancing, then it's going backwards; to pause is to lose. At the same time as the new, smaller gearboxes were being bolted to the back of the engines, the research engineers were already pondering their replacement.

In the winter following the end of the 2000 season, the tendrils of the paddock's grapevine had sensed vibrations that Ferrari's research and development (R&D) department were quietly working on a new transmission; not merely an upgrade of a tried and tested design, but something quite revolutionary. Paddock chit-chat suggested the team were investigating the idea of casting their engine block and transmission housing as a single unit.

Remembering that the transmission is a fully stressed part of the chassis, the idea of producing a single casting for both engine and gearbox is exceedingly exciting, it would make the car stiffer and lighter. No matter how well the engine is mounted to the chassis, or the engine to the gearbox, when the car is disassembled there are always visible signs of fretting between the mating faces, most notably between the engine and gearbox. Any bolted connection will fret in this way (everything moves); it's a tolerated evil, though the extent of any movement is carefully monitored.

Casting a one-piece unit is a fine idea, but doing so leads to another question. Having lost the ability to separate the gearbox and engine block, how were the team proposing to install the clutch assembly? But there were whispers on this too; suggestions that the team were developing a system of controlling the drive that would negate any need for a conventional multiplate clutch.

Grand Prix engineers are continually working to reduce the size and weight of their clutch assemblies. In 1990, a Formula 1 clutch measured six inches in diameter and weighed about two kilos; today we can virtually halve that. A contemporary F1 clutch will rest in the palm of a hand, but the engineers would still prefer to do away with it altogether, regardless of how compact it is. Each year the engine manufacturers look to shave mere tenths of grams from their pistons, connecting rods, crankshafts ... you name it. Imagine how happy they'd be if told they could ditch the entire clutch and flywheel assembly. The very idea that Ferrari were, perhaps, planning exactly such a move was equally exciting news, and precisely how they intended to do this gave rise to many coffee-break debates. Ferrari were saying nothing, of course, why should they?

If they managed to discard their clutch assembly, they would also remove further need of a bell-housing, the hollow section at the front of the transmission used to house the clutch and its ancillaries. And if the clutch is scrapped, so then is the need for a clutch-release mechanism: the release bearing itself, its machined sleeves, the controlling electronics and hydraulics – all gone. Losing all of that would allow for the gear shafts and ratios to be moved closer to the engine, perhaps by as much as 100mm, and that would be another big advantage.

The next question, then, was how they were planning to make/break and control the drive as it passed from the engine, through the transmission and on to the rear wheels.

If there was substance to these reports – and I feel convinced there was – then perhaps it was no accident that the timing of Ferrari's research and development programme coincided with the news that the FIA was intending to revoke the prohibition on sophisticated on-board (hydraulic and electronic) control functions. These had been outlawed at the conclusion of 1993, but come the Spanish Grand Prix of 2001, systems such as traction control, launch control and automatic gearbox strategies would be back in business.

The relaxation of the rules would affect the transmission's final drive, too. Up until Friday, 27 April 2001, the first practice session of the race weekend at Barcelona, the teams were only allowed to alter the hydraulic settings of their self-locking differentials (and so manipulate the percentage of slip acting on the driveshafts) when the car was stationary in the pit lane. It was prohibited to make any alterations once the car had taken to the track. A bit of a strange ruling, and this is how it came about: before the advent of hydraulically controlled diffs, the only way for the teams to alter the characteristics of the transmission's final drive was to bring the car into the pits and physically swap the diffs, one for another.

There would be a selection of four or five on hand, each unit preassembled by the mechanics, built with different ramps, plates and preloads. Out with one diff, in with another, car sent back on track. With a well-drilled crew the whole operation could be completed in fifteen minutes. (I know this from first-hand experience. Back in 1996 my colleagues and I spent three long, very hectic – and extremely cold – days at a tiny test track in south Wales, doing nothing but changing diffs, one after the other. Actually, by the end of the third day we'd managed to get our time down to twelve minutes, thirty-five ... these things become permanently etched on the memory.)

So, anyway, that was what we did to play around with the settings of the final drive during the practice sessions of the race weekends; and not only Benetton – all the leading teams used the same tactics. It was a lot of work but it was fun, at least I thought so; I always enjoyed that up-against-the-clock, now-or-never, do-or-die stuff. Over the next couple of years, however, the designers eventually got the hang of using the car's hydraulics to alter the settings. One engineer, and three seconds with a laptop computer, was all it needed to achieve the same amount of work it had previously taken six mechanics and fifteen minutes' worth of flashing spanners to do.

The FIA pondered things and agreed that the teams could keep their hydraulic diffs, providing they made any adjustments to them only in the pits; in this way there was no chance of the teams using their newly developed systems to enhance the cars' performance either in the race or throughout a flying lap in qualifying. From that standpoint, with the alterations having to be done in the pits, the new system was no different to the old, it merely took less time to carry out the work.

From Barcelona onwards, however, the teams were free to adjust the hydraulic pressures at any time, either by driver-operated switches or by pit-to-car data transmission – another new allowance within the regulations. Providing the adjustments were carried out equally to both sides of the differential, the teams were at liberty to control the hydraulics as they saw fit. And adjust them they did, constantly. Prior to the start of the 2003 season, a slight tightening of the regulations governing electronics saw the banning of two-way data transmission. This somewhat bizarre rule change put an end to the engineers' ability to adjust the on-board electronics while the car was on track. The diff itself, however, remained fully adjustable from within the car.

The driver can select many options, altering the action of the differential from corner to corner; choosing, perhaps, to fully lock the car's diff, removing any independent action from the drive-shafts (like a kart), assisting with rear stability when arriving at a corner under heavy braking. He could choose to unlock the diff, dialling in a degree of slip mid-corner to prevent any snap-oversteer on corner-exit. And there are any number of variables in between, depending on: circuit configuration, weather conditions, driving style, tyres, what have you. The driver can adjust the car using his steering wheel-mounted switches; and even the car can adjust the car, using any number of presets programmed into its on-board microprocessors.

Keeping in mind that conventional, foot-operated clutch pedals have been absent from Formula 1 cars since the mid 1990s; that the drivers now operate the clutch by fingertip control (merely a spring-loaded lever connected to a potentiometer that feeds a signal to the appropriate control box); it seems reasonable to suggest that with adequate development and testing, the already high-level hydraulics and electronics controlling the differential could be tailored to replicate the functions of a conventional multiplate clutch.

It would require some clever design work, naturally. The drive-couplings to the output flanges would have to be manufactured in two pieces, able to be locked and unlocked in the same way that a conventional clutch makes and breaks the drive between a flywheel and gearbox input shaft. Nevertheless, there seems no hard and fast reason why that couldn't be achieved. After all, thirty-year-old technology had enabled two chaps to play a round of golf on the moon (and had managed to return them safely to earth in time for a snifter in the clubhouse bar).

Three decades later, I feel reasonably confident that a team of bright, talented engineers could design a clutch-less transmission system along these lines. A tad cumbersome at first, perhaps; then, as with everything, refined in operation, reduced in size and honed to perfection within a season or two. Maybe they'd prefer not to use the differential internals in this way, but a similar system could be adapted and installed at an earlier point in the drive train. Interesting stuff, many of us were getting very enthusiastic about Ferrari's research and where it might all lead. Then – almost overnight – the tea's-up news service fell silent; nothing more was heard of Ferrari's plans. It was as though any potential uni-casting project and/or clutch-less transmission development programme had suddenly lost favour with the team.

It so happened that this lack of pit-lane news coincided with another proposed change to the technical regulations, this one concerning itself with the longevity of engines. In an attempt to help curb the ever escalating costs in F1, the FIA intended to introduce a rule, effective from the start of the 2004 season, whereby the teams must only use one engine per car, per race weekend. If a team were forced to renew an engine due to a mechanical failure, they would be penalised ten places on the starting grid.

A harsh, somewhat draconian penalty and one to be avoided at all costs. But what if a team, any team, had developed a uni-casting for its block and transmission, and due to gearbox problems were forced to change the transmission's housing? By virtue of being a one-piece item, the team would have no option but to replace the engine, too. But change the engine, for any reason, and it'll cost you ten spots on the grid. Oops! All of a sudden, what had at first looked like a potentially really good idea was now beginning to look like a potentially really bad liability. Most likely it is for this reason that such a masterful piece of innovative engineering seems to have been allowed to wither and die on the vine along with the stories of its possible existence.

A year or so before Ferrari may have been developing their combined engine/gearbox prototype, Williams had been busy working on a new transmission system of their own. Although it was never actually raced, they had shifted it from the design board, built a prototype unit and carried out a series of evaluation tests. The system was a 'continually variable' transmission, an updated and enhanced version of the original DAF/Volvo Variomatic gearbox, in which the speed difference between the input and output shafts is continually adjusted by a series of cones and drive bands. Between bottom gear and top, there aren't really any fixed ratios, the system … well, the system kind of makes its own ratios as it sees best.

After its 1950s debut, the Variomatic came in for considerable (and mostly quite unwarranted) criticism. There were lots of derisory comments in the motoring press concerning cars driven by rubber bands: just wind her up and let her go, that sort of stuff. And for that reason, along, I think, with a general feeling of sheer mistrust over its novelty, this avant-garde transmission system never really took off. On the whole, people don't like change, do they?

Personally, I always thought it was rather a neat idea and presumably the engineers at the Williams research and development department thought so too. It seemed a fine project for a Grand Prix car, a fully refined system should provide a race car with the absolute perfect gear ratio for any given engine speed, circuit condition and level of downforce. Williams clearly believed they were on to something, they continued to research and hone the concept right up to the point where the FIA issued a 'clarification' of the technical regulations, effectively stopping the project in its tracks. Article 9.3.1 (the section of the rule book covering permissible types of transmission systems) now states: 'The minimum number of forward gear ratios is four and the maximum is seven.'

And if the exact wording of that clarification still seems open to a certain degree of serpentine interpretation by the teams, then the FIA's next amendment really gave the Williams 'box a resounding thwack with a coal shovel. Article 9.3.2 reads: 'Continuously variable transmission systems are not permitted.' Ah! Well ... Other than hatching a scheme to make off with every single copy of the regulations and scribbling out the word 'not' with thick crayon – which, let's face it, is not a very practical solution – I think the FIA have rather won the day on that one. Certainly Frank and Patrick thought so, their prototype gearbox was immediately shelved. Shame, really; but again, I think the FIA were acting in good faith, trying to nip things in the bud and so control costs. If Williams had trumped the opposition with their new gearbox, then the rest of the paddock would have had to follow suit, or invent something even more ingenious.

So, there we are, to this day the engineers remain constrained by the wording of the technical regulations to use only manual-type transmissions fitted with between four and seven forward gears; in reality, however, no team uses fewer than six. The teams are at liberty to renew and interchange those four-to-seven gears (more frequently referred to as ratios) as often as they wish. And this is something they do all the time, it's nothing unusual for the ratios in a car's gearbox to be changed for the start of each and every session throughout the race weekend. When choosing the ratios for a particular session, one factor to take into consideration is the prevailing wind speed and direction, both of which the teams are carefully monitoring.

Whenever you visit a track, keep an eye on the flags fluttering above the pits and the control tower. Between sessions, if the flags begin to swing around, changing from a headwind to a tailwind, or vice versa, you can expect to see the mechanics set-to, fervently swapping ratios to compensate for the wind change before the track opens for business. Because of the amount of work involved to achieve this – car up on high-stands, the rear section of the floor and diffuser removed, the gearbox itself unbolted from the engine; then the actual ratio change, followed by the rebuild work – the engineers *must* make their choice of ratios as early as possible after the preceding session has ended. If, just prior to qualifying, one looks in a garage and sees a car still on high-stands, with some rather urgent arm waving and signals being exchanged, it's reasonable to assume there has been some sort of delay in the issuing of the desired ratios.

A seven-speed gearbox allows a little more versatility with regard to ratio selection, but a six-speed unit will weigh less, should be a mite smaller too. Swings and roundabouts. The final decision on which to go for largely depends on the torque and power characteristics of the particular engine the transmission will be working with. If the engine is blessed with a wide power band and an abundance of torque at lower revs (think back to our debate of V8 versus V12) then it will better cope with the inevitable drop in revs that occurs as the driver – or the on-board electronics – selects each gear of a six-speed unit.

On the other hand, engines with a narrow power band and not as much torque, engines that need to operate within a more confined rev range in order to maintain optimum power output, then perhaps a seven-speed gearbox may be the way forward; the additional gear will reduce the size of the steps (the drop in revs) between each gear shift. These days, with everyone using a V10, the choice of a six- or seven-speed gearbox is not so clear cut. Nonetheless, there are differences between the engines. Yes, all the teams use a V10 but the detailing of what is now the standard F1 configuration varies considerably from team to team and each design possesses individual characteristics.

Incidentally, you may have noticed that I've made little comment on the actual gear selector mechanisms of these contemporary paddle-shift transmissions, and deliberately so. I included quite an in-depth explanation of exactly how the system works in *The*

Mechanic's Tale, and it seems somewhat unnecessary to repeat it here. If you have a copy on the bookshelf, by the way, may I take this opportunity to thank you. You're quite obviously a very kind, generous and well-read individual, and if you'd like to swot-up on semi-auto selectors you might like to refer to chapter six.

Here's another little chart I thought you might like. It's pretty self-explanatory, showing the period of time an F1 car remains in each gear immediately before the engine approaches the rev limiter and the green 'shift' light is illuminated on the steering wheel; from this point either the car's electronics or the driver himself will demand the next up-shift. The chart is for a six-speed gearbox during a section of a lap of Monza, 2002.

Two points to note: remember that these figures are not from a standing start, the car is already on a flying lap, consequently the elapsed time for 1st gear is from the time the driver demands full throttle, until the transmission shifts into 2nd gear. The elapsed time shown for 6th gear relates to the duration of time the car remains in top gear before reaching the end of the straight, at which point the car will begin downshifting through the gears.

As with the other charts I've included, the following data is perfectly reliable, but does correspond to a specific choice of ratios, the precise time/speed figures will vary depending on the ratios chosen for a particular circuit, session, prevailing weather and so on. And no, your eyes do not deceive you, a Formula 1 car is perfectly capable of exceeding a hundred miles an hour in first gear!

Gear	Elapsed time	Achieved speed prior to next up-shift	
1st	1.0	98–165kph	59–101mph
2nd	1.23	195	119
3rd	1.11	235	143
4th	1.5	274	167
5th	2.95	317	193
6th	9.0	359	218

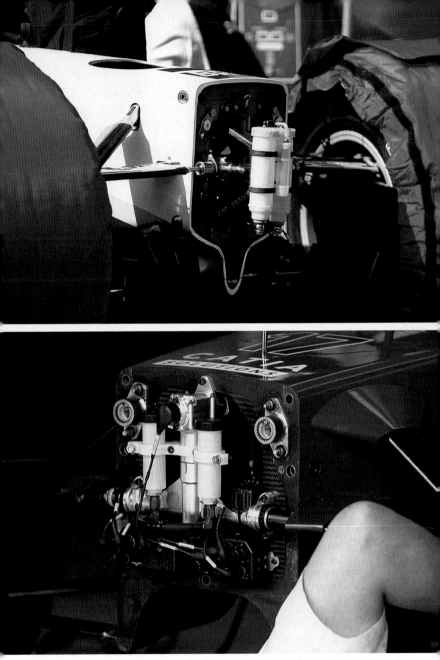

Spot the difference – single keel, twin keel. **TOP** The Williams FW23 with its single, boat-like keel running beneath the chassis. **BOTTOM** The 2001 Sauber, the C20's monocoque included two keels, designed to improve the quality of the airflow immediately behind the front wing (All photographs in this plate section: LAT).

Spot the difference – pullrod, pushrod. **TOP** The 1988 Benetton with its pullrods attached to the top wishbones and the bottom of the chassis. **BOTTOM** The 1990 Ferrari, equipped with pushrods, the suspension links connected between the lower wishbones and the top of the chassis.

TOP The low-nose Benetton and the revolutionary Tyrrell 019 of 1990. The arrival of this landmark Tyrrell signalled the end for what had gone before: the 019 is the direct ancestor of the high-nose, sculptured-keel cars we see today. **BOTTOM** A more detailed shot of the front wing assembly of the Tyrrell 019. The next step in F1's evolution would see the wing's main plane extended to run the full width of the car, between the mounting pylons, increasing surface area and downforce production.

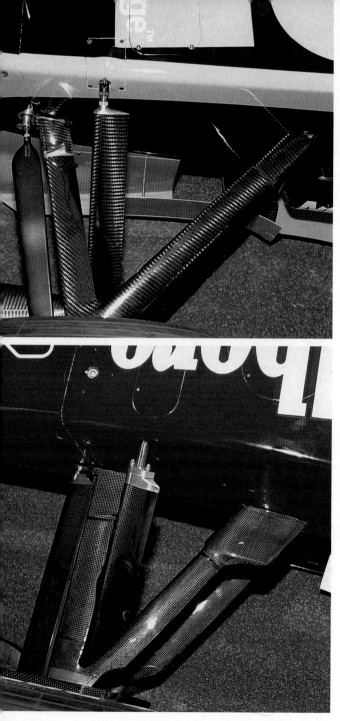

Spot the difference: methods of ride height adjustment.

TOP The ride height of the A23 Arrows is adjusted by turn-buckles, threaded fixings located at the top of each pushrod. **BOTTOM** The F2002 Ferrari uses a series of accurately machined shims, either added or subtracted to alter the length of the pushrod.

TOP The periscope-style exhaust exits, mounted atop the engine cover on the Ferrari, allow the bodywork around the inside of the rear wheels to be pulled in tight to the transmission. Today, all Grand Prix cars are designed in a similar way.

BOTTOM The chimney displaying the Honda logo on the Jordan's engine cover is not an engine exhaust exit, rather its job is to control the air flowing through the radiator matrix.

TOP Looking distinctly more like a solid rocket booster in full flow as opposed to a mere engine failure, it's game over for Giancarlo Fisichella when his car's Honda lets go at Spa, 2002.

BOTTOM Mauricio Gugelmin was uninjured after this dramatic start-line shunt at the 1989 French GP. However, the fact that he managed to get his Leyton House CG891 airborne allows us to see the flat bottom of the chassis and the two exhaust outlets at the rear of the diffuser.

Another start-line shunt, this is Ralf Schumacher's FW24, airborne at Australia, 2002. Thankfully, he too was uninjured. The angle allows us to see the FIA's skid-block running the length of the car, the 'stepped' chassis, and the lack of any exhausts on the line of the diffuser.

The ongoing battle between Bridgestone and Michelin has resulted in their tyres playing an ever-increasing role in the performance of a Grand Prix car. A team's chances of success stand or fall depending on the quality of the rubber supplied to them from race to race.

Today it's all about the transmission's housing. Making the housing both ultra-light and ultra-strong. Ferrari's F2002 made use of an 'investment cast' titanium housing, a ferociously expensive procedure; each housing (just the bare casing) costing somewhere in the region of £120,000 – but the expense doesn't end there. Titanium is beautifully light and strong, but it is an absolute pig to machine, requiring special cutting tools, delicate cuts and extended machining time as a result, you can't rush titanium.

With the signing of former Arrows technical director, Mike Coughlan, McLaren are developing a housing moulded from carbon fibre. Along with John Barnard, Mike was instrumental in developing a similar system for the A19 Arrows. (And – perhaps you won't be too surprised to hear – Alan Jenkins was working on his own carbon gearbox for the fledgling Stewart Grand Prix team at more or less the exact same time. Who was it that said great minds think alike?)

Those early carbon gearboxes suffered from poor reliability. The different rates of heat expansion between the composite materials and the machined aluminium bearing carriers bonded into the housing caused the split lines to fail. The cure was simple but expensive, to change the material specification of the bearing carriers: ditch the aluminium and re-machine them out of titanium, a material that suffers with minimal heat expansion. It did the trick but was something the team had wanted to avoid due to the increased costs. Unfortunately, not all teams enjoy the financial padding afforded Scuderia Ferrari; the sad demise of Prost Grand Prix and, more recently, of Arrows at the conclusion of 2002 is clear indication of that.

Using composite materials to produce a strong, load-bearing construction is nothing new, after all, we've been using it for our monocoques since 1981. If we can make a chassis out of carbon, then there's no real reason why we can't make a transmission housing using the exact same design principles. There are a couple of potential pitfalls (areas that need special consideration); those of excessive temperature burning the resins, and possible oil seepage through the pores and weave of the carbon cloth.

Unlike a monocoque, a gearbox is exposed to all the latent heat beneath the bodywork; this dilemma used to be even more pronounced by virtue of the gearbox's close proximity to the exhaust pipes, but the current trend to exit the pipes atop the bodywork has considerably lessened the problem. As far as fluid seepage is concerned, now the engine oil is no longer stored within the transmission housing, we only have a relatively small quantity of gear oil to worry about. The bonding resins used to cure the carbon fibre are reasonably effective against fluid loss, however, and with the possibility of coating the inside of the housing with additional sealers, the idea of constructing the gearbox from light-weight composite materials becomes increasingly more attractive.

Choices, choices ... which way to go ... What type of transmission should we bolt to the back of the Ferrari engine powering *our* car? Longitudinal or transverse? Titanium or carbon? Well, we know it would be pointless to develop a continually variable gearbox, the FIA would kick us straight out of scrutineering. I *really* like the concept of a uni-casting for both engine and 'box – an awesome idea – but I just know we'd get bitten by the one-engine-per-race-weekend rule. In light of that I think, like Ferrari, we'd do better to steer clear of anything quite so radical. Very sad, nonetheless. Transverse layout? Too wide for these days, the rule amendment introduced for 1998, reducing the car's track by 200mm means we have to use a longitudinal gearbox, as narrow as possible to optimise the airflow around the back of the car.

The final choice, then, is between titanium or carbon fibre for our housing. A tough decision but my intuition tells me, carbon; that's the route both Barnard and Jenkins were exploring before their respective departures from Arrows and Stewart Grand Prix, and it's the route Mike Coughlan is continuing to explore at McLaren. Renault, too, have opted to use carbon fibre for the bell-housing of the R23, their 2003 car. Back in 1981 there were countless cynical comments aimed at the first composite chassis, but with continual refinements it has proved a quite brilliant idea.

I suggest we go for an exquisitely made composite gearbox, equipped with the finest titanium bearing carriers our highly skilled machinists can make. And only *six* speeds (lubricated with proper hypoid oil); we'll rely on the torque and power of the Ferrari engine to compensate for the loss of seventh gear. Having only six speeds will save us a little weight, but of far greater importance, not having seventh gear means it can never fail on us during the last lap of the race. If something isn't absolutely essential – get shot of it; we have no room in our car for frills and trimmings. As to the clutch – to have or have not – I think we should play it safe and go for a conventional multiplate clutch. It would be wonderful to do away with it and develop some trick hydraulically controlled method, but, again, on the grounds of reliability, I think we'd be better off using a well understood, tried and tested piece of equipment. Our engine oil will, of course, be housed in a separate tank, located between the chassis and the engine, allowing our gearbox to remain as small as possible.

I'm not sure if it was the smell of coffee wafting under my nose, the spikes of bright sunlight in my eyes, or someone nudging my arm that finally woke me, perhaps it was a combination of all three.

'Hello, old man,' said Wingrave, 'time to wake up, seven o'clock – morning has broken! Thought you might like a coffee ...?'

I took the cup and mumbled some thanks, still half asleep as I squinted into the sunlight. He was right, morning had definitely broken. Looking out of the lounge windows the transformation was incredible, the long gloom of the night had gone and the thick swirling mist had gone too. It was as though the fog, which had been so clammy and reluctant the evening before, had never existed. The skies were clear and the early sun was growing by the minute.

I glanced at the coffee, out of habit sure that Wingrave would have put milk in it – something I can't cope with, certainly not first thing in the morning. He hadn't, nor did it smell sweet. I took a long swallow and let the caffeine soak in. 'Thanks, George,' I said, this time with more feeling. 'That's a fine gesture!'

Wingrave waved my thanks away, 'Pleasure, old man ... any time.'

'I can't remember falling asleep, sorry about that – I hope it wasn't mid-sentence ...'

'Not a bit of it. We'd been discussing gearboxes for quite a while; I plodded off to the loo about five-thirty, when I got back you'd dropped off.'

I looked around for the others; Wingrave answered before I could ask. 'Carl's taking a shower. And Paul was' – he looked over his shoulder – 'no, correction, Paul *is* back at the reception desk again, talking to his new "friend".'

I washed down the first coffee with another and munched my way through a dish of melon and strawberries; both of which had appeared on the buffet table seemingly by magic.

Stretching and walking over to the windows overlooking the apron, adjacent to the departure building, I saw her ... Concorde. Long and sleek and as beautiful as ever, her ground crew fussing beneath the fuselage, shifting lines and cables, the umbilical cords connecting her to the ground.

Considering she is now well over thirty years old, it's not that Concorde has aged with dignity, it's simply that she hasn't aged at all. Standing there – admiring her sharp profile, her swept delta wings – it struck me that if this aircraft was to be unveiled to the world this very morning, if this was to be her maiden flight, Concorde would still command a standing ovation.

Looking at her now she remains an exciting aircraft, but how stunningly advanced must she have seemed back then? That's the part that fascinates me. Although the aircraft didn't enter regular transatlantic service until 1976, the maiden flight of Concorde, fuselage 001, took place in Toulouse, in the south of France, on 2 March 1969. In point of fact it was scheduled to have taken place the previous day but, ironically, the flight was delayed by twenty-four hours due to heavy fog.

Now, compare the state of Grand Prix technology from that period in history: Jackie Stewart would go on to secure his first world championship crown driving a Cosworth V8-powered Matra, a car built around a fabricated aluminium monocoque. Wings were literally just being toyed with by the designers, but it would take another full decade of progress before the engineers would begin to get to grips with ground effect aerodynamics.

Place Concorde side by side with a 2003 Ferrari chassis, and a certain similarity suggests itself; but, place Concorde side by side with the Matra MS80 (the championship-winning car of 1969), and I can suggest no similarities whatsoever.

I collected a wash-kit from the receptionist and made off in the direction of the shower room. Then, a wash, a brush-up and two more coffees and I felt as good as new. The lounge was much busier now, filling with those passengers brave enough to risk an early morning cab ride out of Manhattan and now preparing to join us on the supersonic flight to Paris.

Paul Kelver had 'negotiated' things so that the four of us could share an entire row of seats – row nine. We boarded at 07:45. I strapped myself into 9C, an aisle seat; Wingrave had the window to my right; Kelver took the other window, leaving Carl Hentschel the aisle seat to my left. Less than fifteen minutes later we thundered down the runway, the front of the aircraft began to lift and moments later we were airborne, soaring up, up, upwards into the endless brilliant blue of a new day.

8

Turning Things Upside Down

'Well, you know, aerodynamics are for people that can't
make proper engines.'
Enzo Ferrari's response to his driver, Paul Frère's suggestion
that his car might be a little un-streamlined

The first conversation I had with Bobby Rahal took place during a
winter test session, a cold Silverstone in 2000, soon after he had
accepted the role of running the struggling Jaguar team. Unfortunately, his tenure was destined to be short-lived. A great pity for
all concerned. But that's another story – one of politics and egos –
and not something I have any real interest in to be perfectly honest.
But, I do believe Rahal did his absolute best for the team, and if
he'd been left in peace to get on with his job, I suspect Jaguar would
currently be in a much stronger position.

When I met Bobby he was still learning the team; learning the
hardware too, feeling his way around the car, piecing together the
different areas of technology – comparing contemporary Formula
1 machinery with that used in America, in the CART series. I asked
him what he thought, how did Grand Prix machinery shape up
against what he was used to – himself a highly successful former
driver and current team owner back in the US.

He smiled and without hesitation said there really was very little
comparison, that F1 and CART are entirely different formulae.
Sure, Formula 1 has way more technology – he indicated the banks
of flickering screens and the myriad Jaguar people milling around
the garage – but that's not to suggest that Formula 1 has the
more exciting racing; the sports are different, that's all. I quickly

discovered Bobby to be a down-to-earth bloke; calm, controlled, a man devoid of even the merest hint of pretence. I guess much of that character stems from the relaxed, yet equally efficient approach that I've found to be a hallmark of the American way.

I asked him which area of a contemporary F1 car seemed the most important, the most critical, where that all-important extra 'tenth' could be found. He paused for a second, weighing things up, then plumped for aerodynamics. As a former driver I somehow expected him to suggest the engine. Nope, not any longer; aerodynamics is where it's at, and that's what we need to work on, he said. And if Bobby Rahal had succeeded in prising the unquestionable aerodynamic genius of Adrian Newey out and away from the clutches of Ron Dennis – something he was so tantalisingly close at achieving – then Jaguar's story would be very different to what it was at the end of 2002.

Rahal's estimation of Jaguar's shortfall was absolutely right – both before, during and after his brief stint at the helm. Aerodynamics continued to be a weak link, both the R1 and the R2 suffered as a result. And on it went, throughout the course of the 2002 season. With the exception of the actual monocoque itself, I believe virtually every aerodynamic surface of the R3 car had been redesigned, re-profiled, and renewed before the final race of the year.

The problem of addressing aerodynamic inefficiencies in hindsight, after the first chassis has been manufactured, is that each area of the car's styling affects another – a change in the flow characteristics of the front wing will to some extent affect the airflow over the rest of the car. Presumably, this knock-on effect is the reason why Jaguar spent much of the 2002 season in constant aerodynamic revisions. If a car's styling isn't right at the start of the year, it's exceedingly difficult to make up the lost time.

Earlier on, I emphasised the need for an abundance of horsepower, that a strong, powerful engine will help overcome shortfalls in other areas of the car. That's true enough, but ideally we don't want to have to mask any shortfalls; we don't want shortfalls at all. We want everything to be working in perfect harmony, and aerodynamics play a vital role in the overall performance of the car.

Asked to name two Grand Prix aerodynamicists, I suspect the names most likely to trip off the majority of tongues would be Adrian Newey and Rory Byrne. These two men have elevated the art form to a whole new level – the majestic lines of their cars have made them living legends. And for good reason, for in their respective stints with Williams and McLaren; Benetton and Ferrari, both have played a commanding role in designing every car that has won every Formula 1 world championship – drivers' and constructors' – since 1992. To the beginning of the 2004 season the pair of them can lay claim to a combined unbroken run of twenty-four world crowns. Little wonder, then, that Ron was so determined Bobby shouldn't take Adrian's skills to Jaguar. Little wonder too, that Jean Todt tries so hard to assuage Rory's professional wants as far as possible.

Blasting around the race track, a Formula 1 car sticks to the ground in exactly the same way that an aircraft doesn't. The aerodynamic forces acting on the wings of an aircraft create lift – a pressure difference between the upper and lower surfaces of the wings. When the amount of lift generated by the wings exceeds the aircraft's weight it will take-off.

In the case of our Formula 1 car, the very last thing we want is for it to take-off. For, although this will certainly focus the driver's attention, it also has the tendency to sap his confidence. What we want is for the car to stay firmly attached to the tarmac. Nevertheless, we can exploit the exact same science to keep our car firmly on the ground, as used by Concorde's engineers to enable us to soar up and away from New York. All we do is turn those same aerodynamic principles upside down; rather than generate lift, we create downforce, what some posh people refer to as 'negative-lift'.

Have a look at the cross-sectional shape of an aircraft wing and that of a race car and you'll notice they are exactly opposite to one another. However, perhaps the wings of Concorde are not a good example to illustrate the comparison, for although the basic aerodynamic principle remains the same, the peculiar shape of her swept delta wings is a response to the specific needs of supersonic flight. Something a tad more traditional will reveal the shape we're looking for; anything really, from a Spitfire to a Boeing 747.

The rule of aerodynamics that governs the production of lift/downforce has been with us since the eighteenth century. Two hundred and seventy years ago a bright Swiss chap, Daniel Bernoulli, published his masterwork, *Hydrodynamica*, in which, along with many other aspects of fluid behaviour, he informed an enthralled readership that a direct correlation exists between the velocity and pressure of a flowing liquid. He explained that when a fluid or a gas passes over the profile of a given shape – in our particular case, air flowing over the upper and lower surfaces of a wing – then the pressure and speed of the flow are interchangeable forms of energy; basically, an increase in airspeed must result in a decrease of air pressure and vice versa.

A quick experiment to show Bernoulli's principle at work is to hold a sheet of paper just beneath your lower lip, then blow across the upper surface of the paper. If all goes well you should notice the paper begin to lift upwards the harder you blow. I must warn you, however, that the visual effects of this experiment are not as stunning as, say, the laser-riddled battle scenes from the *Star Wars* films, but it will give a basic idea of what we're talking about.

From this point on I suggest we only talk in terms of race cars and downforce, it will help to avoid the potential confusions of ups and downs. If we take a cross-section of the upwardly curved wing of a race car, and measure the distance from the front edge (known as the wing's 'leading edge') to the rear edge (the 'trailing edge') we'll find that the distance is greatest between the leading and trailing edges of the wing's lower surface. The shorter distance, therefore, is the upper surface. This is very important.

Incidentally, this dimension between the leading and trailing edges is referred to by aerodynamicists as the wing's 'chord'. And, while we're on the subject of parlance, the width of the wing, the dimension between the endplates fixed to its sides is known as the 'span'. Hardly terms one uses every day – well, unless you work in aerodynamics, of course – but, they might crop up in a pub quiz, and now you're forearmed.

As the car travels forward through the air, the air molecules passing over the wing's lower surface have to travel a greater distance to reach the trailing edge than the air molecules passing over its upper surface. However, as the air molecules acting above and below the wing must both reach the trailing edge at the same time, the molecules on the underside of the wing travel at a greater velocity. As the speed of the air passing beneath the wing increases, so the pressure decreases – just as Bernoulli said it would.

It is this pressure differential between the upper and lower surfaces of the wing that creates downforce – the relatively high-pressure air acting on the upper surface forcing the wing downward. This aerodynamic load is transmitted through the wing mountings and via the suspension to the tyres, effectively pushing them on to the track. And it is this vertical loading that helps the tyres to maintain their adhesion with the tarmac when subjected to the high, lateral forces, as the car negotiates the circuit's twists and turns.

The car's downforce production is further aided by the raked diffuser situated at the rear underside of the car. The diffuser is designed to create a low-pressure area beneath the chassis, helping to accelerate and extract the air flowing beneath the car. The airflow travelling over the car acts on this depression and helps to force the car downward.

The faster the car travels along the track the more downforce a wing will generate; and (to a certain extent) increasing the attitude of the wing, inclining it to sit more square to the airflow will also help to produce more downforce. Raising or lowering the wing in this way is known as adjusting the 'angle of attack'. There is, however, a definite limit to how far a wing can be angled into the airflow. Too much and the wing will 'stall', the controlled airflow separates from the wing's upper surface and all downforce is lost.

The wing's characteristics are understood (one hopes!) and before there is any danger of over-adjusting the angle of attack, the wing will be substituted for a bigger one, and the whole process of fine-tuning the car's aerodynamics starts over.

Although a bigger wing will produce more downforce, everything comes at a price, and the price paid for additional downforce comes in the form of additional 'drag' – the frictional resistance acting on the car as it powers along. Downforce and drag go hand in hand; unfortunately, however, drag increases at a greater rate than down-force.

Road car manufacturers are often extolling the virtues of their latest low-drag streamline-bodied cars; how they have been de-signed to cut through the air like an arrow. And it's true that many road cars do have far superior drag coefficients in comparison to race cars. The overwhelming reason for that is because road cars aren't designed to produce tens of hundreds of kilos of aerodynamic loading.

Its wings and unshrouded tyres result in a contemporary Formula 1 car having to fight three times the restrictive drag of a road car. The aerodynamicists would be thrilled if they were allowed to shroud the tyres, to keep them out of the airflow, but the regulations do not allow that. Consequently, the skill of the aerodynamicists is to manipulate the design of the wings, bodywork and diffuser so as to generate maximum downforce for the minimum drag. And, on the whole, the aerodynamicists are exceptionally clever at doing exactly this. However, no sooner are they congratulating each other on their good work, than the FIA have amended the regulations to further restrict their progress, and it's back to the drawing board.

It's also worth keeping in mind that Grand Prix aerodynamicists are working on designs that will have to operate in far from ideal aerodynamic conditions. Their counterparts in the aerospace indus-try are drawing aircraft with very uncomplicated fuselage shapes; machines designed to operate at altitude, well above the turbulent airflows found near the ground, and away from other aircraft.

Compare that to our Grand Prix car: two or three millimetres off the ground, zigzagging left and right, less than a few metres from the car ahead. The front wing needs to work as efficiently as possible, regardless that the front wheels are located each side of the main plane; the rotating tyres causing colossal turbulence. A little further back and provision has to be made to cool the brakes, and we mustn't forget that air needs to be guided into the radiator ducts to cool the oil and water radiators, too. Towards the rear of the car we find two more rotating wheels and tyres, even wider than the fronts, and these are busy frothing gigantic clouds of turbulent air all over the bodywork; and to make matters worse, somewhere in the same area, the exhausts are belching out the spent gases of 95,000 controlled explosions every minute. Then, waiting directly behind all of this lot and desperately trying to make some sort of coherent sense out of this billowing, swirling madness, sits the rear wing.

Nevertheless, the pay-off for the aero department's unending quest to temper the airflow, improve the downforce and reduce the drag is well worth their effort. The results of their labours are pretty staggering. When travelling at a speed of between 60–70mph the aerodynamics of a Grand Prix car are capable of generating 600kg of downforce. The car, remember, weighs 600kg. Theoretically, therefore, at speeds in excess of 70mph there is sufficient aero-dynamic loading to allow the car to be driven upside down, it would literally stick to the ceiling. But 600kg is nothing: as the car accelerates down the main straight the downforce figures will click higher and higher. At a speed of 120mph the car will produce close on 2000kg of downforce.

Exactly how the different groups of aerodynamicists go about the business of styling their cars is something of a black art, least I've always thought so. A glance at the cars from any recent period of the sport's history will reveal a plethora of different shapes, designs and ideas; though all built to the same regulations, natur-ally. And while it's certainly true that aero work is now more science than gut-feeling, there remains a sufficient variation of ideas to make me believe that gut-feeling and instinct still have their part to play.

In the summer of 1993 I remember asking one of the model makers at Benetton which of the differing nose and front-wing designs – for the, as then, unborn B194 – was performing best in the extensive wind-tunnel tests. He was working on a variety of different profiles, some high nose, some low nose, some intermediate, including one that looked suspiciously like the bill of a duck-billed platypus. 'Have a guess,' he said, grinning from ear to ear, handing me the models to admire and turn over in my hands.

I examined them all before opting for the high-nose design, 'This one?'

'Yes ... and no,' he replied. 'Actually, they're all equally as good, they all perform exactly the same!'

If there's a moral to that, I guess it's merely that there is no mathematically perfect shape in aerodynamics; in terms of reducing drag there are lots of slippery shapes – but none is the slipperiest shape.

More likely, remembering that conversation took place ten years ago, I suspect that was more the case back then than now. Several years down the road I'm sure that advances in both computer-aided design, and wind-tunnel technology have narrowed the number of alternative shapes down quite significantly. And when studying the different car styles, it's worth keeping in mind that aerodynamic design is holistic – the shape of something at the rear of the car may well be the consequence of the shape of something at the opposite end.

I mentioned earlier, in the chapter dealing with chassis manufacture, that there are currently two differing schools of thought governing chassis styling. I suggested we hang fire on the final design of our dream-team chassis until we had a look at the merits of each system, so let's have a look at them.

Following the ban on ground effect styling, the common aerodynamic trend throughout the remainder of the 1980s and into the early part of the 1990s was to keep the nose of the car very close to the ground, the front wing consisting of two separate elements – one attached each side of the nose. However, at the 1990 San Marino Grand Prix, the third race of the season, Harvey Postlethwaite launched the Tyrrell 019. The car featured a significantly higher nose, the left and right elements of the wing supported on diagonal struts, allowing the wing to remain close to the track. The aerodynamic styling of the 019 was a complete break with convention, the concept a result of a collaboration between Postlethwaite and Jean-Claude Migeot.

The idea was to open up the area behind the front wing, helping to reduce turbulence and encourage the airflow to funnel beneath the nose and travel rearward towards the radiators. It was achieved by raising the chassis beneath the driver's legs by six inches and creating a basic sort of keel – similar to the styling of a boat's hull. Just as the leading edge of a boat's keel directs the flow of water around the sides of the hull, so Postlethwaite's keel directed the flow of air around the monocoque.

Finishing the season with a total of only nine points the 019 was no championship contender – though to its great credit it did take second place in Monaco – but the car's lack of laurels was of little relevance to the rest of the paddock; the seed of inspiration had been sown, and new and exciting design concepts were fast germinating throughout the paddock.

That, by the way, is the very reason why teams are so keen to cover their cars from prying eyes and cameras. The competition don't have to get close enough to physically measure something to fathom the secret and possible advantage of some new design or device. Sufficient damage is done should a rival team manage to see something even from a considerable distance. They don't need to learn specific dimensions, all they need is the nudge of inspiration, the 'oh, that's what it is ... now I see what they're doing!' Some secrets are easier to protect than others, of course – very difficult to see inside a gearbox, for example, but most aerodynamic details, by their very nature, have to be exposed to daylight at some point. And such was the case with the front wing of the Tyrrell 019: out rolled the car, a million shutters clicked ... and that was that.

The following season saw John Barnard include a version of the Tyrrell concept on the Benetton B191. Barnard, however, took the idea to its next level. This time, rather than droop two separate wing elements left and right, he designed the front wing to run the full width of the car, supporting a single main plane on two vertical pylons. The upshot of this was to increase the frontal area of the wing by something like 150mm. In the strictly regimented world of Formula 1 aerodynamics, 150mm of additional wing is not to be sniffed at. The additional surface area that this generated, coupled with the increased open area behind the wing's trailing edge proved beneficial, improving airflow beneath the main plane and helping to maintain the air's stability behind the wing.

John Barnard parted company with Benetton halfway through 1991, a move which allowed Rory Byrne to be reunited with his old team – Rory having quit Benetton in the wake of John's recruitment – a clash of conflicting design ideas, I guess. When Rory returned to Benetton's drawing board I suspected he might design the 1992 car based more on the last Benetton car he himself had designed, the B190, a low-nose car. Not a bit of it, Rory too must have seen the potential of the high nose, his B192 Benetton made use of an even higher nose than Barnard's 1991 car.

Up and down the pit lane the trend continued to grow, with similar designs appearing from Footwork (Arrows with a short-lived name change), Brabham, Jordan and Ligier in 1992. Towards the middle of the decade the high-nose concept became the dominant style, and by the end of 1996 it had been universally accepted. With every incarnation, the sculptured keel section of the differing chassis became more evident. When the mechanics had strapped their driver in the car his legs sat significantly higher than his bottom. One of those exceptionally rare instances where the aerodynamic gain outweighs the desire to keep the mass of the driver as low to the ground as possible.

The next significant aerodynamic evolution happened as a result of yet another FIA rule change aimed at thwarting the teams' aero departments. From the start of 2001, the teams were restricted to a maximum of three elements on their rear wings – so gone were those big multi-element rear wings we had been used to seeing unleashed at Monaco, for example – and the front wing endplates needed to be raised a further 50mm.

The front wing works more efficiently the nearer it is to the ground, its close proximity to the tarmac helps to increase the speed of airflow across the lower surface. Raising a front wing by 5mm will make a significant difference ... being forced to raise it by 50mm would make an enormous difference. The general consensus of opinion was that downforce levels would tumble as a result, perhaps by as much as 20 per cent. The crews manning the wind tunnels had some frighteningly long hours ahead if they were to stand any chance of clawing back the lost aero loading.

One problem they faced was that regardless of the high keel, raising the wing by 50mm brought it closer to the underside of the chassis (to a degree, the designers were back where they had started). Once again, the air leaving the wing's trailing edge would flow backward straight into the path of the suspension arms and their inboard mountings. What was needed was some method of creating more room behind the front wing.

The front of the Sauber C20, the Swiss team's car for 2001, was different to any of its predecessors; designed with a fresh aerodynamic style that soon became known as 'twin keel'. In order to open up the area behind the front wing, and thereby clean the airflow, Sauber removed their single keel from the car's centre line, moved the suspension mountings outwards and introduced two keels, effectively creating an inverted U-section behind the wing.

The arrival of Sauber's twin-keel C20 allowed the name 'single keel' to be applied to what had gone before. As usual, the cameras clicked and within minutes of the C20's launch the rest of the F1 paddock were pondering the potential pros and cons of adopting such a system. Nevertheless, even if a percentage of the other teams had wanted, it was too late to copy the idea on to their own cars. The twin-keel detailing was an integral part of the chassis moulding; replicating Sauber's idea would require an entirely new car. No chance of doing that now, the season was up and running, though the aerodynamicists would certainly follow the performance of the 2001 Sauber with renewed interest.

The more pressing task for every team in the pit lane was to try to recoup some of the lost downforce on their own cars, and Sauber was no exception. The wind tunnels ran twenty-four hours, seven days a week. And, once again, I have to say that the results of their constant endeavours to negate the FIA's latest restrictions were absolutely remarkable.

They started the season with 20 per cent less downforce, and, in the winter testing, many drivers were complaining of awful understeer, a direct result of the lost aero loading. Come the fourth race of the season the leading teams had managed to reduce their aero deficiency from 20 to only 10 per cent. But they weren't going to stop at that, oh no!

By the second week of June, mid-season, the time of the Canadian Grand Prix, several people I talked with in the pit lane suggested their aero departments were now merely 5 per cent shy of the downforce figures generated throughout 2000. Impressive? Not as much as this: In September, at the Indianapolis race, engineers from both Ferrari and Benetton were explaining that not only had they clawed back every kilo of downforce the FIA's restrictions had deprived them of at the season's outset, but they had also unearthed an additional 5 per cent. Moreover, not only were the cars now generating more downforce, they were suffering from significantly less drag than before – a consequence of using smaller wings set at less acute angles; both of which are requirements of the FIA's amended regulations.

Throughout 2001 the McLaren MP4-16 had been plagued with understeer problems, the front of their car visibly sliding across the tarmac as Hakkinen and Coulthard fought to match the pace of the Rory Byrne-designed Ferrari F2001. Regardless of the recouped downforce, all teams suffered from understeer, though for most teams the severity of the condition lessened as the weeks ticked by. Nevertheless, McLaren seemed particularly keen to address the problem of front end grip with the design of their next car.

Although the Sauber C20 didn't win any races, the team was extremely pleased with their performance in 2001; Sauber topping off the year with a very respectable fourth place finish in the constructors' championship. And, exactly as happened with the arrival of the Tyrrell 019 eleven years previously, Sauber's aerodynamics were soon adopted by other teams. For 2002 both Arrows, Jordan and McLaren joined Sauber in producing cars that made use of twin keels.

Adrian Newey in particular embraced the idea with open arms, taking the concept to a far higher level than Sauber. By elongating the depth of the keels used on the MP4-17, Newey lowered the height of the front suspension mountings too, using the twin keels to form a much deeper and more splayed inverted U-section than Sauber had devised for their car. These exaggerated keels not only acted as suspension mountings, they also awarded extra protection to the under-chassis airflow, helping to shield the air flowing rearward of the wing's trailing edge from the turbulent air spilling from the wing flaps and front wheels.

The twin-keel concept received a lot of attention when it appeared on the 2001 Sauber, and even more when the idea was adopted by one of the 'big three' teams, something which can only be seen as an endorsement of its potential. Newey and his wind tunnel team had studied the design at considerable length and were convinced they had made significant improvements to the front end grip of their car. The other two-thirds of the big three, however, preferred to stick with what they knew. Geoff Willis – at that time, chief aerodynamicist with Williams – and Ferrari's Rory Byrne both elected to stay true to the proven merits of the single-keel chassis for their 2002 cars. However, when comparing the on-track performance between the MP4-17, the FW24, and the F2002, there is no question which team built the better car.

In the winter of 2001 the Ferrari composite specialists began work on the monocoque for the F2002. Chassis number 217 was the first out of the autoclave. Ferrari have a unique numbering system for their Formula 1 cars. Rather than beginning the production run of each new design from 001, from the launch of their 312B car, back in 1970, they have continued to carry the same numbering sequence from year to year. The last F2001 monocoque to leave their autoclave was chassis number 216; consequently, the first F2002 monocoque in the production run was numbered 217. After his initial outing in the new machine Michael Schumacher's appraisal was succinct: 'In every way the new car is better than the old.'

The F2002 proved instantly quick and throughout the winter months the team strived to ensure the car's reliability would be equally impressive before the opening round of the championship, in Melbourne, Australia. Testing continued until the last moment, but there remained some niggling reliability issues – concerns over the transmission's ability to survive a race distance. Eventually, the team announced they would play safe and enter the tried and tested F2001 car for the first three races, and, in Australia, Michael Schumacher drove the year-old design to one last victory.

Back in Maranello, the team continued to hone the transmission of their new car, and prior to the Brazilian Grand Prix, round three of the championship, the team declared itself happy; although last-minute re-machining work to the gearbox resulted in only one example being ready to race. Ralf Schumacher had won the Malaysian Grand Prix, the second race of the year, and doubtless it was the impressive pace of the Williams FW24 that forced Ferrari's decision to advance the release date of the F2002. It transpired however, that Malaysia would be Williams' only win that season.

The new Ferrari claimed its maiden win in Brazil, the first of fourteen throughout the remainder of the season. McLaren, on the other hand were destined to win but once, David Coulthard driving to victory in Monaco.

Everywhere the Ferrari raced the aerodynamics worked well –

high-speed circuits, low-speed circuits, and no overheating problems. By mid-season Ferrari chassis number 225 had been assembled, the last F2002 of the line. With only nine examples in existence the production run of one of the most successful cars in Grand Prix history was complete.

Considering the success enjoyed by Ferrari in 2002, when the other teams began to design their cars for 2003 it came as no surprise that they should give Rory Byrne's work more than a cursory inspection. Many of the sport's latest creations share similar body styling to the F2002. Toyota, Jaguar, Jordan, and Renault have opted for a Ferrari-style nose: drooped at the front to help keep the mass as low as possible, then lifting upward on the underside, encouraging airflow over the middle section of the main plane. And all the teams have worked to accentuate the tight 'Coke bottle' styling at the rear of their cars, an attempt to duct turbulent airflow away from the lower element of the rear wing.

Likewise, the rear bodywork of many new cars is steeply raked from the top of the airbox to the rear of the engine. With the exception of Renault, this is not a result of super-wide vee angles, but because the latest generation of engines are sitting increasingly lower in the car.

As for our own car ... having pondered the two differing styles, we have to decide which system to use: single-keel or twin-keel. Our composite specialists are standing by, magic wands at the ready, eagerly waiting to adjust our monocoque's aerodynamic styling one way or the other. What do we tell them?

I was a little surprised that Williams didn't produce a twin-keel car for 2003, I got the impression that they were quite keen on the idea at one point, particularly after their chief aerodynamicist, Geoff Willis, parted company with them and headed off to BAR-Honda. However, following the arrival at Williams of Antonia Terzi, a former aerodynamicist with Ferrari, they decided to remain with a single-keel design for their FW25.

Okay, it's easy to suggest that as their new aerodynamicist came to them via Ferrari, she would naturally favour the single-keel concept; personally, I don't think it's anywhere as straightforward as that. Williams would have thoroughly studied the merits of both ideas before deciding one way or the other; it would be illogical to do anything else. Likewise, Ferrari would have done exactly the same; they have also remained with the single keel. The elegantly styled F2003–GA car is a natural evolution of the F2002; and where most of the other teams have tried to replicate this earlier car, Rory Byrne has shifted the aerodynamic benchmark even higher.

I'm going to be swayed by numbers here. Two out of the three leading teams have opted to give the twin-keel concept a miss; I suggest we do likewise.

Whenever I have looked at Concorde's fuselage, I've always been surprised at how small the cabin windows appear, but always assumed this to be a sort of optical illusion. The reality, however, as I discovered by looking out of one – watching New York disappear away behind us – is that Concorde's cabin windows are smaller than those of a 747, *much* smaller; in fact, no bigger than a paperback book.

This may have been *my* first supersonic flight but not for Wingrave. It turns out that George is an old hand at this; his bank sending him on frequent one-day business trips to the dollar factories of Wall Street. 'Well, yes, such luxurious forms of travel are much easier to justify when someone else is stumping-up for the tickets,' he explained. 'Though I have to say, that if time isn't of the essence, I'd prefer to travel up the sharp end of a jumbo – bigger cabin, more room to move around. The net benefit of Concorde is time saved in the air – flight times are cut by more than half.

'Now, going the other way, travelling *to* America, that's a big advantage. The five-hour time difference between London and New York allows me to be drinking morning coffee in Manhattan before I've taken off from Heathrow! But this trip, going to Europe, it doesn't really work. We leave JFK in the morning, and arrive in London – or in our case Paris – at the end of the working day.' He was in full flow. 'The ideal is to fly Concorde to New York, then take the overnight 747 on the way back. Sleep for six hours over the pond and arrive in London next morning. I don't know for sure, but I wouldn't be surprised if that's why Air France managed to upgrade us today. Jolly decent of them – don't get me wrong – but I imagine they usually have fewer passengers going this direction.'

Over on the other side of the aisle, Kelver and Hentschel had remained awake just long enough to experience our take-off out of JFK and to enjoy a glass of champagne. Now they were both very sound asleep; Paul's head lolled on to his friend's shoulder, Carl's chin slumped on his chest.

Throughout the first hour of the flight I kept glancing at the Machmeter at the front of the cabin, the digital display indicating Concorde's speed in relationship to the speed of sound. It's not really possible for the speed of sound to be given a definitive velocity – the actual speed changes depending on air density and temperature. Consequently, the speed of sound is a variable and is referred to as a Mach value. Mach 1 is the speed of sound, but whether Mach 1 is 700mph or 699mph or 701mph is subject to altitude and weather conditions.

As this was my first supersonic flight, I had no real idea of the sensations we would experience as we accelerated through and beyond the sound barrier. By virtue of the fact the aircraft would be travelling faster than sound I kind of assumed there wouldn't be any whopping cacophonic boom threatening to detonate our eardrums, merely because the sound of it happening would never be able to catch us up (and I was actually a little disappointed by this realisation). But I did assume the aircraft would undergo a certain amount of dramatic turbulence. After all, supersonic travel had proved one of engineering's greatest ever challenges; the aerospace industry had worked for years to fully appreciate its effect on aircraft.

I was flying Concorde! A machine designed and built to soar through the stratosphere at 60,000 feet at speeds in excess of 1400mph. And, any moment now, I was going to experience exactly what smashing through that engineering barrier would feel like. It makes the engineering achievements of Grand Prix racing's micro-universe look pretty paltry by comparison, doesn't it? Nine-hundred horsepower ... 220mph ... 19,000rpm. Probably best not to dwell on it too much.

My expectation and excitement built as the numbers on the Machmeter climbed higher: 0.5 – 0.6 – 0.7 up and up ... any second now ... 0.93 ... there was a slight momentary surge of power, almost imperceptible – a second later another – exactly the same. The numbers on the Machmeter held their breath ... then ... 1.0 – 1.1 – 1.2.

I looked over at Wingrave, he looked at me with an expression which suggested, 'yes, I suspected you'd be disappointed ... not very exciting, is it?' What he did say, however, was: 'Have you decided on lunch, old man? I think I'll go for the foie gras marbled with truffles ... and perhaps a glass of their '96 Pomerol to wash it down. What say you?'

I sighed my disappointment and opened the menu, stared blankly at the offerings, then quietly closed it again. The lack of any significant happening as we blasted through the sound barrier was disappointing enough – but the fact we could choose between four different main courses and sample six different Bordeaux wines as we rapidly closed in on Mach 2 ...? Well, I needed a few minutes to get used to the idea, that's all.

9

High-Speed Suspended Animation

'Simplicity is the height of sophistication.'
Leonardo da Vinci

A Grand Prix car does not use a fixed, or 'live' rear axle, a type that remains universal throughout NASCAR, for example. Formula 1 hasn't used this type of axle for decades. That's not a jibe at NASCAR technology, by the way, rather it's to highlight the fact that the use of the fixed rear axle is still prevalent in many forms of motor sport. It's merely a case of different chariots being built to different technical regulations.

The suspension system of a Formula 1 car is an independent arrangement, meaning that each wheel (or 'corner' of the car) is able to move independently, up and down, in respect to the other three. The final drive, the transmission's differential, forms the rearmost part of the gearbox, from there the power is delivered to the rear wheels via two driveshafts. The articulation of a driveshaft – essential to maintain a smooth power delivery while continually tracking any suspension movement – is achieved through two tri-lobe joints, one at each end of the shaft. In essence, a tri-lobe joint is like the wrist at the end of a person's arm ... although it has to be said the human wrist is nowhere near as well engineered.

The tri-lobe joint is a logical progression of the old 'constant velocity' joint. The layout of the tri-lobe joint is even simpler than its predecessor, using (as the name suggests) just three drive 'balls', symmetrically arranged around the end of the driveshaft at 120° intervals and held in position by needle bearings. The drive flanges of the gearbox and stub-axles require some rather intricate integral machining, but it is well worth the extra time and trouble. The end result is a remarkably simple, reliable, and efficient load-transmitting joint.

At each corner of the car, the axle-upright is held between two A-arms – one at the top, one at the bottom. I must admit, however, that although this is their correct name, I haven't actually heard anyone refer to these suspension members as 'A-arms' for donkey's years. Because of an obvious likeness they are more usually known as wishbones.

Like road cars, Grand Prix cars also use roll bars; what the Americans call sway bars (as I'm always being reminded by my colleagues at Speed Channel). Actually, during my days as a young apprentice mechanic, the road car industry in Britain tended to call them *anti*-roll bars (perhaps they still do?). Well, whether we call them roll bars, anti-roll bars or sway bars, we're merely choosing different tags to describe the same thing. Although Formula 1 roll bars are much smaller (and hugely more expensive) than those fitted to any road car, they nevertheless serve exactly the same purpose.

If you're unfamiliar with the concept of roll bars and would like to have a look at one, next time you have a spare couple of minutes poke your head under the rear of virtually any road car (preferably a parked one). That preformed steel rod, about 15–20mm in diameter, bolted to each side of the car – the one that seems to have been added to the suspension as an afterthought – that's the roll bar. More than likely there'll be another one at the front of the car too, though perhaps not quite as beefy.

Okay, I know what you're thinking and I agree; perhaps a roll bar isn't the most exciting thing to look at, but, then again, neither is a twenty-five-year-old single malt Scotch. First impressions can be deceptive, the true beauty of some things will only become evident after a more detailed evaluation.

Grand Prix cars use two roll bars; one at the front, one at the rear. They form adjustable links, connecting the left and right suspensions together. The idea behind a roll bar is to control chassis roll during cornering; this has nothing to do with the torsional rigidity of the chassis, rather it concerns the side-to-side swaying of the car as it rocks up and down on its springs. Basically, a roll bar is an additional spring, designed in such a way that it remains ineffectual providing the vertical suspension movement on both sides of the car remains equal; e.g., bouncing along a straight section of the track. The roll bar only comes into play when one side of the car sees more movement than the other (chassis roll), when this happens the roll bar adds an increased resistance to one side of the car or the other, depending on whether the car is rolling to the left or right; this in turn depends on whether the driver is steering the car left or right.

A Formula 1 car is very stiffly sprung, with the naked eye it is nigh on impossible to see any degree of chassis roll affecting the car, but roll it certainly does and the engineers will monitor and control the amount of roll by interchanging road springs and roll bars, increasing or decreasing their stiffness, often referred to as 'rate'.

The key word here is 'control'; the idea is not to entirely eliminate chassis roll. Adjusting the degree of roll, fine tuning it from front to rear is very useful, something we'll have a look at when we discuss handling and chassis set-up in the next chapter. It's nothing unusual for a team to manufacture a range of between twelve to fifteen roll bars, all of varying degrees of stiffness; and that's just for one end of the car. There will be another set, again twelve to fifteen pieces, for the other end, so thirty-odd roll bars per car. Mind you, it's my experience that only about four of them will actually get used throughout the course of the season, but it's nice to have a really comprehensive choice, I guess. And it's Sod's Law that if the team opted to manufacture a smaller selection of, say, only four different rates, the driver would insist he wanted something in the middle. You're damned if you do, you're damned if you don't!

The Grand Prix fraternity tends to shun the term 'shock absorber', a name familiar to most road car garages and tyre-and-exhaust centres around the world. Apparently, racing engineers don't concern themselves with anything as pedestrian as the mundane problems of absorbing shocks, oh dear me no; the very idea! Instead, their time is spent in the erudite study, analytical calculation and precision damping of suspension oscillations. F1 cars do not *absorb* shocks, they *damp* them; consequently, in racing circles 'damper' is the more familiar name for what is essentially exactly the same as a shock absorber.

Unlike most road-car applications, however, the suspension springs and dampers of a contemporary F1 car are not fixed close to the wheels, in an 'outboard' position, but are mounted 'inboard', housed within the confines of the chassis. The link connecting the damper to the wishbones/axle-upright assembly of each corner is called either a pullrod or a pushrod, depending on the particular system in use.

The differences between the two are rather interesting and I think it well worth our while to pause and look at them in a little more detail. Pullrod and pushrod: have a look at the two photos and you'll soon be able to tell them apart. The wishbones are the two links running parallel to the ground, connecting the chassis and the axle-upright; stretching between the top and bottom wishbones you will see another rod, running at an angle of roughly 45°, if this rod appears to be attached to the bottom wishbone and runs up to the top of the chassis, the car is designed with *pushrod* suspension. Conversely, if the rod seems attached to the top wishbone and runs down to the floor of the chassis, then (yep, you've guessed it) the car has *pullrod* suspension.

In the wake of the ground effects era, towards the middle of the 1980s, the teams began to refine their suspension layouts, doing away with the idea of a single, robust member which served as a combined suspension arm and damper actuator. They began to design lightweight top wishbones, similar to those we see today, and used a small pushrod to operate the damper. Teeth were sucked, drinks were drunk; further design revisions were contemplated, and pullrod suspension surfaced as the new fashion, the system most prevalent during the last third of the decade. The B186, the first Benetton out of the stable, designed by Rory Byrne in '85 and raced throughout '86, used pullrods.

Then, towards the closing stages of the decade the designers pondered and re-evaluated things once more. The pushrod system began to regain some of its former popularity; and 1989 proved a significant year of change. A season which saw leading teams and backmarkers alike torn between the merits of the different designs. John Barnard's Ferrari 640 used pushrods; Neil Oatley's McLaren MP4-5 stayed with pullrods. Ross Brawn's Arrows A11 had pushrods; and Rory Byrne's Benetton B189 remained loyal to his belief in the pullrod.

The following year, 1990, was the real watershed, with ever more teams making the switch to pushrods; even Rory Byrne capitulated: the B190 (and every Benetton subsequently built) made use of them. Now the idea was really on a roll, it wouldn't be long before it was adopted by every team in the pit lane. If memory serves, I think the last F1 car to use pullrod suspension in the 1990s was the Lotus 102, driven by a young and eager Mika Hakkinen in 1992 during the Monaco practice sessions. As I recall, the Lotus mechanics were working around the clock to build him an example of their new car – designated the Lotus 107 – in time for the race itself. The 107 was designed with pushrod suspension, and that pretty much nailed the lid of the pullrod's coffin tightly shut; or at least most of us thought so. Nevertheless, pullrod suspension was destined to make a comeback, albeit briefly, when a couple of designers dusted off their old drawings and revamped the concept for the start of the new millennium.

As with nearly everything that's been designed and refined over the years, both systems have their good and their bad points. As far as the front suspension is concerned, the biggest benefit of using a pullrod system is that the road spring and damper assembly are located at the bottom of the car; their weight as close to the ground as possible (and as we keep mentioning, that's a big plus). The system uses the familiar coiled steel wire road spring, slipped over the conventional telescopic damper. One end of the damper – the main body of the unit – is connected to the chassis by a mounting point bonded within the carbon/honeycomb plies of the monocoque. Same applies to both sides of the car, naturally, allowing the springs and dampers to run vertically inside the cockpit, or, more often, beneath and parallel to the driver's legs.

The other end of the damper, the shaft, is connected to a pivot, known as a rocker, which allows the movement of the damper shaft to turn through 90°. The other end of this rocker is connected to our pullrod, and the other end of the pullrod is connected to the top wishbone/axle-upright assembly. It all sounds a bit '*them bones, them bones*', but I hope you get the general idea.

When the car drives over a bump in the track, the wheel will lift upwards and the pullrod connecting the axle-upright to the damper is pulled up with it (hence the name), making the rocker pivot at the same time, which in turn compresses and works the damper shaft. Now, here's the fun bit: because the pullrod is *pulled* (put in tension, not compression) in order to make the damper work, it can be made reasonably lightweight and flexible; it is more a blade than a solid rod or tube. This is because the pullrod works like a cable, and in essence that's exactly what it is. Here's a quick illustration, think of our pullrod as a tow-rope. Providing we only tow or pull with a tow-rope it works wonderfully well, able to cope with and carry great loads with no problem. But ever tried changing direction and pushing anything with a tow-rope? No, of course not, doesn't work does it, the whole principle quite literally collapses if we take the rope out of tension and try to compress it.

Pushrod suspension operates in a similar way to the pullrod method but this time the springs and dampers are mounted atop the chassis. Just as before, the body of the damper is mounted on the chassis, the shaft connects to the rocker; and the other end of the rocker connects to the top eye of the pushrod. This time, however, the lower eye of the pushrod connects to the bottom wishbone/upright assembly. In this configuration, although the dampers, springs and rockers are mounted on the outside of the chassis, they remain hidden from view by a lightweight carbon panel, profiled to match the car's aerodynamic contours and held in place by two or three small fasteners.

As the car travels over a bump, the wheel is lifted upwards but instead of the connecting rod being pulled, it is instead pushed (put in compression); this pivots the rocker and works the damper shaft. The important thing to remember, however, is that because the pushrod works in compression, it needs to be designed in the form of a hollow but rigid tube. This is the reason why pullrods are so much smaller in cross-section than their pushrod counterparts.

In my eyes, pushrod suspension offers three distinct advantages over the currently unfashionable pullrod system. First, having the springs and dampers mounted on-high makes them significantly more accessible, allowing the mechanics to make a series of rapid changes to the suspension settings during the practice sessions; the low-mounted dampers of a pullrod system are a real pig to work on, changing springs, dampers, bump rubbers and roll bars can take twice as long, and involve three times as much cursing.

The second advantage is that the rigid construction of the pushrod offers improved control over the suspension movement on the downward travel of the wheel, the moment after the car has negotiated the bump in the track and is returning to its normal position; a period known as rebound.

A little earlier I mentioned that two teams at the turn of the millennium had tried to resurrect the pullrod. Well, both teams quickly changed their minds again, but the last team to field an F1 car featuring pullrod suspension was Minardi – fitted to their 2001 chassis, the PS01. The other team to have experimented with it was TWR Arrows, the A21 used it, the car campaigned throughout 2000.

Jos Verstappen was signed to Arrows that year, I caught up with him in the paddock at some point during the summer and asked how he liked driving a car with the pullrod suspension, over the far more popular pushrod system. He quickly shook his head and told me he didn't really like it. He understood the team's reason for including it on the car, namely that of keeping the mass low, and, he said, it worked well along fast straights and sweeping corners, no trouble at all. The problem, he went on, occurred when riding the car over the kerbs, through tight sections such as the Bus Stop chicane at Spa. At places like that, where the chassis was subjected to sudden, dramatic suspension travel, the stability of the car suffered. It was during those brief moments of transition – from bump, to rebound, to bump – just for fractions of a second, before the flex of the pullrod was taken up, the car seemed to go loose on him. I asked if Arrows were planning to persevere with the system on next year's car. He was adamant they'd change it; sure enough, the A22 sported pushrod suspension.

The third benefit of pushrod suspension is that it allows the aerodynamicists to improve the chassis styling, particularly around the tight, sculpted lines of the keel area, beneath the driver's legs. In a pullrod system the suspension springs and dampers are mounted low down, and space has to be made to accommodate them, but by moving them either atop the monocoque or – what is now more usual, *inside* the monocoque, ahead of the driver's feet – the aerodynamicists are free to mould, blend and shape that area as they see fit. In fact, such emphasis is now placed on the aerodynamics in this area of the car that it seems highly unlikely that any team will be able to use pullrod suspension in the future. There is simply insufficient space to mount the components. It would take a series of major changes to the technical regulations governing chassis design to see the system make a return.

Personally, I hope pullrod suspension never rears its damn ugly head ever again. I don't like the system, never have; it's awkward to work on and always strikes me as a clumsy, ungainly layout. It may have looked pretty state-of-the-art on Noah's ark, but ... anyway, I'm just very glad it's gone, that's all.

A point I've tried to emphasise in everything we've discussed so far is that Formula I cars are under continual development, nothing stays set in stone for very long, and suspension systems are no exception to this rule. The past few seasons have seen the introduction of two other significant changes to this area of the car, so let's have a look at them one at a time. Towards the end of the 1990s the leading teams began to experiment with using torsion bars as an alternative to the traditional coil spring.

In the first instance this latest advance was confined to the front of the car, where the suspension mountings form part of the monocoque; the rear suspension, bolted to the transmission, continued to use coil springs. After the usual initial hiccups over reliability, and the engineers had learned exactly how the torsion bars needed to be manufactured, and the drivers had become familiar with and gained confidence in the car's handling, the idea took off like wildfire. From the front of the car the concept was soon adapted to work at the rear, too, requiring the next generation of transmission castings to be redesigned to include provision in the housing for the torsion bars. Now, as with everything that has been seen to work better than what went before, the torsion bar has become the standard springing medium for every car in the pit lane.

The principle behind the torsion bar is simplicity itself, actually it's something we've already discussed a little earlier, when we studied the torsional rigidity of the monocoque. Recall how we hold one end of the chassis, and apply a load to the other end in order to calculate the degree of twist? A torsion bar works on exactly the same basis. Unlike a coil spring which moves, or oscillates up and down, a torsion bar flexes, or twists along its length. Using a series of splines, one end is held fast to the chassis, the other is attached via a reaction arm to the suspension pushrod. As the car rides over a bump in the track, the pushrod moves upward as before but rather than compressing a coil spring, it works against the resistance of the torsion bar, forcing it to twist.

Machined from titanium, different rates of resistance (stiffness) are produced by manufacturing a range of bars that vary in both length and diameter. In order to keep the torsion bar as compact as possible, it is common practice to make each unit in two pieces. In reality it is not a single solid piece (as the name 'bar' might infer), but is in fact constructed from two hollow tubes. One tube fits inside the other, with sufficient free play to ensure there is no friction or interference between the two. The two tubes are then welded together at one end, this leaves the splines of both the outer tube (that connects the torsion bar to the chassis) and the splines of the inner tube (the pushrod connection) at the other end of the finished torsion bar. It is essential that the surfaces of the inner and outer tubes do not rub against each other as any frictional contact between the walls will alter the predetermined working resistance of the torsion bar. This tube-within-a-tube method of manufacture effectively makes the torsion bar half its usual length, reducing what would be a 200mm long torsion bar down to just 100mm.

The past few seasons have seen further refinements to the concept. The latest generation of torsion bars are now wondrously light, weighing just a few grams, considerably lighter than the equivalent coiled wire spring; and their continued inclusion in all forthcoming Grand Prix cars looks set well into the future.

So, there we have it – the torsion bar. Formula 1's very latest, all-singing, all-dancing suspension spring. In light of which, you might be surprised to hear that the idea of using torsion bar suspension is far from revolutionary. When young French engineer, André Citroën, set about drawing the suspension for his new motorcar, the Traction Avant, his design included provision for torsion bar springing both front and rear. However, not only would his new car use torsion bars, it would also feature a front-wheel drive transmission (hence the car's name) and was to be built around a fabricated mild-steel monocoque. The first example of this absolutely groundbreaking (and, sadly, often overlooked) machine rolled off the production line and was purring along the avenues of Paris in 1937. It would take more than sixty years before Grand Prix racing would finally realise the potential benefits of Citroën's suspension designs.

I think the Traction Avant is a wonderful car, but you've probably guessed as much. I have one parked in the barn, one of the first things I bought when I moved to France; a 1957 model, blessed with elegant, swooping bodylines, and one of the last examples of the marque before the company went completely wild and produced the DS (the slightly surreal, hydraulically controlled machine that predated the Williams FW14B active suspension car by thirty-five years). Like the house, my Traction Avant also needs restoring, I keep tinkering with it when time allows, which is not very often; but, its somewhat jaded condition notwithstanding, I still get immense pleasure from merely pulling back the dust sheet, lifting one side of the bonnet and admiring the remarkable, beautiful simplicity of the engineering: André has every right to feel exceptionally proud of his contribution to the automotive world.

The manufacturing process of the wishbones and pushrods has undergone considerable change too. Not so long ago these would have been handmade by the fabricators, each piece produced by welding together aerodynamically shaped tubes. As with the artistry involved in producing the fabricated exhausts, these steel suspension components were beautifully made.

Throughout the 1960s, components such as driveshafts, roll bars and wishbones were plated with bright chromium. Although this tradition was pleasing on the eye, there was a potential for it to create a problem all of its own; the chrome was primarily a protective coating, designed to prevent the steel from rusting, but the fact that it was a plating allowed it to mask tell-tale signs of material fatigue on the steel beneath. Even minute cracks could go unnoticed with the chrome itself remaining unbroken. For the mechanics trying to ascertain the serviceability of the suspension, their task was a little like a doctor trying to check for any broken bones while their patient insisted on wearing a diving suit.

Not only that, but the acid bath treatment which forms part of the chroming process can prove extremely corrosive to any unplated steel; not a problem as far as the outside of the wishbones are concerned, but what about the inner surfaces of the hollow tubing? Regardless of any post-process flushing designed to neutralise the acid, in the weeks and months that followed there was no certain way to ratify the internal condition of these fabricated suspension pieces. They may look as good as new on the outside, but internally be on the verge of collapse.

The teams began to cast around for an alternative and the use of chrome eventually died out altogether. From bright and flashy, the teams gravitated towards the other extreme, now favouring the use of two other finishes: Keyphos and Parco-luberite; both of which produce a hard wearing and rather handsome matt black finish, one that doesn't mask any irregularities in the material or corrode the inner surfaces of the tubing. The idea is that both of these finishes don't so much plate the steel with a covering, rather they impregnate the surface of the steel to a very small degree. Both systems were widely used; some teams favoured one, some teams preferred the other. Williams used the Parco-luberite process on their wishbones, Benetton opted for Keyphos; I think their decisions were based on nothing more than personal preference.

Now, however, the problem of suspension corrosion has ceased to be an issue. Practically the entire suspension system is produced, not by fabricators, but by composite specialists. Wishbones and pushrods are no longer welded, they are made from carbon fibre, laid up in moulds and baked in autoclave ovens.

Carbon wishbones were always going to happen. In 1989, during my job interview with Nigel Stepney, at that time Benetton's chief mechanic, I remember discussing with him the possibility of the teams using composite materials for their suspensions. 'Not yet,' he said. 'So far, no one's been brave enough to commit to it, but give it time ... it'll happen!'

Just a few years later the first composite suspension and steering pieces started to appear. The first part to be introduced at Benetton was in 1996: a carbon steering rack. This was followed shortly afterwards by two carbon trackrods to go with it. (These are the two rods that extend outward from the rack, running parallel with the wishbones to meet the steering arms mounted on the uprights.) I can recall a chap from the drawing office bringing one over to show me – the first one to be produced. He was genuinely thrilled with it; gushing that it had just been released from the R&D department, following a series of demanding tests. It had been pulled, pushed, vibrated and load tested in every possible direction; subjected to more punishment than it would see in the course of three race distances. The prototype piece had passed muster with the stress engineers; the draughtsman's project had been given the green light – a batch would be produced. I held his prototype trackrod in my hands; it was as light as a pencil.

I freely admit to not fully sharing his wide-eyed excitement. I suspect several other mechanics felt the same way judging by the array of anxious faces when these revolutionary composite pieces were taken out of the laboratory and first bolted to an actual car and put to the ultimate test – driven at speed around a race track. The tension broke into a series of relieved jokes when the car returned to the pits in the same condition it had left. I can now, more readily, appreciate a little of how McLaren's mechanics must have felt when Barnard's original composite car pulled out of the pits and set off down the pit lane to commence its first installation lap.

Nevertheless, irrespective of any personal feelings of trepidation, I must report that both the carbon steering rack, its trackrods and all the various wishbones and pushrods, which arrived periodically after that, all worked, to the best of my knowledge, without any problems whatsoever. At least they did throughout my years with the team. Of course I can't vouch for anything that may have happened after I left them to it.

The designers were extremely keen to do away with steel suspensions. Apart from the obvious weight saving, the other advantage of using composite materials to produce the wishbones is that it allows them to be moulded to virtually any shape. Fabricated steel wishbones are limited to a simple airfoil or teardrop shape (in cross-section), and, once again, because of the increased importance now placed on aerodynamic detailing, the teams wanted considerably more scope than that.

An interim solution was to take a fabricated steel wishbone and let the composite chaps mould a carbon fibre shroud around it. This assuaged the aero department to a degree, but the drawback was that the suspension parts became even heavier than before, now constructed from both steel *and* composite materials.

There was only one real solution: to go the whole hog, machine the moulds and allow the composite department to produce the entire piece from carbon. As a cautionary move (because they are subjected to the least suspension loading), the top-front wishbones were the first to be manufactured from composite materials. When this proved a success the designers pressed onward, remaking the suspension in sequence of loading. Next to change were the top-rears, then the bottom-fronts, then the pushrods. The final wishbones to be lost to the fabricator's art were the bottom-rears as these carry the greatest loads.

Also, by virtue of their close proximity to the exhausts, it's essential to protect the rear wishbones, both top and bottom, from exposure to the excessive heat under the bodywork. Remember, that if carbon fibre is overheated, the bonding resins will burn off, reducing the wishbones or pushrods to mere useless plies of cloth ... not good at speeds in excess of 200mph. The rear wishbones and pushrods are wrapped in heat-reflective gold foil, and adorned with several temperature sensitive stickers, allowing the team to monitor and safeguard the levels of heat the wishbones are exposed to, each time the car takes to the track.

I should point out that the increased freedom of design that these composite wishbones lend to the aerodynamicists is heavily controlled by the technical regulations. The FIA want it clearly understood that the suspension components of the car are exactly that: suspension components, *not* aerodynamic devices. Remember that the regulations absolutely forbid the teams to use any form of 'movable aerodynamic device'. This primarily refers to the use of adjustable wings, allowing the downforce to be regulated while the car is moving, and/or any kind of sliding skirts (harking back to the ground effect era) whereby the underside of the car can be 'sealed' to the track. This regulation also governs the barge-boards; these too must be rigidly fixed on their mountings, unable to droop below the stepped plane (as purely unintentional as this movement may be), and so influence, in any small degree, the airflow on the underside of the car.

Well, as far as the wishbones and pushrods are concerned, there can be little doubt that they are 'movable' – they're supposed to be, they're part of the suspension! Therefore, in order to satisfy the FIA that these pieces are most definitely not movable aerodynamic devices, the teams have to design them in such a way that they cannot under any circumstances produce any downforce; basically they must cut a neutral path through the air, this is the reason why their profiles don't more resemble small winglets. However, although the aerodynamicists are unable to use the wishbones to the extent they'd like, extremely careful consideration is given to their shape, helping to reduce drag to an absolute minimum. To this end it's becoming increasingly common practice these days for the trackrods to be encased within hollow sections of the top wishbones, totally removing them out of the airflow.

The other aspect of the suspension system that we haven't yet mentioned is tyres; a significant degree of the car's suspension movement is achieved through the engineered malleability of the tyres' sidewalls, and the major contribution that tyres add to a car's overall performance can be easily overlooked.

The tyres provide the direct link between the eight- to nine-hundred horsepower and the race track, having to convey this colossal energy to the tarmac with the minimum of wheel spin. At the start of the race, plumes of white smoke and squealing tyres may look impressive but they certainly don't make the car quick off the grid – exactly the opposite in fact. What we're trying to achieve is a controlled launch, perfect traction.

Not only do the tyres have to grip under hard acceleration

and cope with the even higher forces of retardation under heavy braking, they're also responsible for endowing the car with its ballerina-like poise and nimbleness as the drivers constantly flick the steering left and right during cornering.

Bearing these things in mind it's obviously important for the teams to make a careful decision when entering into partnership with a tyre manufacturer. That said, when Goodyear finally pulled the plug on their involvement in Grand Prix racing at the conclusion of 1997, the choice was made easy for the teams – Bridgestone became the industry's sole supplier.

It's possible that the timing of Goodyear's departure was prompted by the FIA's decision to ban traditional racing 'slicks' and mandate the use of grooved 'dry weather' tyres for the start of the 1998 season. As usual, the FIA were looking at ways to reduce the cars' speed, and increase the potential for more overtaking manoeuvres. The new regulations required the tyres to include grooves around their circumference, so reducing the amount of rubber in contact with road. It was hoped that this, combined with a 200mm reduction to the cars' track (the width of the car, measured between the outer faces of the tyres), would raise the centre of gravity, reduce adhesion, and so, slow cornering speeds.

Not so long ago there were two differing philosophies governing tyre manufacture. A company would either concentrate on tyre compound, working to perfect the ideal chemical mix for each circuit – this was Goodyear's great strength. Alternatively, the engineers would tend to concentrate their efforts on tyre construction, the inherent flexibility of the sidewalls and carcass – and this was Bridgestone's area of expertise.

Following the FIA's requirement for grooved tyres, however, the importance of the surface compound was somewhat diminished, with the emphasis now on the tyre's construction. The new regulations had played straight to Bridgestone's strength. Well, whatever the reason, Goodyear decided to call it a day and have played no further part in Formula 1 from that day on. Nevertheless, I believe it would be folly to dismiss a possible future return. I suspect we haven't seen the last of them, at least I certainly hope not. Times change; managements and policies change too.

For the following three years Bridgestone were looking good – quite literally they couldn't lose a single race. It was a situation that was never going to last for ever, someone would have to take up the challenge sooner or later. It was Michelin that finally took the plunge. After sixteen years away from F1 they agreed terms to supply five teams in 2001 – Williams amongst them. For their part both Ferrari and McLaren stayed with Bridgestone. Michelin readily accepted they had a difficult job on their hands: the continuous advances in construction technology and the alchemy of complex compounds had made redundant much of their previous expertise. A sixteen-year sabbatical makes for a lot of catching up.

Bridgestone, however, were way too wise to sit back in the hope of watching Michelin stumble. The Japanese concern were well aware of the potential danger that these past masters posed to their position of dominance. Just like them, Michelin's engineers also placed great emphasis on the tyre's construction. Neither company, however, could afford to specialise on just one facet of their product – those days had gone. Only a tyre endowed with excellent construction *and* compound would suffice.

The development work from both tyre suppliers became very intense and as the pre-season testing drew to a close and the teams headed off to Melbourne for the opening round of 2001, there was considerable speculation as to how much improved the tyres would be compared to the previous year. Some said lap times might fall by as much as a full second per lap; others suggested the figure would be close on two seconds. I don't think anyone expected three and a half seconds, nearly four. But that's exactly what happened. The performance gain was staggering!

It was incredible. Such an improvement merely by bolting on a different set of tyres! It would prove impossible for a team to find such an advantage in any other way (apart from filling the fuel tank with nitrous oxide, of course, and I suspect Max may frown on that). After a full season of tweaking and manipulating the chassis to its absolute maximum potential, a team may uncover another half a second … but a simple tyre change had produced seven times that!

Now it becomes clear why the importance of tyres must never be underestimated. Black round things, they ain't. Tyres have always been important, naturally, but now more than ever the engineers are consulting with their respective tyre partners before finalising any suspension design. It used to be the case that the tyres arrived, were bolted to the car and the engineers adjusted the settings of the suspension and steering geometry to suit. No longer good enough, I'm afraid. The stakes are much higher. A winning chassis will have a symbiotic relationship with its tyres: team and tyre supplier must be united as never before.

In the winter of 2001 (in a move which, in hindsight, seems to have been a stroke of pure genius), Ferrari agreed to supply Bridgestone with all its chassis, engine and transmission data. In turn, Bridgestone agreed to disclose to Ferrari all information concerning its tyre compound and construction techniques. A team of Ferrari engineers would be permanently based in Japan, while Bridgestone's engineers would be free to roam the laboratories of Maranello.

Meanwhile, McLaren–Mercedes, who at that time were also a Bridgestone team, decided they couldn't agree to such an open exchange and jumped ship; Ron Dennis agreeing terms with Michelin. The question is, did Ferrari suspect that this would be McLaren's reaction to their own proposed deal with Bridgestone? Well, whether they did or not, the upshot was, that of the sport's three leading protagonists, Ferrari and Bridgestone were now able to reap the rewards of an exclusive relationship; one of trust and rapid technical progress.

The suspension layout and steering geometry of the Ferrari F2002 were specifically designed to complement its Bridgestone tyres – tyres that had been specifically designed to complement the chassis. As Bridgestone developed something new, be it construction or compound, so Ferrari would redesign their carbon fibre suspension components; adjusting their car's basic geometry layout to suit the tyres.

Come end of play in Suzuka, Ferrari had won fifteen of the season's seventeen races, and clinched another constructors' championship, bringing their total number to twelve (three more than Williams, and four up on McLaren). As for Michael Schumacher . . . when he crossed the finish line in Magny-Cours he'd not only won the Grand Prix, he'd also matched Fangio's record of five drivers' championships – a record that had stood the test of time for forty-five years of continual competition.

There's no question that the bespoke Bridgestones played an enormous role in the success of the F2002, a view which Ferrari themselves have been more than happy to support. Michelin, on the other hand, found its resources compromised, having to design its tyres around the differing chassis requirements of both Williams and McLaren. That was never going to be easy. Of the two races that Ferrari didn't win in 2002, one went to Williams, the other to McLaren.

As to our choice of tyres and suspension, the pieces we'll need to manufacture for our car; I believe there are really four decisions to make. First and foremost we have to decide between Bridgestone and Michelin.

It is clear that Ferrari have experienced wonderful success with Bridgestone – in terms of race victories they had a phenomenal run of success in 2002 – though it's worth remembering that no other Bridgestone-shod team looked close to winning.

For their part, Michelin, having suffered terribly at the hands of their Japanese rivals, were absolutely determined to turn things around. And turn things around they did: 2003 proved infinitely better, with two of their teams, McLaren and Williams, remaining in the fight for championship honours until the end of the penultimate round, the US Grand Prix, held at Indianapolis. By that stage of the season Ferrari remained the sole Bridgestone runner in the race for both the constructors' and the drivers' championships.

However, after Indianapolis had played itself out, Williams found themselves without any further hope of winning the drivers' championship, and McLaren's fight for the constructors' trophy was also over. At the end of the 2003 season Bridgestone had, yet again, beaten their French opposition to both world crowns.

Michelin may have lost out to Bridgestone but they had made huge improvements. The question is, going into 2004, can Michelin sustain this new-found pace and keep Bridgestone on the hop? One thing is for certain, throughout the off-season, the winter of 2003/2004, both companies will be working flat out to gain the technical advantage.

And where exactly does that leave us with regard to our own choice of tyres? We must be aware that our choice of tyre supplier with always be a gamble; over the last two years the shift of superiority in the ongoing tyre war has swung both ways, often from race to race. Now, more than ever before, the strength of a Grand Prix team stands or falls on its choice of rubber. I believe we have to think laterally.

I suggest we try this: we opt for a partnership with Bridgestone, but rather than trying to get them to develop a tyre that suits our chassis – which, as a brand new team, let's face it, is not going to be high on their list of priorities – we ask them to supply us the same compound and construction they are producing for Ferrari. We can be sure that these are going to be extremely good, tyres that have received the finest attention to detail in both design and production. Then, we ask Bridgestone's engineers to help us as much as possible with suspension and steering geometry. Allow their engineers to lead us, let them tell us exactly what our suspension needs to achieve to get the best from their tyres. We make our car suit their tyres. We're never going to prise Bridgestone and Ferrari apart, so we need to capitalise on their close partnership.

Second; do we go for pushrod suspension or pullrod. Pushrod, right you are! A fine choice. Besides, remembering that we've already opted for a high, single-keel design for our monocoque, we couldn't really fit pullrods even if we'd wanted to – which we don't.

Third; do we opt for coiled wire road springs or torsion bars? Torsion bars are the future – compact and very light. Other than cost, I can see no advantage in choosing coil springs, and I don't want cost to be an issue. I want winning races to be the issue.

Fourth; do we use carbon or steel wishbones and pushrods? I suggest we opt for carbon. It's true that we might suffer some initial unreliability (and I truly hate the thought of that), but if we're going to be competitive then I believe we have little choice. Steel bones are too heavy and the aerodynamicists will never forgive us. Besides, the practice of manufacturing composite suspension pieces is becoming increasingly commonplace. We should opt for carbon but before producing anything we will make certain to check with the composite specialists, the chaps actually making the things; that they are as happy with the designers' ideas as the designers are themselves. To be honest, this happens most times anyway. It would be a terribly conceited fool who thought their work to be above consultation with the myriad hands-on experts around him. And we're not looking to employ fools – conceited or otherwise.

These days almost everything seems to be made of carbon fibre, and the desire to use composite materials wherever possible extends to the brake discs and pads too. The idea of using carbon for manufacturing Grand Prix brakes was the brainchild of designer Gordon Murray – back in the 1970s – at that time working as technical director with Bernie Ecclestone's Brabham team.

Murray's flash of inspiration was triggered by a magazine feature concerning the carbon brake discs under development by Dunlop Aviation's engineers for – surprise, surprise – the Concorde supersonic jet. By ditching the traditional steel brakes in favour of ones made of carbon the Dunlop engineers had managed to shave 500kg from the aircraft's undercarriage, that's more than 80 per cent of the total weight of our F1 car.

The carbon discs in use today have undergone a series of major developments from those first raced by Brabham back in 1980. Gordon Murray's original design consisted of a ring of carbon blocks inserted into a milled steel disc. Now, however, the entire disc is produced from carbon. Nevertheless, because the carbon discs have to withstand a core temperature of around 600°C and a surface temperature of over 1000°C, they aren't manufactured using the same process as for other composite parts, such as the monocoque or the wishbones; nor can they be made from similar pre-preg cloth – the bonding resins would instantly ignite at these temperatures.

The disc manufacturing process remains the sole preserve of a handful of highly specialised companies, is both wondrously complex and very long-winded. Each disc takes approximately six months to make (yep, six months!), and a Grand Prix race distance will reduce it to a piece of useless scrap in under two hours.

Now, let me state here and now that I'm far from an authority in such scientific procedures. (Indeed, the whole process strikes me as frighteningly similar to the formation of a new solar system from randomly shifting star-stuff passing through the fabric of the universe.) But I'll willingly tell you what I know … forgive me if it all seems a bit vague. The latest generation of carbon discs are created in super-heated ovens pressurised with methane (actually perhaps furnace might be a better word). Inside the furnace a delicate lattice-work of carbonised rayon slowly accumulates a build-up of carbon atoms through a process known as vapour-deposition (that's the bit of the manufacturing technique that takes the majority of the production time – well, you can't rush carbonised rayon vapour-deposition, now can you)?

The resultant material produced by this seemingly fantastical method is then solidified by subjecting it to a series of additional temperature increases over further sustained periods. Then you take a deep breath, cross your fingers, open the oven door and – bingo! – out jumps a brake disc. And the leading teams will work their way through two, maybe three car sets per race weekend, with each car set – four discs and eight pads – costing in the region of eight to ten thousand pounds. Right, now I feel like I'm back in the saddle again.

The carbon discs have very good coefficient of friction, which means they make for great brakes. But it's important to keep them at their optimum working temperature; the teams give considerable attention to monitoring and adjusting this throughout the weekend. Before reaching the car, each new brake pad is drilled and fitted with a small temperature probe, coupled into the car's telemetry system. This allows the teams to monitor the temperature of both the inside pad and the outside pad of each corner of the car. The temperature of each brake disc is monitored by four infrared sensors, again one per corner; the sensors fixed atop the axle-uprights, pointing directly at the inside face of the disc. Brake temperatures are controlled by adjusting the size of the ducting fitted to each corner of the car and by interchanging a series of blanking plates, controlling the amount of airflow over the surface of the discs.

Although these carbon discs are exceptionally good at stopping the car, the myth that they are *vastly* superior to steel brakes (at least the latest generation of steel discs and composite pads) is just that – myth. When working with Benetton, I can recall a test session we conducted in Monza (with Alex Wurz as our driver), where we carried out several back-to-back tests with various brake discs, carbon versus steel. The reason for conducting the test, by the way, was due to a possibility of the FIA banning carbon discs at some point in the near future; something the team wanted to be prepared for, despite the fact that the ban never happened. As far as the difference in braking performance was concerned, there seemed remarkably little between the two. As far as the difference in financial cost was concerned . . . well I never saw the actual invoices, but I suspect they were several light-years apart.

No, the major reason for preferring carbon discs over steel is not one of stopping power – it's one of weight. Exactly the reason why Dunlop Aviation developed them in the first place.

A carbon disc and its two pads will tip the scales at approximately one kilogram, its steel equivalent, on the other hand, will weigh close on four kilos. A quick calculation shows a car set of steel discs will add twelve kilos to the mass of the car. Any reduction to the car's mass is advantageous, but savings on brake weight are worth more than ever. Mounted on the car's axles, the brake discs rotate at the same speed as the wheels; the resulting rotational forces generate a gyroscopic effect which, depending on velocity, makes the steering increasingly heavy and the car less responsive to the driver's steering input.

You may remember a similar experiment in science class at school ... when holding the axle of a spinning bicycle wheel? If not, then you should give it a go, the results are rather impressive. Try this on a swivel chair and you'll discover that a simple spin of the wheel will generate sufficient energy to effortlessly turn in circles. The less the mass, the less the gyroscopic effect; as far as our car is concerned this makes for more nimble, more responsive handling.

I'm reluctant to say 'centrifugal force' to describe this effect because my science teacher told me that *centrifugal* force doesn't really exist, it's an *apparent* force, but not an *actual* force. She insisted that what we really wanted to say was '*centripetal* force'. Centripetal force is an actual force, she said – centrifugal is not.

I was too young to formulate the opinion at the time, but now, with the maturity of the passing years, I've come to the conclusion that hers is not the ideal personality to get stuck with on a desert island. What's really needed in a situation of desert island survival, of course, is a troop of Washington Redskins cheerleaders – all keen on spear fishing and all with doctorates in the particular branch of chemistry that specialises in the distillation process of tropical fruit. And a few decent novels to help while away the long summer nights, obviously. I mentioned this to George and he agreed. The only thing George didn't want on a desert island was tinned pineapple – said he had bad memories of tinned pineapple and would rather not get involved again. Forgive me ... I digress.

The other reason for wanting to keep the weight of the brakes to a minimum is because their location results in them falling into that undesirable area of race car engineering known as 'un-sprung mass'. This is bad. Engineers don't like un-sprung mass. It keeps them awake at nights. Un-sprung mass is the combined weight of all the parts of the car that cannot be controlled by the suspension. Anything that is controlled by the suspension is called sprung mass. Here's how to tell the difference: if something bounces up and down on the car's springs, then it's sprung mass; if it doesn't, then it's un-sprung mass.

Basically, un-sprung mass is anything connected to the outer mountings of the suspension wishbones: axle-uprights, stub-axles, steering arms, wheel bearings, brake discs, brake pads, calipers, wheels, tyres. It's important to keep the un-sprung mass to an absolute minimum, because the lighter these parts are, the less inertia they will have, and the less the tyres will lose contact with the tarmac when the un-sprung mass is subjected to the vertical acceleration and deceleration caused by the bumps and dips of the tarmac, as the car negotiates its way around the track.

That said, however, I don't want to give the impression that good brakes play second fiddle to low un-sprung mass. Efficient, reliable and, above all, powerful brakes are absolutely vital, not just as an essential safety feature of the car, but because they are an intrinsic part of the car's overall performance. It's well recognised that the most reliable method of overtaking the opposition is not to out-accelerate them but to out-brake them. Stay off the brake pedal for as long as possible, run deeper into the corner, brake late, dive up the inside, exit in the lead and power off in pursuit of the next victim.

Well, that's the theory of it; it doesn't always quite work like that it practice, of course. The staying-off-the-brakes-and-going-deeper bit is easy enough, it's the rest of the manoeuvre that's the tricky part. How often do we see drivers dive down the inside carrying way too much speed, lock the brakes and overshoot the apex; only to see their intended prey shake their head in bemusement, hand out the cockpit giving a cheery wave as they footle on their merry way?

Back in the old days, when I worked as a mechanic in one of Ferrari's dealerships, an old lag once told me: 'Working on Ferraris is easy – no problem! Anyone can rip a V12 engine apart; in a matter of a couple of hours the thing can be reduced to a pile of oily bits and pieces. The difference between a professional mechanic and an amateur, however, is not just that the engine will work when it's all put back together, but that it will work *better* than before. Getting yourself in trouble is easy; getting yourself back out of trouble . . . that's something else entirely.' Very true. And exactly the same is true with regards to out-braking one's opposition. It's easy to go barrelling in, but making it stick, pulling off the manoeuvre . . . that's entirely different.

When a driver hits the brakes from high speed, he will initially apply a very high pedal pressure, basically stamping down his foot. The huge downforce generated by the car's aerodynamics presses down on the tyres allowing the rubber to grip the track. This, coupled with the car's high drag, will produce deceleration in the region of 4.5g, more than double that of flat-out acceleration, courtesy of the engine's horsepower.

As the car's velocity decreases, so the downforce acting on the tyres decreases; requiring the driver to reduce pedal pressure and so prevent the wheels from locking. It is at this point that the driver gets to show his talent, as he continually plays with the pedal pressure, searching for maximum retardation without locking the wheels.

Up until the end of the 1993 season, the teams were at liberty to use antilock brakes (ABS), a system similar to that used in many of today's road cars. Electronically controlled pressure regulation, a fluid distribution system capable of continually monitoring and adjusting the pressure supplied to each of the car's four calipers.

When the cars were fitted with ABS all the drivers needed to do was stamp on the brakes, the microprocessors did the rest. By monitoring the signals supplied by the four wheel-speed sensors, the computer would keep the brake pressure applied until the split second a wheel began to slow to the point of locking. At this point, the ABS system reduced the pressure to that corner of the car; then, as the wheel began to speed up again so the brake pressure was reapplied – on, off; on, off; on, off. If you've driven a road car with ABS and felt the brake pedal appear to throb beneath your foot, what you've felt is the system continually recalculating and resetting the brake pressures.

The ABS system worked extremely well, faultlessly as far as I'm aware. However, the FIA banned the system for the start of 1994. From then, and continuing to this day, the full responsibility of brake control was back in the hands (or, more accurately, the foot) of the driver. I think the argument against the use of ABS was that it detracted from the driver's skill behind the wheel; that the great efficiency of the ABS system lessened the driver's worth, made the show less spectacular.

I don't know about that; there are many people who think racing is primarily about making car A outperform car B. Besides, with or without ABS, I still believe the driver plays a more than highly significant role. What I do know for certain, however, is that the only reason the teams equipped their cars with ABS was because it certainly *did* enhance the car's braking. Equipped with ABS the cars had more efficient brakes and as a direct result of that produced faster lap times. It made the chariots more competitive.

Nevertheless, the rules are the rules and everyone must play to the same rules. ABS is no longer a part of the industry's arsenal, and so the onus falls on the drivers to do the best they can with the imperfect technology at their disposal. And, you may be surprised to learn, they actually do replicate the ABS system to a degree. Working with their engineers to learn what's required, and by judiciously adjusting the force they apply to the pedal when braking, the best drivers in the business have trained themselves to produce a limited form of ABS-style cadence, modulating the pressure up to five times per second. They'll certainly never beat the efficiency of the outlawed system, of course, but there's no doubt that the technique certainly helps.

The brake system of a contemporary F1 car is extremely straight-forward; the regulations governing this area of design are very strict and leave almost no room for creativity. The maximum diameter of any disc must not exceed 278mm and its thickness must not exceed 28mm. Only one disc per wheel is allowed; and only two pads per wheel. Only one caliper per wheel is allowed, its material of manufacture is specified; it must have no more than six pistons and each piston must be circular in cross-section. And Article 11.5.1 says: 'No braking system may be designed to prevent wheels from locking when the driver applies pressure to the brake pedal.' That's the bit of the rule book that consigns our beautiful ABS system to the scrap heap.

In light of these technical restrictions, I believe we have no option but to join the club and buy all our brakes as proprietary items. Nevertheless, one thing we can do is to ensure we mount the calipers as low as possible, keep the mass low; this is easier to achieve at the rear of the car because the steering is fixed. If we imagine the brake disc as a clock face, we should aim to locate the rear calipers at six o'clock. This isn't so easy at the front of the car because the calipers will foul the bottom wishbones when the driver moves the steering; even so, we must do the best we can. Ideally, the calipers should be mounted behind the front axle centre line (to get the weight closer to the middle of the car), and as low as possible. On the left-hand side of the car the caliper should be located at approximately five o'clock; and on the right-hand side at approximately seven o'clock.

Mounting the calipers in this way may give rise to problems when we try to bleed the air from the brake system's hydraulics. The bleed nipples should really be mounted vertically, the highest point of the caliper, to allow any trapped air to rise upward and escape through the nipple. This is a high consideration on road car designs. If we experience any problems with trapped air and poor bleeding, however, we'll merely unbolt the calipers from the axle-uprights; place specially machined blocks between the pads (to act as the disc, preventing the pistons from pumping their way out of the calipers), rotate the calipers so the nipples are vertical, and bleed the brakes with the calipers held away from the car.

All the brake fluid lines are flexible, Aeroquip-type hoses (not rigid copper or steel as used on road cars) so we have a certain amount of freedom to move the calipers without needing to disconnect any fluid lines from the car. Sure, it's a bit of a scene to have to bleed the brakes in this way, but well worth the trouble in terms of the benefit to weight distribution. Anyway, our mechanics are trained professionals, they know what they're doing – the drivers trust them with their lives.

And that's really all we can do with regards to enhancing the brakes. Well, I guess there's nothing to stop us building our own furnace, hanging up some rayon webbing and having a go at knocking out a few of our own brake discs. After all, once we've thumbed our way through the instruction manual how difficult can carbonised rayon vapour-deposition actually be? Besides, even if we fail to get the hang of it, we can always use the furnace to warm up some steak-and-kidney pies should we find ourselves working late at the factory.

The captain switched on his intercom and told us we were more than halfway home, and that we had reached our maximum altitude – at a groundspeed of 1350mph we were cruising over the Atlantic Ocean at 59,000ft. This is twice as high as any jumbo flies, and well above the level of any meteorological disturbances. There is no rain, no lightning storms, not a single cloud to be seen. Nevertheless, the view out of the window was exquisitely beautiful. Outside the aircraft, stretching away in all directions lay a seemingly endless expanse of rich, intense blue, almost purple. This is the planet's stratosphere, the last protective layer dividing earth from the infinite inky blackness of space itself. And the lack of any weather disturbance made the flight absolutely stable, it was as though we weren't moving at all.

As soon as lunch was served my appetite tried its hardest to return – it seldom deserts me for very long – and it forced me to eat a little scrambled egg flavoured with truffles. It seems truffles were in season. The eggs must have helped because my appetite then persuaded me to try a few scallop dumplings and fresh sorrel sauce. Both Wingrave and I then managed to polish off a plate of French cheeses and two more glasses of the '96 Pomerol. And by the time we'd done the same to coffee and some raspberry macaroons, I felt my old self again. And through this whole wonderful experience, Paul Kelver and Carl Hentschel slept on.

'And, so, George, old chap, there we are. That's what our dream-team Formula 1 race car will look like. It will have a beautifully slick, single-keel carbon fibre chassis; it will cut through the air like a dart and create oodles of downforce.

'It will have the very latest Ferrari V10 bolted to its back face, or, at least, the very latest V10 Ferrari are prepared to give us, maybe a year behind their own. It will have a wonderfully compact six-speed composite transmission, with a conventional multiplate clutch.

'Composite brakes; Bridgestone tyres – assuming they'll agree terms to supply them to us; composite pushrod suspension fitted with torsion bars. And before we attach any ballast it will weigh a mere 450kg. We have to account for the mass of our driver too, of course, and assuming he'll tip the scales at an athletic 75kg, the total weight of our car-driver combination will be 525kg; giving us a very useful 75kg of ballasting to play with in order for us to reach the "legal" minimum racing weight of 600kg.

'All we have to do now is load it on the transporter and take it to a track. There we have to set it up; bolt the driver in; and see how it all works when driven around a few laps of the circuit.'

10

Down a Bit ... Down a Bit More ...

'Understeer is when they hit the Armco with the front of
the car; oversteer, on the other hand, is when they hit the
Armco with the rear of the car.'
Jock Clear – chief race engineer, BAR-Honda

When running the cars in anger, the overriding concern for every-one is to prevent the car from sliding off the track and skitting through the gravel trap; and, in a worse case scenario, finishing any such off-road excursion by slamming into the Armco or tyre barrier. In terms of optimising the car's performance this is generally considered a bad thing. The main consideration is the driver's safety, naturally, that goes without saying (not to mention the resulting lost track time and financial cost incurred in having to rebuild and rectify any mechanical damage). A gracefully controlled power slide on corner-exit is one thing but a car that is continuously losing adhesion with the tarmac and 'breaking free' is no good to anyone.

We want the car to stick to the track and we want its handling characteristics to be predictable, both of which are linked to the car's overall level of grip. There is never enough grip. Lack of grip is a constant driver whinge, everyone wants more; the tyre manufacturers and chassis engineers are always looking at ways to increase their car's traction. The greater the level of adhesion between car and track, the faster the car can work and the lower the lap times will be. A Formula 1 car relies on two different forms of grip: aerodynamic grip, achieved, as we've already discussed, by harnessing the beneficial effects of airflow and air pressure as the car drives along; and mechanical grip; courtesy of the harmonious relationship between the suspension, tyres and the surface of the track.

To a certain degree the car's mechanical grip is enhanced by the engine's electronic management systems: traction control (during normal running) and launch control (at the start of the race). I say 'enhanced' because these electronic controls do not in themselves create *additional* mechanical grip. Traction control does not alter the suspension's spring rate, adjust roll bar stiffness, lower or lift the ride-height, or vary the tyre pressures. Traction control *optimises* the available grip already designed within the physical make-up of the car. The difference is subtle yet significant, and one that is often misunderstood.

Traction control works by carrying out a series of fine adjustments to the power delivery from the engine to the rear wheels, which, in essence, is exactly what the driver does with his throttle pedal. The overwhelming advantage of letting the computer do the work, however, is that the electronics are capable of monitoring, and correcting this power delivery at an infinitely faster rate than any driver can ever hope to achieve.

In terms of net gain – exactly how much faster the car works when using traction control – well, it's possibly not as much as one might imagine. In dry conditions, for the first couple of laps on new tyres, the time advantage will be minimal, absolute fractions of a second. Sure, fractions of seconds matter, of course they do, but my point is we're not talking two, three, four seconds per lap – figures some people have suggested to me – even in pouring rain the advantages are nowhere close to that.

I talked with Ferrari's technical director, Ross Brawn, asking, amongst other things, for an average 'per lap' time advantage of using traction control. It was towards the end of 2002, a time when Max Mosley had announced his intention to do away with traction control from the outset of the following season. The FIA president was apparently convinced that this move, along with several other technical restrictions, would help to spice up the racing, while at the same time helping to control its ever-escalating costs. The president's news caused much unrest, certainly at the sharp end of the pit lane. Primarily, I suspect, because Max had announced his intentions to significantly alter the sport's engineering capabilities without the leading teams' endorsement.

Nevertheless, after some political jostling a date was set for its removal, July 2003, the weekend of the British Grand Prix. It was a worrying few months for the leading constructors. However, there must have been many noteworthy happenings and heated telephone conversations behind closed doors, for at the end of the day the much publicised ban came to naught, the major teams stood united and the idea of any attempt to remove traction control seemed merely to melt away. It was a significant moment.

Ross Brawn is an outstanding engineer, his pit lane achievements are legendary. Not only that, Ross is a fascinating chap to talk with, and regardless that the ban failed to materialise, his thoughts on traction control and a potential ban make interesting reading. Of particular note are his prophetic comments concerning the rise of Michelin and the close contest that unfolded towards the end of the 2003 championship.

'It is probably true that with new tyres on a qualifying lap the benefit of TC (traction control) is low, perhaps 0.1s or 0.2 dependent on the track. The gains are much bigger on a long run. Rear tyre degradation is controlled and reduced, and it could mean 0.5 to 1.0 towards the end of a stint. In the wet the benefits are more to do with direct performance as opposed to tyre degradation; it could be 0.5 to 1.0 per lap.

'The fact that is not generally understood is that the car and the engine are developed to take advantage of TC. For instance, our engine characteristics are different now to what they were in the non-TC era. The current engine can compromise drivability for performance because the TC will cope. This affects bore/stroke ratio; cam timing; throttle mechanism; induction and exhaust system design, etc.

'This is what causes the huge frustration when some teams tell

Max that they can "turn it off". It can be done but the teams who have taken the system and car to the next level are particularly shafted – and those who have not had the ambition or the capacity to develop, their cars are less affected.

'I don't believe that removing TC will make any difference to the quality of racing, reduce the costs, increase overtaking, or change the way the cars appear on the track. Some parties are presenting the argument that the public are fed up with "computers driving the cars". If this is the perception, then we have done a poor job of presenting the technical side of Formula 1 because this is simply not true.

'It will certainly give the media plenty of fodder regarding innuendo, suspicion, accusation, and this will certainly liven things up, although, as you know from our Benetton '94 days, it can be very unpleasant for those accused.

'What bugs me is that people are not looking at pre-post Barcelona 2001. Did the reintroduction of TC make any fundamental difference to the racing? – No. Did it get rid of the suspicion and innuendo? – Yes. I suspect we will have the same pre-post Silverstone 2003 when TC is banned.

'The problem is that it is being presented as one of the reasons why we did not have a close championship in 2002, and a lot of the public and media are being conned. Still, what seems to be important is the perception, not the reality (that's PR). Other people need to make that judgement, but this chopping and changing is a terrific waste of money and resources at a time when we are trying to be more prudent.

'If we have two or three teams fighting each other, that will make the difference, and it's hard to see how this change will have encouraged this. Still, if we slip a little and Michelin improve, then the decision to remove TC will be promoted as the reason why we have a more exciting championship!'

A computer's reaction time is immeasurably faster than any living creature; they calculate faster, they formulate the solution faster, they respond faster. Without electronic assistance all any driver can do is attempt to replicate any banned function as best as possible. It stands to reason that some drivers will do a better job than others, but there is no question that the potential of every car in the pit lane must suffer as a result.

That said, however, technical restrictions are nothing new to the industry. Engineering constraints are continually being imposed on Grand Prix racing, and the sporadic banning of this or that piece of technology has been a feature of the sport from day one. High wings; ground effects; toluene fuels; turbos; active suspension; qualifying tyres – the list goes on and on. It's frustrating to those that have worked so hard to develop and refine these systems, naturally, but that it happens is certainly nothing new. Perhaps, then, the engineering challenge is better viewed as one of trying to build the best car possible from what one's allowed to use at any given time? And, at the end of the day, I guess that's how I feel about it ... kind of.

Others, however, may not feel that way. I believe the current enthusiasm of the major car manufacturers to participate in Grand Prix racing is fuelled by a desire to exploit F1's technical heritage. They want to use the sport as an engineering training ground, a test bench for new technology, and a bejewelled showcase to high-light their scientific prowess. And in so doing they'll hope to shift umpteen more cars from their forecourts, too.

With the likes of Ferrari, BMW, Mercedes, Renault, Toyota, Ford and Honda investing untold billions of dollars in the sport, I suspect the rule makers may have to tread lightly if they are to prevent these massive corporations from upping sticks and moving camp. At least five of the manufacturers have already organised themselves into a consortium, designed to protect their mutual future interests in the sport and, as far as I'm aware, are fully prepared to quit Formula 1 and form their own breakaway series within the next five years. That's serious stuff.

On a more personal level, I suppose the question of technology and motor racing must be subjective. What does motor racing mean to you, what aspect of the challenge excites you? There's no right or wrong answer, least I don't believe so. Leaving aside the obvious need to cap unacceptably dangerous speeds, is the thrill of racing to be found in the search to make one car faster than the next, or is it observing the drivers battling against the (curable) inefficiencies of their cars? For those that believe the driver is the most important factor, then the end of the path must surely lead to a contest that excludes any technical advantage, total parity of equipment; a racing formula where everyone uses the same make of chassis, the same type engine, the same supply and compound of tyres.

The good news is that such a series already exists. International Formula 3000 is founded on this very basis; the entire field uses identical Lola chassis designed to the exact same dimensions as the current Formula 1 regulations; all equipped with Zytec 3.0 litre V8s and all on the same specification Avon tyres – and the tyres are true slicks. For those that fancy the idea of such a controlled formula of racing I would certainly recommend giving International F3000 a go. It's worth having a look, compare the two, see what you think.

As to F1's predicament, I readily appreciate there are two sides to the coin, and, I agree, there is something entertaining in watching drivers scrabble for grip. Nevertheless, in what is widely perceived to be the pinnacle of international motor sport, I can't help feeling that any future electronic restrictions would be a little like taking the poles away from a pack of elite downhill skiers and seeing which one copes best without them. Truth is, though the actual skiing might look more spectacular, they'll all be slower.

Anyway, enough from me on this subject, we could sit and debate the pros and cons of technology in motor racing for ever and a day – how about we let Jock Clear, senior race engineer with BAR-Honda have the last word:

'I don't know about you, Steve, but the whole "driver aids" thing pisses me off. Remember the old 1920s cars, the ones with ride-on mechanic, etc.? Those cars were equipped with a lever on the steering wheel to advance and retard the ignition. The driver had to do this while speeding up to keep the engine running cleanly. Well, we no longer have to do that because some clever German devised a distributor with a vacuum advance/retard mechanism.

'My point is: do we want to go back to that? No, of course not, so where do "driver aids" stop? The fact is we can't un-invent technology. Also, we don't want Joe Public realising that the car he drives to work is equipped with higher specification technology than an F1 car!

'The bottom line is that with or without traction control the skilful drivers will still win and the less skilful ones will not. As far as making F1 more exciting to watch, that should be done with aero and tyres, not limiting the technology! I'm in favour of getting rid of launch control, that should go, I think; but that is not a reversal of technology, it's just limiting the use of such technology.'

All Formula 1 cars will lose adhesion with the tarmac and break free from time to time, it makes no difference if they are built by Ferrari, Minardi or any team in between, none is immune, it's part and parcel of racing. The sport's challenge to a team is to design and build a car capable of navigating a series of corners with more stability and carrying more speed than that of the competition; the challenge on offer to the driver is to retain control over the car while pushing it to the very boundary of its limitations, to drive it so hard it teeters on the absolute edge but never allowing it to fall off.

The TV pictures of cars circulating the tracks at phenomenal speeds can be very deceptive. They look so smooth, so stable, the cars often appear as though fixed to the circuit on rails. The reality, however, is that Formula 1 cars are constantly dancing on a finely honed razor's edge of adhesion; they are like mustangs, forever poised, waiting for the slightest provocation to show any inexperienced or overconfident driver just exactly who's boss. If the driver misjudges his braking point by so much as a couple of metres; if the car is allowed to carry just a fraction too much speed into the corner ... in less than the blink of an eye the car has gone. Sometimes the driver can catch it, flick the steering, catch the slide and carry on, sometimes he can't and ... WHAM! Wheels, suspension, wings and ten thousand unidentifiable fragments of carbon are cascading in all directions.

Touch wood, the driver will be perfectly fine apart from looking a tad bewildered; on his long walk back to the paddock he will have a chance to reflect on things, to ponder if, in hindsight, it was possibly not such a wise move to try and negotiate Suzuka's 130R without a quick lift of the throttle. It looked like a stunningly quick lap ... right up to the point he wrote the car off.

There's no denying that any shunt is annoying, but that drivers will occasionally, inevitably do so, is not such a bad thing, providing, that is, it only happens during the practice sessions, not the actual race. That sounds somewhat contradictory so allow me to clarify what I mean. Although the aftermath of an accident creates work and expense for everyone, the fact that the driver has exceeded the car's limitations at least proves he is trying his hardest to deliver a respectable lap time.

The driver is the last link in the team's chain; the efforts of hundreds of others rest on his shoulders, and there can be nothing more soul-destroying for a team than having a driver on board who is not giving of his absolute best, leaving his team-mates to witness the potential of their beautiful car being completely wasted. So, the occasional faux pas by the drivers will be forgiven; you will notice, however, that championship-winning drivers do not make a habit of it. Stupidity, on the other hand, is something else completely, and a continuous string of self-induced mistakes will not be tolerated for very long.

The drivers need to learn the skill of *feeling* the limit, the point just before the car lets go, they have to nurture that mysterious sixth sense which tells them exactly how far they can push the car without actually crossing the boundary. I've always been fascinated by this sixth sense business. I think it's something we all possess and that we use in different ways depending on personal circumstance. You may remember how I described mechanics as being able to *feel* when something is right or wrong, a sensation passed from the bolt, stud or nut, through the spanner and into the hand. And we've all experienced the feeling that someone is watching us, sensed their eyes boring into the back of the head, turn around and there they are. I've also heard of soldiers sensing that imminent danger is lurking close at hand, a reasonable enough assumption in times of combat, sure; but yelling for their comrades to stop walking, seconds before entering a minefield, that's something else.

As far as racing drivers are concerned, that 'something else' tells them their car is on the absolute edge, the 'knockings' as it's sometimes referred to. I've asked every driver I've worked with if they could describe for me their awareness of being right on the edge, and all have said pretty much the same thing. That they become an extension of the car, the car fits them like a glove, and when driving flat out the four corners of the car transmit recognisable signals, messages travelling through the car and into the body as it pounds along the track. Not just the obvious sensations such as the turning resistance of the tyres felt through the steering rack, but infinitely more subtle, delicate signs. A slight shift in the stability of each corner, the malleability within the carcass of the tyre, the change in movement of its sidewall as the weight of the car loads each wheel.

And things become infinitely more sensitive in the rain, of course; adhesion is much lower with a wet track, the grip level is changing from lap to lap, more often from corner to corner; traction is at a premium and the limit of the car is far more unpredictable. When I asked Michael Schumacher to explain his awareness of the car when driving on the edge, he again described how he felt the slight shifts of adhesion from each wheel, how these tiny signals travel through the car and into his body: 'It's as though the four corners of the car are talking to you,' he said, 'you just have to interpret the messages.' And is it the same in the wet, I asked. 'In the wet everything is much more sensitive; in the wet the car doesn't talk to you – it whispers – you have to listen much more carefully.'

One evening, over a pre-dinner drink at an event hosted by BMW

North America, I broached the same subject with Gerhard Berger. I told him what Schumacher had said to me and asked for his thoughts. Gerhard mulled things over for a few moments then concluded that Michael's was perhaps the best, the most accurate explanation he had come across. 'Yah, that's good,' he smiled. 'In the wet the car whispers to you ... I think Michael has it pretty much spot on, I like that!'

During the practice sessions, when the mechanics are rapidly wheeling their car back within the cosy sanctuary of the pit garages, how often have you seen the driver lift his hand out of the cockpit and perform a little mime while talking to his engineer over the radio? It happens all the time, they all do it. The driver, gloved hand held parallel to the ground, uses it to indicate how the car is reacting over the bumps, dips and corners of the circuit; stabbing his fingers forward to indicate the front of the car, swinging his wrist side to side to explain how the rear of the car is working.

These actions are always accompanied by a stampede of vocal explanations too, thoughts stream from the driver like water bursting a dam, his brain still computating quick enough to handle decision-making where information is arriving at speeds in excess of a hundred metres per second. The more urgent his hand signals, the wider the driver's eyes, the worse the car is handling. You don't need to hear the conversation, his body language speaks volumes.

And while the driver is in full flow, gesticulating and downloading his impressions of the car, his patient, long-suffering engineer will be watching, listening, nodding, scribbling notes, translating jabbed fingers and wide eyes into potential set-up changes to camber, ride-height, suspension, and front wing. But not only that, the engineer will also be working to keep his driver's confidence on a high; keep him motivated, keep things moving forward. Lose the driver's confidence in the car (its predictable handling and its ability to only improve) and the whole house of cards collapses.

This continual interplay twixt driver and engineer is all part of the ongoing search for the seemingly ever-illusive 'balance'. The perfect balance. It's a little like the quest for the holy grail, everyone searches for it, follows the clues and slowly works towards it . . . but it always *just* manages to elude them. If the car is working perfectly, then the driver should be able to push a tad more, and when he does so the car develops another little handling problem; cure that, go a bit quicker, and something else needs fixing. Lower the net over a butterfly, and watch it innocently flutter to the next bush.

Either that or a team never gets close to finding their car's balance all weekend: the car was an unpredictable pig on Friday, it remained so throughout Saturday, and continued to be a pig until it finally flung itself into the barrier on Sunday afternoon . . . THWAK! Job done. Time to pack up and head off to the airport for a beer. As a general rule of thumb, however, if the driver's not complaining about some aspect of the car's handling, then he isn't driving it fast enough.

Without any reservation, I'd say that out of all the questions I get asked, the most frequent request concerns a desire to better appreciate the difference between understeer and oversteer. Out of every ten e-mails or letters, that question will appear in six of them, in one form or another. Engineers, drivers, writers and broadcasters alike, we all talk about the handling and the balance of race cars in terms of understeer and oversteer, and yet we're all as guilty as one another for not giving adequate explanations of what it all means to those we're attempting to inform. However, I must say, I think Jock's quote at the top of this chapter hits the nail bang on the head; not only very amusing, it's also very accurate.

The balance of a race car is a reference to its on-track behaviour, its general stability and its ability to negotiate all three stages of a corner – the entry, the apex and the exit – as fast as possible, as predictably as possible. Now, we've seen how often compromise must play its part in race car design, but here, in the world of chassis set-up, it really comes to the fore. Everything about the set-up of a car, its aerodynamic settings and its mechanical settings is a compromise; there can never be a perfect solution.

The reason for this is because a Formula 1 circuit consists of a series of different challenges – slow corners, fast corners, long straights, tight chicanes – and each demands a particular set-up to optimise the car's performance; and the optimum set-up for a slow corner is certainly not the same as for a fast corner. The perfect solution to this conundrum would be to alter the car's set-up from corner to corner as the car circulates the track, but the technical regulations forbid the teams to make any changes to the suspension or aerodynamics while the car is running on-track. Indeed, such is the FIA's insistence that the suspension settings must only be adjusted in the pits that, unlike some of the junior formulae, Grand Prix drivers are even forbidden to adjust the roll-bar stiffness via a cockpit-mounted lever.

Understeer and/or oversteer will not affect the car as it accelerates along the straights (at least we hope not, if it does then we really are in phenomenal trouble), these conditions only come into play as the driver attacks a corner.

Let's discuss understeer first and let's also assume our driver is barrelling along the straight, approaching a right-hand corner. He turns his steering wheel to the right, the front wheels respond and move accordingly (so no actual problem with the steering mechanism), but the car itself doesn't respond to the direction change. Rather than turn to the right the front tyres break adhesion with the tarmac and the car merely carries on as before, travelling in a straight line. In a split second the car has overshot the apex of the bend and is now heading towards the gravel trap and the dreaded tyre barrier is looming ever closer.

If you've ever driven a road car in snow or ice, then you've almost certainly experienced understeer at some stage; hit the brakes, the wheels lock, turn the steering wheel (which feels very light), and nothing happens – the car just refuses to obey any instructions. Well, whether driving the family runabout or a state-of-the-art

Formula 1 race car, that's understeer. The driver turns the steering wheel but the car *under*-steers. In a race car it isn't necessary to actually lock the wheels to produce understeer, although the drivers certainly do so from time to time.

By the way, if you've heard or read of engineers discussing 'tyre slip-angle' and thought it all sounded a bit daunting, what they're referring to is nothing more complex than the difference – measured in degrees – between the direction the front wheels are facing and the direction the car is travelling (basically its longitudinal axis). I guess it would be feasible to take an overhead shot of a car as it negotiated a corner, draw these two intersecting lines on the photograph, take your protractor (assuming Scoggins hasn't had it away) and calculate the car's slip-angle. I don't quite know why anyone would want to, but it could, nevertheless, be done.

Oversteer, on the other hand, is the exact opposite of understeer. Our derring-do driver approaches the same right-hand corner, he turns the steering wheel to the right but this time, rather than the car carrying on in a straight line, the rear tyres break adhesion with the tarmac and the back of the car 'steps out' and attempts to overtake the front. The extreme of this condition will see the car spin through 180° as it travels past the corner apex and heads, backwards, into the gravel trap. The tyre barrier looms closer, just as before, it's just that this time our driver can't see what's coming.

Okay, there we have it, but remember that the above examples are somewhat brutish, given in the hope of achieving a clear distinction between the two. In reality, a whole range of understeer/oversteer exists as a Grand Prix car negotiates its way around a lap. Moreover, a car doesn't suffer from just one condition or the other, it is subjected to both, and not only at different points around the same lap, but at different points of the *same* corner.

There is always the potential for the car to swap ends at the approach to the entry of the corner, as the driver slams on the brakes and the mass of the car transfers towards the front (this is all part of the reason why we've tried so hard to move the mass of the transmission closer to the middle of the car). If the car survives this initial heavy braking and sufficient speed is reduced before the corner entry, it may then suffer from understeer as the driver initially turns in to the corner; followed by snap-oversteer as he hits the throttle and attempts to power the car out of the corner. Look at some of the in-car camera shots during the TV broadcasts, and you'll notice how the driver's hands are forever flicking the wheel, left right left, constantly correcting the steering, reining the car back into line. Naturally, some cars handle better than others; those whose drivers seem to be having an easier time in the cockpit actually are having an easier time: smooth is quick.

Again, as with almost everything we've discussed, a comprehensive examination of how the technical director, engineers and mechanics go about reducing their car's tendency to understeer and oversteer – how they, along with their drivers, search for the perfect balance – could fill several volumes. Nevertheless, to bypass the subject would be quite wrong and I won't do that. How and what the teams adjust on their cars during the race weekend is important (of course it is), and even a less than complete study of chassis set-up will greatly enhance an appreciation of what's happening in the garages during the practice sessions, when the mechanics are seen beavering away in the pits.

An immense amount of fine tuning is carried out on the cars, many small adjustments requiring the cars to be sitting absolutely flat and square on the ground, perfectly level. However, because the floors of the pit garages are normally made of poured concrete, as opposed to accurately machined blocks of inspection-quality granite, it is necessary to make a 'flat patch' for each car. This consists of four plates or corner-weight scales, one resting under each wheel of the car; the plates are adjusted up and down until all four are level in respect to one another. All suspension measurements are taken with the car resting on this flat patch.

Of primary importance is the car's 'ride-height' – the distance between the underside of the car and the surface of the track. We want the car to run as close to the track as possible but not so close that its underside continually scrapes along the tarmac. Running the car very close to the ground will increase the velocity of the airflow travelling rearward between the underside of the car and the tarmac. This *increase* in airspeed produces a *decrease* in pressure beneath the car, enhancing downforce production. Naturally, the FIA know this too, of course, and in an attempt to force the teams to raise their cars' ride-height and so reduce downforce (and therefore lower cornering speeds), they insist the teams secure a legality skid-block or 'plank' to the underside of the lowest part of the car (the reference plane).

At one time each plank was etched with a serial number at manufacture and its thickness recorded by the FIA (it had to have a minimum thickness of 10mm). Anytime during the race weekend the FIA were at liberty to check this dimension. If any section of the surface area had reduced in thickness in excess of 1mm – a result of abrasion from contact with the tarmac – the car was deemed to be outside the regulations and could well have been excluded from taking any further part in the event or the results of the race itself. The ruling seemed extremely harsh and its inter-pretation made little allowance for any accidental damage caused to the plank by riding the car over the kerbs or running over debris on the track.

Now, however, the regulations governing plank wear have been somewhat refined, serial numbers are no longer necessary. The planks are measured at three specific points along their length, and allowance is made for any incidental scrapes and scratches. Nevertheless, the planks are still required to have a nominal thick-ness of 10mm, and any car fitted with a plank that measures less than 9mm is still at risk of exclusion.

As the teams themselves determine their cars' ride-heights, the onus of responsibility is on them to ensure the planks do not rub and wear on the tarmac and fall foul of the regulations. It's a little like Russian roulette: How low do you want to go? How low have Ferrari dared to drop their ride-height? How about Williams and McLaren? Should we lower our car just one millimetre more?

It's clear that a very fine line exists between enjoying the benefits of running the car as low as possible and suffering the potential penalties of running it just a tad too low. Yes, it's a gamble, but help is at hand to make the bet as safe as it can be. To help the engineers pinpoint the limit of risk-free adjustment, the cars are fitted with two laser ride-height sensors, mounted front and back. One sits beneath the keel of the chassis, the other at the rear of the diffuser. Throughout the course of every lap these lasers will measure the ride-height at both ends of the car and feed the information, via the on-board telemetry system, back to the engineers in the pits. These days the telemetry system works in 'real time', which means the information is constantly transmitted, a continuous stream of information, giving the engineers an un-ending supply of data.

The car's optimum ride-height will vary from track to track, much depends on the undulations of the circuit, some of which are in considerably better condition than others. The tarmac of Magny-Cours, for example – home of the French Grand Prix – is in perfect condition; impeccably smooth, like driving on a prize-winning billiard table. On the other hand, Brazil's Interlagos is more like driving on a prize-winning collection of mine craters. The worse the state of the circuit, the higher the ride-height will have to be in order to keep the plank legit.

An average ride-height setting will be in the region of 32mm at the front, 65mm at the rear. When watching the cars on TV you might think that these figures seem too high; often there is next to no visible clearance at all between the bottom of the car and the track. And you'd be perfectly right in thinking that. The above figures are what's known as the static ride-height, when the car is sitting quietly in the pit garage or on the starting grid prior to the race. When the car is moving, however, and the tremendous aerodynamic load is generated by the wings and bodywork, these ride-heights will drop dramatically. As the car powers along the main straight the ride-height will reduce to 12mm at the front,

15mm at the rear. Still too high, do you think? Correct again, you must have the eyes of a hawk! Although certainly much lower, these latter figures do not take into account the thickness of the FIA legality plank, we have to subtract another 10mm from them to arrive at the true ride-height, so now we're down to 2mm at the front, 5mm at the rear.

These cars are extremely sensitive to aerodynamic change, and the engineers will ask the mechanics to make *very* small alterations to the ride-height in order to fine tune the trim of the car. A change of 1mm would be a big jump, and it is by no means unusual for the mechanics to raise or lower the car by as little as a quarter of a millimetre. Consider exactly how small that is. Each page of the book you're reading is roughly 0.1mm thick, so if you squeeze three pages together, the paper held between your finger and thumb will be just a fraction thicker than a typical ride-height adjustment. Hard to believe isn't it? It still fascinates me that a driver – any driver – can feel the effects of such a minuscule alteration, and appreciate the difference it's made to the balance of his car. Even more so when I see those 'super slow-mo' replays of the cars slamming over the kerbs, with their wheels bouncing six inches in the air . . . Well, whatever; they say they can and I guess that's why they earn the big bucks. Who are we to argue?

Depending on the particular design, these alterations are made in one of two ways; either by adding or removing one or more machined shims from the top of the pushrods, or by adjusting turn-buckles, also located at the top of the pushrod. Two solutions which achieve the same result – to increase or decrease the overall length of the suspension pushrods. The majority of teams use shims; it's neater (aerodynamically) and arguably a more precise method, but you can still see turn-buckles on some of the cars.

Change to the camber angle of the front suspension is another adjustment one frequently sees the mechanics carrying out during the sessions. Measured in degrees of a circle, camber angle concerns the vertical attitude of the tyres (whether they appear to lean inward or outward) in relation to the chassis. When you look at an F1 car from the front, you will notice that the top of the wheels and tyres leans inwards, this is called *negative* camber. If the top of the tyres were to lean outwards then they would have *positive* camber; and if they were perfectly vertical they would have zero camber. All F1 cars have negative camber; an average setting for the front suspension of the car is somewhere between 1.5° and 3.5°.

Adjusting the degree of camber built into the car will alter its steering characteristics and affect the heat and potential grip of the tyres. This is because adjusting the camber will move the position of the tyre's 'contact patch', the relatively small section of the tyre that makes contact with the track: The more negative camber the car is given, the more the contact patch moves towards the inside shoulder of the tyre. Moreover, increasing the camber may help to improve the response of the front of the car, making it react faster to any steering input, especially during initial turn-in, and may give a little more mid-corner grip. Conversely, if the driver is complaining of oversteer on initial turn-in, then reducing the front camber could help to eliminate the problem somewhat.

Adjusting the front camber will also help to control the temperature of the tyres, something that can be especially useful in provisional qualifying when it's important to get the tyres up to their optimum working temperature as quickly as possible. Have a look at the front camber on the Ferrari during a Friday qualifying session, then compare the same car during the race itself. It depends on the particular circuit, of course, but often you'll notice that Ferrari run with significantly more camber during provisional qualifying runs.

Building the car with increased camber will generate more heat within the contact patch of the tyres, although much of this temperature increase is achieved by shifting the heat-spread across the surface of the tyre. For example, the heat-spread across a tyre running with negative 2° camber might be 70–75–80 (outside-middle-inside) Celsius; whereas the heat-spread across the same tyre running with negative 3° camber might be 60–75–90 Celsius.

The temperature of the outside shoulder dropping ten degrees, while the inside shoulder increases by the same amount. Adjusting the heat-spread in this fashion is fine for short durations but will prove detrimental to the longevity of the tyre over sustained distances, leading to localised hot spots and blistering of the rubber.

As recently as the early part of the 1990s, these camber adjustments were achieved by altering the length of the threaded section of the spherical bearing joints screwed into the top wishbones. These served as both inboard mountings (attaching the wishbone to the chassis), and outboard mountings (connecting the wishbone to the axle-upright). The mechanics would unbolt the top wishbone from the upright, slacken the locknut and wind the joint further in or out depending on whether the car needed more or less camber. The suspension was rebuilt, the car placed on the flat patch and checked; the adjustment process was somewhat hit-and-miss and it could take two or three attempts to achieve the desired setting.

A later refinement was to fit the spherical bearing of the outboard mounting to the top wishbone via a small, machined block. The block was spaced away from the wishbone by a number of shims; adding or subtracting shims would alter the final length of the wishbone and so alter the camber. Exactly the same method, in fact, that's used to adjust the car's ride-height.

The drawback to both of these methods is that the tracking (the car's steering alignment – toe-in or toe-out) needs to be checked and adjusted after each camber change. The reason for this is because any camber adjustment will move the upright either closer or further away from the chassis, and, as the steering trackrod is also attached to the upright, moving the position of the upright inevitably alters the steering alignment. Annoying but there we are ... that's life.

(And remember this: camber adjustment will alter the tracking, but adjustments to the tracking will *not* alter the camber. I hope that gels with you because I can readily appreciate that it might seem a tad illogical at first glance. I also hope it gels with you because, sadly, unlike our bread baguette/torsional rigidity analogy, I'm completely stumped for a simple way to demonstrate this somewhat curious relationship between camber and tracking. It holds true for all cars, however, so if you still want a little guidance with the concept, all I can suggest is that next time you visit a race track, ask the kindliest-looking bunch of mechanics to show you their car.)

Anyway, back to our Formula 1 car. In light of the fact that the tracking needed resetting following any camber adjustment, the engineers designed a third solution; a method which is still in use to this day. Now, the leading teams use an interchangeable range of steering arms (not trackrods – rather the plates that bolt atop the axle-upright). These steering arms, or camber plates as they are also called, bolt atop the uprights and form the mounting points for the top wishbones and trackrods.

The wishbone mounting is in a slightly different position on each of these steering arms; swapping one for another will alter the position of the upright, so adjusting the camber. All very good and all very neat. But here comes the trick bit: by carefully mapping the relationship between camber adjustment and its effect on the steering alignment, the engineers have been able to design these pieces whereby the mounting for the trackrod remains fixed at its original point, allowing the tracking to remain unaltered irrespective of the new camber angle.

The machining on these pieces is very accurate, and the engineers can be reasonably certain that each steering arm will give a precise and predictable change in camber, with no appreciable change in tracking. Consequently, the pieces are numbered with the degrees of camber they will produce when fitted to the car. If the engineer asks for negative 2° camber, the mechanics will merely unbolt the original steering arm, exchange it for the appropriate replacement, add a dab of Loctite, re-torque the nuts and send the car back to the track. A well-drilled crew can carry out a camber change in under two minutes.

You'll have noticed that the camber settings on the rear of the car haven't featured very much. Although the camber angle of the rear suspension is still important, by virtue of the fact that the steering geometry at the rear is fixed (we don't have four-wheel steer in F1, the regulations don't allow it), the rear of the car is not as sensitive to camber change. An average figure for the rear camber will be in the region of zero to negative 1.5°. The figures are appreciably lower than the front settings because less camber will help to improve traction, and we're using rear-wheel drive (oh, four-wheel drive is also banned, by the way). Less camber may give better traction but it comes at the expense of mid-corner grip. Everything is swings-and-roundabouts (I guess that's just another way of saying compromise?). Thus, what we gain in one hand we lose from the other, but, on the whole, drivers can live with over-steer more than they can with understeer and we want all the traction we can get our hands on.

The difference between the degree of camber built into the front suspension and that at the rear is very noticeable. Have a look at any of the cars (although the Bridgestone-shod teams tend to run more camber than their Michelin counterparts) and you'll soon spot how upright the rear wheels look in comparison to the fronts.

By the way, I don't want to dismiss the great importance of tyres and tyre compound with regard to the effectiveness of the set-up. We can adjust steering geometry and tyre pressures, of course, but if we want to play with the compounds, the only thing we can do is substitute one set of tyres for another.

The tyre suppliers are allowed to produce two different dry weather compounds for each team. For ease of identification the two options are called 'hard' and 'soft' but as the exact compound of the rubber will vary between circuits – depending on the grip quality and abrasiveness of the tarmac – the terms hard and soft are rather incomparable from race to race. For example, the hard compound at one race may become the soft compound at the following race, the tyre suppliers complementing this with an even harder compound than was issued at the previous race. Or they may produce two new compounds, both considerably softer than those used at the previous race, but one will still be harder than the other and again the two compounds will be known as hard and soft. I hope you followed that!

Our eventual choice of which compound to use will depend on how well the tyres work with the car and how many laps we intend to run in between fuel stops. In general terms, the softer compound will offer the car more grip but the tyres will degrade faster than the harder compound. Conversely, the harder tyres will not be as 'sticky' but will (should!) outlast the softer option. Also, at a tortuous track such as Monaco, where overtaking is virtually impossible, do we risk choosing the soft option to help generate as much grip as possible during qualifying; so putting us further up the grid, but then discovering that the soft option degrades too quickly during the race, forcing us to pit more often? Yep, it would be nice to use both compounds, soft for qualifying and the harder option for the race but, unfortunately, the rules don't allow for that. The teams have to decide on their choice of compound before Saturday qualifying begins and they have to stick with that option for the remainder of the weekend.

Exactly how much wing the cars will use depends on the nature of the track; it becomes a compromise between downforce and drag. Long sweeping high-speed sections require no wing at all; the cars only benefit from their downforce during cornering. Consequently, the engineers have to decide what's of more value: to run less wing (and so produce less drag) and maximise the car's straight line speed; or to run significantly more wing, pay the drag penalty along the straights but increase cornering speeds.

I would choose Monza and Monaco as the two circuits to highlight these extremes. Have a look at the aerodynamic settings on any of the cars as they hurtle along the straights of Monza and you'll notice that its rear wing is very unobtrusive; the top element will be almost horizontal, producing minimum downforce but sapping the least of the engine's precious horsepower as a result.

Conversely, a car built to run on the twisting, winding streets of Monaco will have wings sprouting all over its bodywork, anywhere the regulations will allow. The rear wing will look like a barn door. Horsepower advantage is not the major issue here, the low-speed nature of the track demands downforce, as much assistance as possible to help the cars stick to the track as the drivers throw the steering left and right.

Let's have a look at how the teams attempt to reduce or 'dial out' problematic understeer and oversteer. It's useful to remember that both conditions are interlinked (less of one condition results in more of the other) and both are caused through a loss of grip – understeer: the front tyres break free; oversteer: the rear tyres break free.

To help control understeer/oversteer problems we must manipulate the suspension and aerodynamics so as to create additional grip at the troublesome end of the car. We can do this in three ways; we can concentrate on the troublesome end directly, try to create more grip there, or – what may not seem quite so obvious – we can work on the opposite end of the car, and *remove* some grip from there. The third solution is the more usual: attend to both ends of the car at the same time.

To create an example, let's assume our driver is complaining of excessive understeer; he turns into the corner and the car carries on in a straight line. The majority of drivers dislike this condition more than oversteer because it makes them feel so helpless – turn the steering wheel and the car doesn't want to respond.

While chatting over drinks at various hotel bars, Sam Posey has often told me how much he hates driving a car with excessive understeer: 'The front of the car just washes away,' he says, 'the driver's input into the car, his control over it, simply vanishes … it's just a horrible feeling!'

The basic problem is that there is insufficient aero grip and/or mechanical grip, the latter caused by the front of the car being too stiffly sprung. What we need to do is create more overall grip at the front end, and there are several things we can do to help. We can crank the front wing up a little, to try and increase the downforce at the front. This will give more aerodynamic grip by pushing down harder on the front tyres. We could drop the front tyre pressures a tad, not much, maybe half a pound, this will induce some additional 'give' in the sidewalls, helping to produce a little extra mechanical grip. We can fit a softer roll bar to the front suspension, helping to induce more chassis roll at the front of the car, or, we can fit softer springs to the front suspension, something that will also induce more chassis roll.

Conversely, we can carry out exactly the opposite of these adjustments to the rear wing and suspension – reduce the downforce, up the tyre pressures a pinch, stiffen the springs and roll bar. Taking aero grip away from the rear and increasing the stiffness of the rear suspension will increase the car's tendency to oversteer, effectively offsetting its tendency to understeer.

Oversteer is more user friendly than understeer – the back of the car steps out but the driver retains control over the steering. If the rear of the car steps out to the right, he will also steer the front of the car to the right, correcting the slide by pulling the car back into line (says Steve, making it all sound so wondrously simple!)

The methods of helping to control excessive oversteer are the reverse of those used for understeer. Increase the level of aerodynamic grip (more rear wing), a sniff of pressure out of the rear tyres, and soften the rear springs and roll bar. And, just as with understeer, we can carry out the opposite adjustments at the front of the car; less front wing, a half pound more pressure in the front tyres, and stiffen the suspension.

If we can appreciate that the equal and opposite conditions of understeer and oversteer are inextricably intertwined, and that the car will suffer from varying degrees of both at different points around a lap of the circuit, we can more clearly understand why we can never fully cure one condition or the other. Reducing one condition merely adds to the severity of the other. The technique is to work towards achieving a compromise where neither understeer nor oversteer is too extreme; a situation where both are tolerable. A fine balance. Remember, keep your eyes on the driver's hand signals as the car returns to the pits, that'll give us a pretty good indication of how well we're doing.

A few minutes after five-thirty in the evening, Paris time, our pilot switched on the seat-belt lights, and flight AF001 began its approach into Charles de Gaulle. We had been airborne for just three and a half hours. The skies were cloudless but winter had already darkened the city. As we dropped lower the outside blackness became dotted with the orange and red glitter of street and car lights; the aircraft dipping to the left, making its final corrections before lining up with the runway.

A muffled roar enveloped the cabin as the air streaming around the fuselage encountered the wheels of the undercarriage. Then, with only the briefest of squeals from below, we were on the ground. Our speed was lost in seconds, within no time at all we were slowly taxiing towards the stands of Terminal 2.

Breezing through passport control, we stood inside the white glare of the Customs hall waiting for our luggage. The immigration officers, all sporting remarkably short hair, looked blankly out of their cubicles, giving each passport no more than a cursory glance, as the line of passengers trooped past.

'Okay, chaps,' I said as my old green Samsonite trundled its way along the conveyor belt. 'I guess this is where I say goodbye. Thank you for your company, it's been ... well, it's been memorable ... to say the least!'

Wingrave heaved an enormous brown leather suitcase off the belt. Red-faced from the effort, he turned to me. 'Steve,' he said, 'before you head off, tell us ... after all that effort building our car ... how will we do? Could we possibly win any races?'

Could we win any races? I looked at Wingrave and the others, all waiting, expectantly. *Would* we win any races? What should I say? I thought of the teams encamped in the pit lane, the *real* teams. Minardi: involved in Grand Prix racing since 1985, close on three hundred race starts, not a single race victory to their name. Arrows:

four hundred starts, raced in F1 from 1978, sadly no longer a going concern; the team's entire history passed without one winner's cup adorning the trophy cabinet. BAR, Jaguar, Sauber, Toyota: three hundred race starts between the lot of them – not one win.

With their near total dominance over the sport for the past twenty years, the odds of sneaking a race win past the noses of Ferrari, McLaren and Williams are not merely remote, they are almost non-existent. Nevertheless, each and every race weekend, the rest of the teams arrive. They pitch camp, unpack their cars and work like dogs to try and win. Would we win any races? I looked my three friends straight in the eyes. 'Yes,' I said. 'Yes, we'll win a race – either that or we'll die trying!'

Actually, as it turned out, that wasn't quite goodbye. We shared the journey from the station beneath the airport to the Gare du Nord. It was here that we shook hands and parted company. I asked where they were headed. 'Pagani's, Great Portland Street – terrific Italian. Do you know it?' asked Kelver. I said I didn't, but as the only Great Portland Street I knew was in London, not Paris – as far as I was aware – I suggested they might be in the wrong country.

'We'll dash to the cheese shop, then board Eurostar ... should make the seven-thirty to Waterloo,' said Hentschel.

They set off in the direction of the metro; Kelver and Hentschel humping the great leather case between them. Wingrave paused, then turned. 'See you on the river, old man,' he said enigmatically. With a final wave he casually folded and stowed our meeting in his top pocket, and was gone.

11

Coffee in Saint Germain des Prés

> 'If you are lucky enough to have lived in Paris as a young
> man, then wherever you go for the rest of your life, it stays
> with you, for Paris is a movable feast.'
> Ernest Hemingway

Since moving to France – more accurately, since shuttling between
Europe and the States – I've taken to spending an increasing amount
of time in Paris. Charles de Gaulle airport out in the northern
suburbs is but a twenty-minute train ride from Gare du Nord
station. Each time I return from America it becomes ever more
difficult to pass up the chance of a brief sojourn in the heart of
what is truly a very beautiful city.

I've grown especially fond of life in and around Saint Germain
des Prés. After the Great War this quarter was a popular haunt
with 'the lost generation'. Many gifted (and soon-to-be extremely
famous) young writers, artists and poets made their home here,
including Ernest Hemingway and F. Scott Fitzgerald. For much of
my adult life I'd harboured the notion that this small enclave must
be somewhat elitist, its residents arrogant and pretentious. Exactly
what I'd based that notion on, however, completely escapes me;
was it merely because a few creative souls used to meet here for a
drink and a sandwich? A pathetic prejudice if so ... nurtured
through ignorance and little personal experience. It's the only
defence I can offer, and it's no defence at all.

Walking around the labyrinth of narrow roads of Saint Germain –
its tiny streets strung like cobwebs – the only impression I'm left with
is that the place is merely a fun corner of a cosmopolitan city. Sure,

there are a few flamboyant establishments to hand, Les Deux Magots and Le Café de Flore stand side by side on the main boulevard. But for every chic restaurant, there are ten more unassuming places; crammed at midnight, tranquil in the early morning.

On the corner of rue Jacob and rue des Saints-Pères stands the modest restaurant where – now more than seventy years ago – following a brief, private viewing in *les waters* of chez Michaud, Hemingway managed to assuage Scott Fitzgerald's fears that the measurements of his manhood were in some way less than adequate. It seems that Fitzgerald's then wife, Zelda, had intimated as much and the whole business was deeply troubling the poor chap. The restaurant no longer carries Michaud's name, but it still does good business; I should go in for lunch one day, perhaps they have a plaque on the wall commemorating the event.

During hot weather, the most relaxing time of day to experience Paris is first thing in the morning. There are a couple of reasonably good hours straight after breakfast, too; but that whole sorry period skulking between the end of lunch and nine in the evening is to be avoided like the plague. No air, too congested, and way too many people sporting hiking boots and backpacks. Paris is not K2 – it's Paris – it's a major European capital, a city offering every amenity a reasonable person could ever want. Cafés abound, they're on every corner of every street, it isn't necessary to lug sufficient supplies and equipment for a three-week fieldtrip. What is it with these people?

I like to begin my days in Saint Germain with coffee in Le Pré aux Clercs, a somewhat threadbare café just off the square adjacent the abbey. The bar is zinc-topped and proper and it's important to be there at no later than six-thirty, just as the sun creeps over the rooftops. This is the time to catch it, the best time of the day, as the glass doors running the length of the café are opened. I sidestep to the bar, dodging the towers of wicker chairs, five-high, stacked and dumped there the previous evening. At this hour the inside of the bar still carries a little of the night's chill, but it won't last long. A new day is under way, Paris is waking up.

Not so long ago I used to hate such early rises (when working as a race mechanic I was habitually poor at getting the hang of dawn starts) but now, with my days divided on opposite sides of the Atlantic, my body is permanently unable to decide which time zone to stick with. All it knows for certain is that come five in the morning it must be time to wake up. And so I do, as regular as lightly-oiled clockwork. It annoyed me at first, but now I've grown used to it and it doesn't bother me a jot. In fact, I quite like it.

The first cup of brutally strong coffee is down in two gulps, the next takes a little longer. I like to sip water in between swigs of coffee; it's a habit I've picked up from watching the locals. It brings an entirely different sensation to the palate, something reminiscent of fresh tobacco. I love the taste – the smell too – although the idea of smoking so much as a single cigarette makes me feel thoroughly ill.

After ten minutes, standing room at the bar has gone; the place is full. Regulars stopping for a quick coffee, a beer or a shot of cognac on their way to work. The counter is the place to be; prices are half if you're prepared to lean against the zinc – everyone does.

I've always thought of coffee as a simple drink, yet I'm amazed at how exceedingly complicated and ostentatious some people have managed to make it. Take a handful of ground beans, force hot water through them, collect the liquid in a cup. How complicated can that be? I remember visiting a coffee shop in Melbourne and being astounded at the different ways it could be served: espresso, cappuccino, iced-cappuccino, latte, mocha, choco-mocha, latte-choco-mocha; double-latte-choco-mocha-sausage-egg-'n'-blueberry. Okay, I made that last one up, but ... what on earth's going on?

Admittedly, I was a tad tired and grumpy, having just landed in Australia after a thoroughly nasty twenty-four-hour flight, and I'm sure the girl behind the counter didn't really deserve the haranguing I gave her, but she got it all the same. 'Just a cup of coffee please – black – no sugar.' She gave me her best, superbly well-rehearsed patronising look, you know: eyes wide, head tilted, the whole nine yards, before informing me that she sold twenty-three different 'appellations' of coffee, available in four different sizes: regular, medium, king-size ... 'Just sell me a cup of coffee you pretentious cow, you don't need to make an epic out of it! Just coffee – normal coffee – in a cup, no milk, no sugar. It's so bloody simple – it's just coffee poured into a cup! Look, it's easy. Sell me the same coffee you remember your mother pouring for you when you were a little girl. Think back to a time before you were brainwashed by all this marketing crap; think back, grasp reality and sell me the same coffee *you* remember, *I* remember, the whole world remembers. Don't pretend you don't know what coffee really is – it's supposed to be a drink not a fashion accessory ...!' Finally, she grudgingly sold me a 'regular' size serving of her fresh-roasted-filter-coffee-of-the-day. I duly apologised for my outburst ... well it was a tad o.t.t. She told me to piss off. I guess that kind of made us even.

Back in Saint Germain the streets are already filling, the moment of the new morning is passing, within thirty minutes the day will be set. At exactly five to seven Madame arrives from the back kitchen of Le Pré aux Clercs, pail in one hand, mop in the other, cigarette screwed between pursed lips. She curses the men's feet as she slops water around the floor; moving the chairs, making space for the boxes of vegetables piling in from the grocer's van – daily supplies for a hundred meals. It's time to go. For me this place is done; until ten o'clock tonight it's now merely another bar.

Turn right out of Le Pré aux Clercs, up to the square and right again, a minute's walk at most stands my favourite: Le Bonaparte. Resting against the counter, paper open, my fingers burning on the hot cup, I can see clear across the square to Les Deux Magots, the first café in the quarter to be blessed by the morning sun. Its clientele pay a healthy premium for drinking there, it's only fitting they should be the first to catch the warmth of the new day.

While I sip and read and ponder, the barman behind the counter, shirtsleeves rolled, is engrossed in halving and squeezing an entire box of oranges. The juicer whirrs constantly. Occasionally he swaps the bottles below the spout, he stores them beneath the counter, each brimming with fresh juice: recycled Evian bottles, most missing their labels. More oranges go under the chopper, the juicer whirrs again.

I remember standing against the bar in Budapest's airport with a couple of workmates, some chaps from McLaren too, waiting for our homeward flight to be called after the '92 race weekend. The chap behind the counter was doing the exact same thing: halving and squeezing oranges. Funny how these things spark memories. It was an exceedingly hot afternoon that day, and I remember seeing James Hunt walk through the door with Murray Walker. We were waiting for the same flight, a charter to London; I think pretty much the whole of the paddock's British contingent was on it. Murray looked perfectly normal ... like Murray really ... open-necked shirt, briefcase, what have you; but James was wearing nothing but a pair of red shorts. He carried a ticket, a passport and a packet of cigarettes. That was it. There wasn't even a pair of flip-flops to spoil the perfect minimalist look.

The thing that really made the event stick in my mind, though, was that James was absolutely at ease with himself, perfectly comfortable. This was real for him, no stunt or affectation designed to impress or shock, this was *genuine*: James Hunt, former world champion driver, current commentator for the BBC; work done for the day ... going home. Take me, leave me; do what you bloody well want, just don't give me a hard time about your own petty hang-ups. He became a hero of mine that day. Sadly, his heart gave out the following summer and that was that. He was only forty-five. Mind you, he'd certainly packed a lot of living into those years.

Back in Le Bonaparte, juicer still hard at work, I manage to capture my wandering thoughts. What does the day hold in store ... what should I do? Perhaps a stroll across the river, an hour or two exploring the Louvre. Isn't it curious why some people see things better with their head leaning to one side? They do it a lot in the Louvre, you know, as they stand admiring the Mona Lisa.

Not straight away. They take the whole thing in first; head upright, bottom lip protruding, then, when searching for more detail, their heads begin to lean. I wonder if Leonardo painted her enigmatic smile with his head resting on his shoulder? Maybe he did.

It doesn't open until nine-thirty, the Louvre, plenty of time to amble back to the hotel. A shower, a bite to eat; then off. Get in early before the boots and backpacks front-up, with their cameras and sports-bottles of electric-blue-hydro-restorative-lactose-enriched energy drinks. Essential stuff, no doubt, if one's to survive the morning in an air-conditioned museum. Makes one wonder how the troops in the Somme ever found the stamina to wage such colossal battles, with only rainwater to quench their thirst, scooped from the bottom of bomb craters as they prayed to be granted another minute of life.

One more coffee … there's no great rush, then I'll head back to the hotel. There's only ten, fifteen minutes remaining before the morning, the *real* morning vanishes. No point in staying after that.

And, so, there we are; that's me done. I always envisaged this to be a journey of three parts; and we have reached the end of part three. Over the years, some people have suggested how unusual it is that a mechanic should change lanes and choose to work in the media. Fair enough, I guess. A few, however, have gone so far as to suggest that it's surely impossible that 'practical people' (by this I suppose they mean mechanics) could possess the necessary predisposition to contribute anything of merit. They have suggested this to my face, you understand, quite unabashed. They wait expectantly as though I should stroke my chin, sagely, and nod in agreement. Really, I suppose, those who suggest such rubbish deserve not the oxygen that debate affords their gross stupidity. But I will say this: compared to my years spent working in the pit lanes of the world, I find writing to be a comparatively effortless profession. The pages write themselves; it's all I can do to keep up. Changing a problematic engine with less than an hour to go before the formation lap is flagged under way – now that's where real pressure is.

Nevertheless, it remains true that not many race mechanics have opted to publish the musings of their profession; you can count them on the fingers of just one hand. Four. And out of this pitiful number both Alf Francis and Ermanno Cuoghi elected to give their stories to journalists. The only other F1 mechanic who has written his own words is Tetsuo Tsugawa, an immensely likeable chap; one I had the privilege of working alongside at Benetton throughout 1990. His last year with the team was my first. Tetsuo now works as a journalist for the Japanese media, travelling the world as part of the F1 circus.

Out of more than fifty continuous years of Formula 1 competition we have but four first-hand accounts of life deep inside the pit lane. Not much to show for five decades of international motor racing, is it? I wish it were otherwise. I would love to read of life inside those problematic Jaguar pits; what it was like to work on that troublesome 2002 car, the R3 (by the end of the season I think the team had redesigned every component but the monocoque itself). There's some truly frightening work loads right there!

A real insightful breakdown of the politics surrounding the team would make pretty interesting reading too. Bobby Rahal hired and given carte blanche to get things sorted; who, within a matter of months, is himself ousted to make way for Niki Lauda to get things sorted; who is then ousted a mere fifteen months after that, presumably for not getting things sorted ... fast enough! You certainly have to make your mark in that job, not a second to lose; no time for tea breaks in that office ... and don't let the revolving door smack you in the backside on the way out.

However, the 2003 season was conducted amid far greater stability in terms of the team's management and their car's handling: the R4 has worked far better than its predecessor, and with Mark Webber behind the wheel the whole team seems totally rejuvenated.

There's another terrific story waiting to be told, of course: Ferrari's return to glory; the wondrous Schumacher dynasty, when trophies rained from the skies, church bells rang and the townsfolk of

Maranello danced in the streets. If I was a betting man I'd put half a billion lire (sorry, these days I guess that should be two euros) on either Ross Brawn or Nigel Stepney writing that up one day – come their retirement. I wish there were a hundred other books by mechanics and engineers – truly I do. Lamentably, however, I strongly believe that the trend of little-to-no communication between the pits and the race enthusiast will continue.

A couple of years ago in the museum at the Williams factory, at Grove – while recording a segment on the FW14's active suspension – a mechanic I've known for many years accused me of being a turncoat. He wasn't bitter, he remained light-hearted and friendly, but I was left in no doubt that he saw my revised role (that of standing in front of the camera explaining how the cars worked, as opposed to shielding them from view), as a blatant 'switching of sides'; this coming from a chap that works for a rival team. Along with my colleagues at Benetton this was a mechanic whose cars we'd competed against for ten years! We may have been on-track rivals but we were both F1 mechanics – kindred spirits, I guess. That's how I thought of him and it was certainly how he *used* to think of me. Now, however, I had left the fold; taken up my pen and opted to stand in front of the camera. In his eyes I had swapped allegiances, and he made a specific point of highlighting that fact. As I say, not vindictive, but things had changed between us; he made that crystal clear.

Grand Prix people tend to keep themselves to themselves. They elect not to write of their profession, in exactly the same way that cats elect not to talk to their owners. Both prefer to go about their business in silence, viewing the outside world with quiet disinterest. Life goes on beyond their private domain, but it holds no fascination for them; it is a land filled with watching eyes, a land that stretches on for ever. It is the world beyond the closed doors of the chariot makers.

Index

A-arms (wishbones) 161, 163, 171, 208–9
ABS *see* antilock brakes
access holes in chassis 31–2, 56, 59
adhesion *see* grip
adjustments to suspension 206–9
aerodynamics 142–59
    airflow 145–6, 148, 154
    carbon fibre monocoques 44
    chassis design 50
    development 28–9
    downforce 28–9, 144–6
    exhaust layout 106
    grip 190–1, 212–13
    ride height 204, 206
    suspension systems 167, 173–4
    wings 145–8, 149–51
Aeroquip hoses 187–8
aerospace industry *see* aviation industry
air supply temperature 74
aircraft aerodynamics 144–5
airflow *see* aerodynamics
Alboreto, Michele 74–5
Alfa Romeo 50
aluminium chassis 37–9
antilock brakes (ABS) 185–6
architecture 10–11
aromatics in fuel 63
Arrows 137, 214–15
    A11 164
    A21 166–7
    A22 167
artistic merit of exhaust systems 101–2
Audi R8 74
Austrian Grand Prix, 2003 94
Auto Unions 120
autoclaves, composite materials 41, 42, 47
Avgas (aviation gas) 61
aviation industry 40, 42, 73, 140–1, 147,
    180
axles 160

back-to-back tests 110, 182
bag-tanks (fuel cells) 52–3, 54, 56–7
balance, car handling 200–1

ballast 32, 189
BAR 215
Barnard, John 39–43, 125, 151
bearing carriers 137, 139
Belgian Grand Prix (2001) 12
Benetton
    B186 164
    B189 164
    B190 164
    B191 151
    B192 151
    B194 149
    B195 122–3
    carbon fibre components 171–2
    engine oil reservoirs 126–7
    exhaust systems 101–2
    fuel in pits 51, 62
    leaving 4–5
Berger, Gerhard 199
Bernoulli's principle 145–6
Birdcage *see* Maserati Tipo 60
bladders 56–7
bleeding brakes 187–8
BMW, V10 engine manufacture 92–5
bodywork
    aerodynamics 147, 156
    integrated in chassis 37–8
    screws 122–3
    on space-frame chassis 35, 36
bonding resins 41–2, 47, 181
box section monocoques 37–8
'boxer' engines (flat engines) 81, 85–7
Brabham 50, 180
brake systems 180–8
    ABS 185–6
    calipers 187–8
    carbon 180–2
    disks and pads 180–4, 187
    fluid lines 187–8
    importance 184
    mass 182–4
    specifications 187
braking technique 185
Brawn, Ross 96, 122–3, 191, 192–3

Briatore, Flavio 112–13
Bridgestone tyres 175–8
BRM, H16 engine 81
Brunner, Gustav 44
bulkheads 53
Burti–Luciano 12
butterfly valves 111
Byrne, Rory 105–6, 122, 144, 151, 156, 164

C20 Sauber 152–3, 154
calipers, brake system 187
camber angle
  front 206–9
  interchangeable steering arms 209
  rear 209–10
  tracking relationship 208–9
car construction 51, 58–60
car manufacturers, power over sport 194
carbon brake components 180–2
carbon fibre
  advantages over steel 172–3
  aerodynamics 44
  chassis construction 39–48
  male/female moulding 42, 43–4
  'pre-preg' cloth 47–8
  steering systems 171–2
  suspension systems 171–3, 180
  technical regulations 40
  transmission housing 137–9
  unidirectional cloth 41
CART series 142
castings, transmissions 128–9, 132
centre of gravity
  ballast 32
  cylinder configuration 85
  engine position 89–90
  FIA regulations 175
centre mounting, engine and
    transmission 120–1, 127
Chapman, Colin 35–8
chassis
  access holes 31–2, 59
  carbon fibre/composites 40–8
  construction process 46–8
  engine relationship 70–1
  Ferrari numbering 155
  number made 49
  rigidly fixed engines 89
  roll control 161–2
  roll increasing 213
  space-frames 35–6
  tyre relationship 177
chassis design 32–50
  see also torsional rigidity

aerodynamics 149–50
  considerations 31, 45–6
  future directions 44
  handling 33–4
  history 34–44
  model milling 46
  monocoque concept 37–8
chemistry of fuel 63
'chord', wings 145
chromium coating 170–1
circuit differences 205, 211–12
Citroen, André 169–70
Clark, Jimmy 81
Clear, Jock 190, 195–6, 200
clutch assembly 128–9, 139
clutch-less transmissions 132
CNC milling machines 46
cockpit size 24
coil springs 168
collectors
  exhaust systems 104
  fuel feed 54–5
composite gearboxes 139
composite materials see carbon fibre
compromise
  balance 200–1
  fuel cell size 57
  monocoque design 31–2
  over/understeer 213–14
  V10 engines 85, 87
computers
  antilock brakes 185
  chassis design 46
  suspension systems fabrication 102
  traction control 191, 193–4
Concorde 98
  aerodynamics 144–5
  appearance 140–1
  carbon brake disks 180
  flight 188–9, 214
  speed 157–9
configuration, engine cylinders 80–2,
    85–6
constant velocity joints 160
construction process
  car building 99–101
  monocoques 46–8, 49
Constructors' Championship
  Benetton 4
  BMW 92–3
  McLaren 115
  prestige 49–50
continually variable transmissions 133–4
contractors, parts manufacture 42–3, 50
Cooper Climax 120

Cooper, John 120–1
cornering
    over/understeer 190, 200, 201–3, 213–14
    roll control 161–2
costs
    attitudes 88
    brake disks and pads 181
    engines 97
    increased budgets 23
Cosworth
    fuel development 61–2, 64
    V8 engines 82–3, 84
    Zetec -RV10 engine 84
Coughlan, Mike 137
Coulthard, David 109–10
Coventry Climax engines 120
crank shafts 81–2
crash structure 119
cylinders
    number in engine 79, 80, 81–3, 84–5
    number influencing sound 107
    offset distance 103
    offset (vee) angle 80–1, 85

DAF/Volvo 133
dampers (shock absorbers) 162–3, 165–6
De Tomaso 50
DeNike, Kimberly 14–15
Dennis, Ron 23–4, 39, 71–2, 112–13
'diff' cap 119
differentials, FIA regulations 129–31
diffuser exit exhaust systems 104–5
diffusers, aerodynamics 146, 147
downforce
    aerodynamic development 28–9, 144–6
    deficiencies 153
    diffuser exit exhaust systems 104–5
    drag 147–8
    FIA regulations 173–4
    ride-height 203–4, 205
    wings 152, 211–12
drag 147–9, 211
drive coupling 60
'driver aids' technology 194–6
drivers
    aerodynamic position 151
    attitude of teams 26–7
    braking skill 184, 185, 186
    car awareness 196–9
    changing attributes 23–5
    communication with engineer 199–200
    confidence in cars 105
    deaths 74–5
    diffs adjustments 131

discomfort 88–9
    importance 70, 71
    psychological stress 24
    relationship with car 26
    size and strength 24, 25, 32
driveshafts 160–1
Duckworth, Keith 70

ecologically friendly fuels 62–3
electronic management systems 191
electronic pumps 55
engine oil reservoirs 125–7, 138, 139
engines 70–98
    cataclysmic failure 73
    centre mounting 120–1, 127
    chassis relationship 70–1
    costs 88, 97
    crank shafts 81–2
    cylinder configuration 80–2, 85–6
    cylinder mass 85
    cylinder number 79, 80, 81–3, 84–5
    cylinder offset (vee) angle 80–1, 85
    cylinder/exhaust connection 103
    efficiency 76
    FIA regulations 132
    flat bottom plate 90
    frictional power loss 85
    installing 87
    manufacturers 91–6
    normal aspiration 72, 75–6, 82
    performance data 83–4
    position in car 89–90
    progress 26, 27
    reciprocal motion versus rotary 77–9
    reliability problems 93–4
    rev speeds 76, 83–4, 93, 95
    rigid fixing to chassis 87, 89
    shortfall masking 143
    size 96
    torque 83
    traction control 192
    turbocharged 27, 72–5
    twin turbos 75
    V8/V10/V12 comparison 82–5
    valves 79
    vibration 88–9
Estoril circuit, Portugal 61
exhaust systems 86, 101–16
    butterfly valves 111–12
    collectors 104
    diffuser exits 104–5
    driving turbochargers 73–4
    harmonics 108, 110–12
    outlet position 104–6, 108
    over-the-top exits 105–6, 108

pressure waves 107–8
primaries 103–4
secondaries 104–5
'song' 107, 109–10
extreme pressure lubricant *see* hypoid
 lubricant

F1 Racing magazine 6
fabricators 102–3, 170
Fangio, Juan Manuel 24
Farina, Giuseppe 22
Fédération Internationale de
 l'Automobile (FIA) regulations
 aerodynamics 28, 147, 152, 153, 173–4
 antilock brakes 186
 attitudes 194
 braking systems 186–7
 car width 86
 chassis material 40
 crash structure 119
 crash test requirements 45
 engine configuration 79–80
 1 engine per weekend rule 76, 132
 engine turbocharging 27, 72
 exhaust systems 111
 four wheel steer/drive 210
 fuel composition 27–8, 61, 62–4, 65–6
 fuels systems 56–7, 58
 grooved tyres 175
 legality skid-block 90, 204
 movable aerodynamic devices 173–4
 number of engines used 76, 132
 number of tyre compounds 211
 on-board control functions 129–31
 on-track changes 201
 racing weight 32
 reference plane 90–1
 technical restrictions 27–8
 traction control 191–3
 transmissions 133–4
 turbocharged engines 27, 72
 width of cars 106
 wings 90–1
female/male moulds 42, 43–4
Ferrari
 051 engine 95–6
 126C4 43
 640 164
 641 107
 Bridgestone relationship 177–8, 179
 chassis numbering 155
 exhaust outlets 105
 F300 105
 F2002 137, 155–6, 177–8
 fuel in pits 62

success 27, 71
test teams 49
transmissions 123
uni-casting project 128–9, 132
V10 engines 84, 95–6
V12 engines 82–3, 84, 107
Ferrari, Enzo 50
Ferrari, Scuderia 82, 95, 123
FIA *see* Fédération Internationale de
 l'Automobile
filtration, engine oil 127
financing *see* costs
finishing race 94
fire 51, 58
five-axis mills 46
fixed rear axles 160
'flat' engines (boxer engines) 81, 85–7
flat patches 203
flex resistance *see* torsional rigidity
Fluckiger, Max 92
Forghieri, Mauro 30
four-to-seven gears ruling 134
France 4–6, 216–21
frangible couplings, fuel lines 58
frictional power loss, engines 85
front end grip 154
front wing designs 149–51, 152
fuel cells (bag-tanks) 52–3, 54, 56–7, 66
fuel composition
 performance improvement 61–2, 64
 regulations 27–8, 61, 62–4, 65–6
 smell 62
 suppliers 64, 67
fuel consumption 55–6, 66–7
fuel systems 52–67
 access hatch 59
 bag-tank construction 54, 56–7
 bulkheads 53
 collectors 54–5
 delivery hoses 52–3
 early 58
 fuel mass 57–8, 66
 installation 56, 58–9
 lines and couplings 58
 location 58
 mechanical pump 55, 60
 monitoring consumption 55–6, 66–7
 primary pumps 55
 safety 56–7, 58
 sloshing control 54
 water injection systems 60–1
fully-stressed members 37–8, 89

gas chromatographer 65
gear oil 126–7

gearboxes 118–20
  composite 139
  four-to-seven gear ruling 134
  housings size 127
  installation 124–5
  ratio selection 134–5, 136
  shift timings chart 136
  Variomatic 133
Giacomelli, Bruno 82
glue, Locktite 87–8
Gonzalez, Froilan 24
Goodyear tyres 175
Grand Prix, Belgium 2001 12
grip
  see also oversteer; understeer
  adhesion loss 196
  aerodynamic 190–1, 212–13
  increasing 212–13
  mechanical 191, 213
ground-effect cars 28, 39
gyroscopic effects 183

H16 engine, BRM 81
handling 33–4, 190, 200, 201–3
hard and soft tyres 210–11
harmonics
  damping valves 111–12
  exhaust systems 108, 110–11
Head, Patrick 28, 50
heat see temperature
Hentschel, Carl 19, 48, 67–9, 97–8, 117,
    140–1, 158, 215
Hercules Incorporated chassis 42–3, 50
high-nose designs 149–51
Hobbs, David 9
Hockenheim, 1994 fireball 51, 52
holistic car design 32
Honda, fuel development 64
Honda RA168E V6 engine 71
honeycomb aluminium 39, 41, 47, 48, 119
horsepower
  BMW versus Ferrari engines 95–6
  car design 70–1
  engine design 76–7
  fuel system 60–2, 64
  normally aspirated engines 75, 84,
    95–6
  torque relationship 83–4
  tubocharged engines 71, 72
hoses, fuel delivery 52–3
housings
  gearboxes 118, 125, 127
  transmissions 137–8
Hunt, James 220
hydraulic diffs 129–31

hydraulics, brake system 187
Hydrodynamica (Bernoulli) 145
hypoid lubricant 126

Inconal alloy 103
independent suspension 160
induction systems, turbocharged 72
injection systems
  atomised water 60–1
  mechanical pump 55, 60
inline engines 80, 85, 87
inline gearbox 124–5
interchangeable steering arms 209
Interlagos, Brazil 205
International Formula 3000 195
Issigonis, Alec 126
Italian Grand Prix, Monza
  1988 71–2
  2002 93, 94

Jaguar
  aerodynamics 142–3
  endurance racing cars 36
  R3 222
  R4 222
  team 215, 222
Jakeman, Michael 53
Jano, Vittorio 30
Jenkins, Alan 125, 137
JFK International airport 17–18, 68–9,
  97–8
Jones, Alan 28

K-nuts, self-locking 87, 88, 89
keel designs 150, 151, 152–4, 156–7
Kelver, Paul 19, 48–9, 67–9, 97–8, 116–17,
    140–1, 158, 215
Kevlar mesh 57
Keyphos coating 171

Lauda, Niki 222
launch control 191, 196
Lausitzring circuit, Germany 74
leading edge of wings 145
legality skid-block 204
Life Racing Engines 82
lift, aerodynamics 144–5
live rear axles 160
locking diffs 131
Loctite 242 'nutloc' 87–8
longitudinal transmissions 124–5, 138
Lotus
  25 36–8, 58
  43 81
  102 164

107 164
  monocoques 36–8
  Team 38
low emission fuels 62–3
lubrication system 89–90

Machmeters 158, 159
McLaren, Team 39
McLaren International
  carbon fibre use 39–43, 137
  exhaust systems 107–12
  Hercules partnership 42–3
  merger 39
  monocoque development 39–43
  MP4-1 40–3
  MP4-4 71–2
  MP4-5 164
  MP4-5B 114–15
  MP4-7 115–16
  MP4-15 109–11, 116
  MP4-16 111
  MP4-17 106, 111
  MP4–16 153–4
  MP4–17 154
  Paragon facility 112
  preserved old cars 113–16
  tyres 177, 178
  Woking headquarters 112–16
magazine writing 6
Magny-Cours, France 205
male/female moulds 42, 43–4
Manhattan 10–16
Mansell, Nigel 24
manufacture of transmissions 123–4
March chassis 50
Marta chassis 50
Maserati Tipo 60 (Birdcage) 35
mathematical jargon 30–1
Matra MS80 141
mechanical grip 191, 213
mechanical pump, fuel system 55, 60
mechanics see race mechanics
The Mechanic's Tale 6, 135–6
Michelin tyres 176–9
Minardi 214
  PS01 166
Mini, transmissions 126
mistakes in car building 60, 100
moments (forces) 121
Monaco circuit
  course conditions 211, 212
  fuel consumption 66
  pit lanes 107
monocoque-engine-transmission
    principle 118–19

monocoques
  see also chassis
  first concept 37–8
  origin of word 33
Montoya, Juan Pablo 93, 94
Monza circuit 211
Mosley, Max 191–2
mould tooling 41–2
multiplate clutch 139
Murray, Gordon 180

naphthene 63
NASCAR 160
negative lift see downforce
New York 10–16
Newey, Adrian 106, 111, 144, 154
1950s cars 23–5, 35
1960s cars 35–8
1970s cars 38–9
1980s cars 27–8, 39–44, 71, 149–50
1990s cars 113–16, 126, 150–1
normal aspiration/turbocharged
    comparison 72–3, 75–6
nose designs 149–51, 156
nuts 87, 88, 89, 99
Nuvolari, Tazio 25

Oatley, Neil 111
oil reservoirs 125–7, 138, 139
On Track magazine 6
on-board control functions 129–31
ovens 42, 47, 181
over-the-top exit exhaust systems 105–6,
    108
oversteer 190, 200, 203, 212–13
overtaking 184

P81/P82 BMW engines 92–5
panel screws 122–3
parco-luberite 171
Paris 216–21
periscope exhausts 105–6, 108
petrol see fuel
Piquet, Nelson 61–2
piston engine alternatives 77–9
pistons mass comparisons 85
pit lane refuelling rig 52–3, 66
pit lanes 51, 62, 107, 203
plank see legality skid-block
polar moment of inertia 121
Porsche, Ferdinand 120
Posey, Sam 9
Postlethwaite, Harvey 150
power see horsepower
pre-approved fuels 65

'pre-preg' carbon fibre cloth 47–8
pressure differentials, wings 146
pressure waves, exhaust systems 107–8
primary pipes, exhaust systems 103–4
primary pumps, fuel system 55
Project 4 39
Prost, Alain 71
psychological stress on drivers 24
pullrod suspension 163–7
pumps
  engine oil 125–6
  fuel system 55, 60
pushrod suspension 163–7, 206

qualifying 207, 211

race mechanics 51–2
  attitudes to media 223
  fuel consumption monitoring 55–6,
    66–7
race retirement 94
race shops 51
racing weight 32
Rahal, Bobby 142–3, 222
ratios, gearboxes 134–5, 136
rear axles 160
rear crash structure 119
rear wheel airflow 106
rear wings 148, 152, 211–12
reciprocal motion pistons 77–8
records
  drivers championships 178
  highest engine rev speeds 93
  most victories in a season 71
reference plane 90
reliability
  BMW V10 engines 93–4
  Ferrari engines 95–6
  McLaren MP4-4 71
  performance relationship 76–7, 94
Renault R23 138
Renault Sport engines 73
reservoirs, engine oil 125–7, 138, 139
resin, carbon fibre composites 41–2, 47,
  181
revs (engine speeds) 76, 83–4, 93, 95
ride-height
  adjustments 206
  aerodynamics 204, 205–6
  FIA legality skid block 204
  measuring 203, 205
  variation with track 205
rig *see* pit lane refuelling rig
rigidity *see* torsional rigidity
rocket fuel 61

roll bars (sway bars) 161–2, 213
rotary engines 78–9
rubber engine mountings 88, 89
rubber fuel cells 57

safety
  crash test requirements 45
  early race cars 24–5, 35
  fuel system 56–7, 58
  turbocharged engines 72
Safety Car 67
Saint Germain des Prés 216–21
Sauber 215
  C20 152–3, 154
scavenge pump 126
Schumacher, Michael
  Benetton to Ferrari move 84
  car awareness 198
  drivers championships 178
Schumacher, Ralf 12, 94
screws, panels 122–3
secondary pipes, exhaust systems 104
secrecy, car design 110, 116, 150
Senna, Ayrton 71–2, 113, 114–15
seven-speed gearboxes 135
shape
  see also aerodynamics
  car development 38, 39, 44
shift timings chart 136
shock absorbers (dampers) 162–3, 165–6
single casting transmissions 128–9,
  132
single keel designs 152, 154, 156–7
six-speed gearboxes 135, 136, 139
skid-block *see* legality skid-block
smell of fuel 62
soft and hard tyres 210–11
sound
  exhaust systems 107
  number of cylinders 18, 107
  speed of 158
Spa circuit 66
space restrictions, car design 86
space-frame chassis 35, 36
'span', aerodynamics 146
Spanish Grand Prix
  2001 129
  Barcelona 1998 105
spares, cars and chassis 49
speed of sound 158
speeds
  engines revs 76, 83–4, 93, 95
  shift timings chart 136
Speedvision 7–9, 13
sponsorship 67, 88

spot-checks, fuel samples 65
springs
  coil 168
  suspension systems 163, 165–6, 168–9
  torsion bars 168–9
stainless steel (Inconal) 103
steel
  chassis frames 34–5
  corrosion protection 170–1
steering
  interchangeable arms 209
  over/understeer 190, 200, 201–3, 212–13
  rotational forces 183
  systems 171–2, 177
  tracking 208–9
Stepney, Nigel 96, 171
Stewart Grand Prix
  carbon fibre housings 137
  engine oil reservoirs 126–7
Stewart, Jackie 141
straight engines 80, 85
strength of drivers 25
strength-to-weight ratio, chassis 36, 40
stressed members 37–8, 89
styling 143, 149–50, 156
'sucking' 73
supercharged engines 79–80
supersonic travel 157–9
suspension systems
  adjustment 33, 206–9
  camber 206–9
  carbon fibre 171–3
  coil springs 168
  independent 160
  manufacture 102
  protective finishes 170–1
  pullrod/pushrod 163–7
  ride height adjustment 206
  torsion bars 168–9
  tyre relationship 177–8
sway bars (roll bars) 161–2

t-cars 49
TC see traction control
teams, employing drivers 26–7
technical regulations see FIA regulations
technology, limiting use 194–6
temperature
  brake disks/pads 182
  carbon fibre suspension 173
  engines 73–4
  tyres 207
test rigs 37–8
test team cars 49

testing
  back-to-back 110, 182
  crash test requirements 45
throttle lag 74, 75
tired chassis 34
titanium 137, 139
toluene fuel mixtures 61
torque
  engine comparisons 83
  nut tightening 87
torsion bar springs 168–9
torsional rigidity
  access holes 31
  aluminium monocoques 36–9
  composite monocoques 42–3, 45
  engines 89
  importance 33–4
  measuring 37–8
  space-frames 38
  transmission system 118
Toyota 215
  ATS 44
tracking, camber relationship 208–9
traction
  see also grip
  importance 190–1
Traction Avant (Citroen) 169–70
traction control (TC) 191–2
trailing edge, wings 145–6, 151, 152
transmissions
  centre mounting 120–1, 127
  clutch-less 132
  continually variable 133–4
  engine oil reservoirs 127
  housing 137–8
  installation 118, 124
  manufacture 123–4
  Mini 126
  single casting 128–9, 132
transverse gearboxes 124–5
tri-lobe joints 160–1
Tsugawa, Tetsuo 222
tubs see chassis; monocoques
turbocharged engines
  FIA banning 27, 72
  power 71, 72
  problems 73–4, 75
  theory 72–3
turbulence, tyres 148
twin keel designs 152–4, 156–7
twist resistance see torsional rigidity
TWR (Tom Walkinshaw Racing) see
  Arrows
tyre slip-angle 202
Tyrell 019 150–1

Tyrell, Ken 50
tyres
  aerodynamics 147, 148
  compound variations 210–11
  degradation 192
  importance 174–5, 176–8
  manufacturers 175–6, 178–9
  pressure 213
  temperature 207

un-sprung mass 183–4
underside flatness 90
understeer 153–4, 190, 200, 201–3, 212–13
uni-casting transmissions 128–9, 132
unidirectional carbon fibre cloth 41
unlocking diffs 131

V6 engines 71
V8 engines 82–3, 84–5
V10 engines
  becoming industry standard 82–7
  BMW 92–5
  Ferrari 95–6
  performance data 84
  sound 18
V12 engines 18, 82–3, 84–5
valves 79, 108
vapour deposition 181
variable geometric length exhausts 111
Variomatic gearbox 133
Varsha, Bob 7–8
'vee' configuration 80–1, 85, 86–7
venting, fuel delivery 52–3
Verstappen, Jos 166–7
vibration 88–9
Villadelprat, Joan 5
Volvo 133

W12 engine, Life Racing Engines 82
Walker, Murray 220
Wankel rotary engines 78–9
water injection systems 60–1

weather conditions
  drivers' senses 198
  fuel consumption 66
  traction control 192
weight
  brakes 182–3
  cars 32, 189
  chassis 36–7, 42–3
  distribution 121–2
  drivers 32, 189
  lightness doctrine 122–3
  strength-to-weight ratios 36, 40
  un-sprung mass 183–4
wheels
  camber angle 206–9
  locking 185, 202
width of car regulations 106
Williams
  BMW partnership 92–4
  continually variable transmission 133–4
  Frank 50
  FW006 50
  FW07 28
  FW10 3
  FW24 93–4
  FW24 155
  single keel designs 156–7
  tyres 176, 178
  using other car constructors 50
Willis, Geoff 156
Wilson, Frank 7–9
wind changes, gear ratios 134–5
wind-tunnel technology 149, 153
Wingrave, George 19, 48–9, 67–9, 97–8, 116–17, 139–40, 157–8, 159, 189, 214
wings
  aerodynamics 145–8, 149–51
  downforce 28
  FIA regulations 90–1, 153, 173–4
  positioning 90–1
  stability 71
  variation with circuit 211
wishbones (A-arms) 161, 163, 171, 208–9